SCANDALOUS

SAINTS

Frederick Heese Eaton

Preface

When Frederick Heese Eaton died at age 79 in 1993, he left a Will directing that the bulk of the residue of his estate be used to publish and distribute this book.

This book is being sent to you as a result of that bequest. While parts of it will be offensive to many readers, it was Mr. Eaton's request that this book be distributed to as many newspapers, radio stations, television stations, and college libraries in the United States as possible.

Although the views expressed in this book do not reflect the opinions of the Administrator of the estate or his attorney, it has been published and distributed to fulfill Mr. Eaton's last wishes and distribute the message he felt so strongly about in the manner he prescribed.

Ron Hongell

Ronald Hongell, Administrator of the Estate

David E. Shell

David E. Shell, Attorney at Law
Ukiah, California

Introduction

Frederick Heese Eaton was born in Illinois on December 17, 1913. Little information is available about his youth or his life prior to his marriage to his wife, Hildur.

Mr. Eaton spent most of his adult life as a publisher, printing and distributing booklets that he wrote, often under pen names. From what can be surmised, Mr. Eaton's earlier works were written while living in the town of Santa Rosa, California and then later in a small cabin in the rural community of Hopland, California (approximately 120 miles north of San Francisco along Highway 101).

Mr. Eaton's earlier works include several "How to" booklets such as "How to Make Champagne" and "How to Make Beer". In addition to his collection of "how to" books, Mr. Eaton also published a series of booklets on natural cures for various illnesses. Compiled from what appears to be information supplied by his father, Dr. John B. Eaton, he printed a series of treatment books such as "Herbs for Coughs & Colds", "Herbs Used in Treating Cancer", "Vitamin Treatment of Diseases", "Herbs Used for Asthma", and "How to Avoid Tooth Decay".

Other works included "The Hidden Path to God", and other manuscripts revolving around the Bible, in all its translated forms. These works sometimes appear to be an in-depth, literal analysis of the Bible; at other times a humorous interpretation of Mr. Eaton's viewpoint. Some manuscripts have never been published as far as known.

Mr. Eaton's devotion to the task of printing and distributing his knowledge and beliefs among a large segment of the population inspired him to direct in his Last Will and Testament that a large portion of his estate be used to print and distribute this work, "Scandalous Saints". The reader is left with the opportunity to read it and form his or her own conclusions.

Table of Contents

CHAPTER I. WHERE DID SAINT LOT GET HIS SULTRY HAREM? . . . . Page 1

CHAPTER II. THE SAINT WHO MARRIED HIS SISTER . . . . Page 8

CHAPTER III. A LADY SAINT IN THE KING'S BEDROOM . . . . Page 15

CHAPTER IV. THIS SAINT WAS INSPIRED TO COMMIT MURDER . . . . Page 20

CHAPTER V. WHAT DID THE SNAKE REALLY DO TO EVE? . . . . Page 24

CHAPTER VI. DID SAINT NOAH ACTUALLY HAVE A FLOATING ZOO? . . . . Page 33

CHAPTER VII. THE NAKED SAINT AND THE JUGS OF VINO . . . . Page 37

CHAPTER VIII. SHOULD A QUEEN MARRY HER OWN SON? . . . . Page 43

CHAPTER IX. WHAT SAINT REUBEN DID TO HIS FATHER'S PRETTY MISTRESS . . . . . Page 50

CHAPTER X. WHY THIS HOLY MAN GOT HIS DAUGHTER-IN-LAW PREGNANT . . . . . Page 54

CHAPTER XI. THE SAINT WHO DALLIED WITH HIS BOSS'S WIFE . . . . Page 58

CHAPTER XII. THE HOLY SAINT WHO WAS BORN OF INCEST . . . . Page 63

CHAPTER XIII. THIS SAINT FILCHED THE TEN COMMANDMENTS. . . . . Page 70

CHAPTER XIV. A HOLY MAN'S MANY UNHOLY LAWS . . . . Page 82

CHAPTER XV. WHICH SAINT RAPED 32,000 GIRLS? (WITH SOME HELP, OF COURSE) . . . Page 97

CHAPTER XVI. THE SAINT WHO PRACTICED GENOCIDE . . . . Page 104

CHAPTER XVII. WHY THE SUN STOOD STILL FOR SAINT JOSHUA . . . . Page 110

CHAPTER XVIII. THE SAINT WHO ROASTED HIS OWN DAUGHTER . . . . Page 116

CHAPTER XIX. THE SAINT WHO CUT HIS WIFE IN PIECES . . . . Page 120

CHAPTER XX. THE STRONGMAN WHOSE WEAKNESS WAS WOMEN . . . . Page 128

CHAPTER XXI. A GODLY MURDERER AND WIFE STEALER . . . . Page 139

CHAPTER XXII. HOW THIS HOLY MAN AVOIDED EXECUTION FOR MURDER . . . . Page 148

CHAPTER XXIII. THE SAINT WHO RAPED TEN WOMEN ON A ROOFTOP . . . . Page 152

CHAPTER XXIV. HOW SAINT SOLOMON GOT HIS THOUSAND WOMEN . . . . Page 158

CHAPTER XXV. WAS KING SOLOMON THE WISEST MAN ON EARTH? . . . . Page 162

CHAPTER XXVI. THE PROPHET AND THE PRETTY
        YOUNG WIDOW . . . . Page 168

CHAPTER XXVII. ISRAELITE SAINTS WHO ATE THEIR
        CHILDREN . . . . Page 173

CHAPTER XXVIII. SOME SAINTLY PORNOGRAPHIC
        PROPHECIES . . . . Page 179

CHAPTER XXIX. SUSANNA AND THE LECHEROUS
        ELDERS . . . . Page 185

CHAPTER XXX. WHO DISRUPTED THIS LADY'S
        VIRGINITY? . . . . Page 193

CHAPTER XXXI. THIS SAINT SAID THEY WOULD
        ROAST IN HELL . . . . Page 199

CHAPTER XXXII. THE HOLY MAN WHO WAS A
        HYPNOTIST . . . . Page 206

CHAPTER XXXIII. "CUT OFF YOUR HANDS," THIS
        SAINT COMMANDS . . . . Page 214

CHAPTER XXXIV. A FAKE EARTHQUAKE AT THIS
        GODLY FUNERAL . . . . Page 222

CHAPTER XXXV. SAINTS WHO MURDER FOR MONEY
        . . . . Page 227

CHAPTER XXXVI. A HOLY SCHEME TO GET MONEY
        FROM NON-JEWS . . . . Page 234

SCANDALOUS SAINTS

CHAPTER I.   WHERE DID SAINT LOT GET HIS SULTRY HAREM?

"You're the most beautiful woman I've ever known." He held her close. "Give me your lips."

She smiled, clinging to him tightly with her naked arms. She closed her eyes and pressed her lips to his . . . . .

A current romance? No. This happened four thousand years ago near the shores of the Mediterranean Sea.

Sometimes we moderns imagine that love and sex were invented recently, along with The Pill, but not so. Love was life's most thrilling adventure thousands of years ago when the Bible saints walked this earth. And you'd be surprised at the unconventional things those saints did with love and sex too. Of course, you are never told about the scandals the saints got into, so this book was written to expand your mental horizons, as they say.

The fact of the matter is that many of the much revered Bible saints were less than saintly. Not only that, but may of the laws and teachings those saints promulgated were completely outrageous; certain laws that the clergy never discuss. But we will examine those unusual laws herein too for your edification. And we will expose the wild and scandalous lives of these "saintly" people, who are held up as examples to show us how to live uprightly, when they didn't live uprightly themselves.

Take for example the early Bible saint named Lot, who was the nephew of Saint Abraham. He is called "righteous Lot" in the Bible New Testament, and those words were written by none other than the highly revered apostle Saint Peter, outstanding Judeo-Christian chosen by Jesus Christ himself. At 2 Peter Chapter 2 and Verse 7 of the Bible we read; "righteous Lot, greatly distressed by the licentiousness of the wicked."

All right. We'll see how distressed "righteous Lot" really was by the immorality going on then. Now this is going to be a very sexy story. If you're religious or somewhat on the prudish side then brace yourself. You're going to learn a lot about the sex lives of the saints before you finish this chapter.

Perhaps you remember the Bible story of the man called Lot; how he lived in a city called Sodom. Then one day Saint Lot was visited by two men. Thereupon a gang of rapists assaulted Lot's house and attempted to drag out Saint Lot's two male visitors to have homosexual intercourse with them. Usually we hear of rapists attacking women, but in this case the rapists wanted men.

Then the Bible tells us; "And Lot went out at the door unto them, and shut the door after him and said: 'I pray you, brethren, do not so wickedly. Behold now, I have two daughters which have not known a man (i.e., never had sexual intercourse). Let me, I pray you, bring them out unto you, and do ye to them as is good in your eyes; only unto these men (my visitors) do nothing." (Genesis Chapter 19, and Verses 6 to 8 in the Bible.)

In other words, in Saint Lot's eyes women and daughters were less valuable to him than men. Throw them to the rapist wolves. But leave his male visitors alone, (Do you suppose Saint Lot was interested in these men for the same reason that the mob was? It surely looks that way from here. Saint Lot liked the men more than he liked the women.) Saint Lot may some day be known as the patron saint of homosexuals.

Also Saint Lot invited the homosexual rapists to "Do to them (his daughters) as is good in your eyes." In other words, "If you're not satisfied with normal sex relations, then have anal sex with them or oral sex relations, as homosexuals do; it's okay with me. But here they are. Rape them at your pleasure." This is a queer standard of morality that the Bible, and more particularly the Judeo-Christian New Testament, holds up for people to follow, don't you think? With "righteous Lot" as the saintly example.

Well, the homosexual rapist mob didn't want Saint Lot's daughters any more than Lot did. They wanted the visiting men. "And they (the mob) pressed sore upon the man, even Lot, and came near to break the door." (The Bible tells us at Genesis 19:9) According to the Bible account, then Lot's visitors blinded the mob with tear gas or mace or pepper (the story doesn't say which), and this left them staggering about sightless and helpless outside.

Here the Bible story claims that Lot's visitors, notified their host of the impending destruction of the city of Sodom and surrounding areas. They urged Lot to flee from there with his family. This Saint Lot did the next day, taking his wife and two grown daughters with him. It is doubtful that Lot fled Sodom because of any supernatural warning, however. He left town because he feared another attack by the mob, which might seek to take revenge on him.

Shortly thereafter fire fell from the sky on Sodom and the other cities in the area and they were destroyed, according to this story. Meteorite showers striking the earth are well known, and this event occurring at that time gave the saintly Bible writer a chance to insert an account of a warning first being given to Lot by God. Today the Bible God does not give warnings to his followers about impending disasters; they die like everyone else in floods and earthquake. Therefore we must conclude that the Bible God did not give any warning to his follower Lot either.

We must also remember that Saint Moses, who allegedly wrote this tale, lived some 400 years after this event. during that 400 years, the tale having been handed down from generation to generation chiefly by word of mouth, made embellishment with miracles almost inevitable. Stories get better with the telling.

Moses' Bible says: "And he looked toward Sodom and Gomorrah and toward all the land of the plain, and behold, and lo, the smoke of the country went up as the smoke of a furnace." (Genesis 19:28)

The Bible also tells us that Saint Lot's wife lagged behind him to watch the destruction of Sodom, and she was caught by the fringe of the blast, which fried her to a pillar of salt. So Lot was left without a wife. This is an important point to keep in mind as we consider the next sizzling episode of this story.

HOW CAVEMAN HAVE THEIR FUN

The tale continues (and I give it to you the way it is written and will analyze it fully afterward, because it needs analyzing.) Moses' Bible says:

"And Lot went up out of Zoar and dwelt in the mountain, and his two daughters with him; for he feared to dwell in Zoar. And he dwelt in a cave, he and his two daughters."

"And the firstborn (daughter) said to the younger, "Our father is old, and there is not a man in the earth to come into us after the manner of all earth (i.e., have sexual intercourse with us.) Come, let us make our father drink wine, and we will lie (sexually) with him, that we may preserve seed of our father.'" (Genesis 19:30-32)

Hey, now! One excuse was as good as another when the girls wanted to do what they wanted to do. This smoldering Bible story continues:

"And they made their father drink wine that night. And the firstborn went in, and lay (sexually) with her father. And he perceived not when she lay down nor when she arose." (Genesis 19:33)

Since the old man didn't know "when she lay down nor when she arose," the old man must have been lying there with all his clothes off, stark naked, because if she had to wrestle his clothes off him first, she might well have aroused him out of his drunken sleep.

Well, the firstborn daughter now wanted her sister to try it too. The Bible tells us: "And it came to pass on the morrow that the firstborn said unto the younger, 'Behold, I lay (sexually) yesternight with my father. Let us make him drink wine this night also; and go thou in an lie with him, that we may preserve seed of our father." (Genesis 19:34) Anyway, it was a heck of a lot of fun, she undoubtedly told her sister. So the younger sister was anxious to have sexual intercourse with the old man too. This was a new game for these girls to play, apparently, and they were getting a big kick out of it.

There is some question as to whether a woman can rape a man without his cooperation. But maybe old man Lot was not a drunk as his daughters thought he was. Maybe Lot was drunk with one eye open, and was just as anxious to have some fun as his daughters were. Lot was obviously a bi-sexual, and willing to take women when he couldn't get men.

The Bible tale continues: "And they made their father drink wine that night also. And the younger arose, and lay (sexually) with him, and he perceived not when she lay down, nor when she arose." (Genesis 19:35)

Anyway, that's how the Bible reports it. But in those days they had trouble getting writing materials, and besides that they had no printing presses and everything had to be hand written. So they naturally left out a lot of conversation that went on between the Bible characters.

However, we can just imagine what the girls actually said, and it was probably something like this:

"Well, Sis, I made it with Pops last night, and now it's your turn," said the older girl.

"Gee, I wonder how I'll like it?"

"Oh, you'll like it all right. I thought it was the most wonderful experience I ever had," Evelyn told her.

"Well, if it's so good, why don't we do it every night?" asked her younger sister.

"That's a good question," Evelyn replied. "But the simple fact of the matter is, if wo do that, we'll run out of wine."

"Oh, darn!" Miriam exclaimed. "I knew something would come up to spoil it."

"But Pops had plenty of wine tonight," Evelyn reminded her. "And you haven't had sex him once yet. Why not try it first and see how you like it?"

"Why shouldn't I like it? You said you thought it was the greatest."

"Okay, I hear Pops snoring back in the cave after drinking all that wine. He's asleep, so now it's up to you to go in there and make it with him." Evelyn didn't want to be the only pregnant unmarried girl in the family.

"All right, I'll do it!." And with that, Miriam took off every bit of her clothing until she was naked.

"You're beautiful, Miriam," her sister smiled. "Any man would be anxious to have sex relations with you."

"And to think poor Pops is stoned drunk and can't enjoy my beauty," she grinned. "Well, here goes everything. And if I don't get pregnant, it won't be my fault."

Turning, Miriam walked naked into the cave where her father lay sleeping. And Miriam succeeded with her project, as the Bible tells us: "Thus were both the daughters of Lot with child by their father. And the first born bare a son, and called him Moab; the same is the father of the Moabites unto this day. And the younger, she also bare a son, and called his name Ben-ammi. The same is the father of the children of Ammon unto this day." (Genesis 19:36-38)

Oh, this was absolutely naughty, and it's in the Bible too? But this is what the Bible tells us at Genesis Chapter 19 and Versus 28 to 38. However, this story doesn't fit the facts of biology which we understand today. Neither does it fit into the normal pattern of human conduct.

Here you have the account of a man having sexual intercourse with his two nubile daughters. The sexual intercourse took place only on two successive nights, and not more, according to the Bible. Yet both daughters immediately became pregnant. The big question is, from a biological standpoint is this likely to happen?

First of all, let's review some simple facts of biology and human sexuality. Today we know that a woman is only fertile for one day out of a month. Added to that, the man's sperm may remain inside of her and be able to fertilize her egg for about two days. So Saint Lot could not have sexual relations with his daughters only twice and got them both pregnant unless he happened to hit them both on their very brief fertile periods. This is no small trick to accomplish.

More than that, it is extremely unlikely that these two women would have their fertile periods just one day apart. Add to that the fact that no woman is fertile every month of the year, and many women are fertile only half of the months of the year, even though they may have their periods each month. So the likelihood of these women being fertile on two successive days is further reduced.

Saint Lot of course did not know this when he cooked up that story to tell his relatives after they discovered that Lot's daughters were both pregnant, though unmarried and living with Lot. Neither did the others understand the fertile periods of women at that time. They therefore believed Saint Lot's alibi which blamed his daughters for the sexual intercourse with him which resulted in their pregnancy.

However, the facts of the case as stated by Moses' Bible show Saint Lot, a widower who had recently lost his wife, living in a cave with his two grown daughters. There were alone. They lived miles from anyone else. Lot needed a wife, and his daughters needed husbands. Here is a recipe for sexual intercourse and incest. The facts show that Lot and his daughters must have had sexual intercourse not just two times as Saint Lot claimed, but many, many times. Otherwise, Saint Lot could hardly have got the two women pregnant.

So this is how Saint Lot got his sultry harem. Can you imagine a middle-aged man living in a cave with two beautiful and willing young women? They must have worn him out.

But just think a bit now. Have you ever heard of women getting a man drunk and then having sexual intercourse with him? You haven't? Neither have we, except for this fiction in the Bible. Women don't do that sort of thing. But we have all heard of men getting women drunk and then having sexual intercourse with them while they were in a drunken sleep. This happens all the time. It is so common that mothers always warn their daughters of this possibility. Women are very easily overcome by alcoholic drink; much more easily than men.

What could have happened is that Saint Lot may have plied his daughters with plenty of wine and then had sexual intercourse with them while they slept in a drunken stupor. Either that or the girls freely volunteered to have sex relations with their father. As Saint Lot's story says because they were all short of sex partners at that time and were undoubtedly physically distressed by that situation.

We, of course, recognize the sexual distress they must all have been under. Yet no matter how understanding we may be of their plight, we can hardly call Lot "righteous" as Saint Peter does in the Bible.

However, suppose we accept Saint Lot's wild tale of being raped by his two nubile daughters while he was stoned drunk and unconscious on two occasions. And suppose we concede that by some almost impossible sets of coincidences both girls became pregnant after only one act of copulation each. This still would not qualify Lot as being a "righteous" saint, because Lot admitted he was a repetitious and confirmed drunkard. And Saint Paul positively says in the Bible at 1 Corinthians Chapter 6 and Verse 10 that no "drunkards . . . . shall inherit the kingdom of God." So either way the Bible saints contradict each other when Saint Peter calls Lot "righteous," and Saint Paul shuts him out of God's kingdom, and these two saintly Christian apostles were both supposed to be inspired by the same God.

Drunkenness, causing incestuous pregnancy, and then deliberately lying about it, are hardly righteous virtues, even though St. Peter in the Bible considers Lot to be righteous. And what do you think of a father who offered to turn his daughters over to a howling rapist mob? This guy Lot wasn't even a real man, let alone a righteous saint. Lot was indeed a scandalous saint.

CHAPTER II. THE SAINT WHO MARRIED HIS SISTER

When we were taught about the Bible saints we of course were told that they were righteous. They all obeyed God's laws and lived upright holy lives. So when we learned of Abraham we were told that he was the father of the faithful. He was an example we should all follow. In the Bible, God is quoted as saying: "Abraham obeyed my voice and kept my charge, my commandments, my statutes, and my laws." (See Genesis Chapter 26 and Verse 5.)

So after bragging up Abraham's saintly life, let's look at the Bible record and see just how saintly Abraham really lived.

The first place in Moses' Bible that we hear of Abraham is in Genesis Chapter 11. Here it states: "Now these are the generations of Terah; Terah begat Abram, Nohar and Haran; and Haran begat Lot. . . And Abram and Nahor took them wives; the name of Abram's wife was Sarai; and the name of Nahor's wife, Milcah, the daughter of Haran." (Genesis 11:27,29)

Here we learn that Abram (Abraham) married Sarah (Sarai) but we are not told about Sarah's ancestry. We are told that Abraham's brother Nahor married Milcah, his niece.

Why were we not told here who Sarah's parents were? There was an obvious reason. Her parentage was very scandalous, and it is not revealed in Moses' Bible until much later in the story of Abraham. Eight chapters later.

In the Bible Saint Abraham finally tells us of Sarah's parentage in his own words in Genesis Chapter 20 and Verse 12: "Indeed she is my sister . . . and she became my wife."

So there the scandal was out. Saint Abraham married his own sister. Holy altar smoke, it was incest! (I wonder if their daddy knew what they were doing to each other when they were youngsters?)

Right at the very start of his career Abraham engaged in immorality by committing incest with his own sister, and persisted in it, keeping her as his wife and having a child by her. Diabetes, which is the hereditary curse of the Jewish race, may be directly traceable to this incest between Abraham and his sister Sarah. The entire Jewish race is supposed to be decended from Abraham and Sarah, according to the Bible Record.

Nobody can reasonably say that Abraham did not now what he was doing when he committed this incest. We don't need Moses to bring us laws on tables of stone in order for us to know that incest is wrong. Natural human experience teaches us that.

This same natural law was obvious to Abraham. He was a cattleman, and the son of a cattleman. He had often observed that when cattle were inbred, that is, bred incestuously, they often produced freaks and runts. They therefore knew that inbreeding humans would produce the same unfortunate results. And yet Abraham wilfully persisted in his improper incestuous conduct with his own sister for a lifetime. They thought it was fun, and it was.

In the face of that, Moses' Bible brazenly upholds such unrighteous conduct by claiming that God said: "Abraham obeyed my voice and kept my charge, my commandments, my statutes and my laws." (Genesis 26:5) When he wrote that, Moses was just deceiving the Israelites; trying to induce them to obey his laws.

ABE'S NEXT IMMORAL ACT

As though this incest wasn't enough immorality, Abraham had to go on to greater projects. This incest apparently pleased Saint Moses' God for the Bible tells us: "Now the Lord (Jehovah) had said unto Abram, 'Get thee out of thy country, and from thy kindred, and I will make of thee a great nation, and I will bless thee, and make thy name great; and thou shalt be a blessing. . . And Abram took Sarai his wife, and Lot his brother's son, and all their substance that they had gathered, and the souls (slaves) that they had gotten in Haran; and they went forth to go into the land of Canaan; and into the land of Canaan they came." (Genesis 12:1, 3, 5)

It matters not that Abe's father Terah and he had been on the long trip to Canaan for many years already. (Genesis 11:31) At this point the Bible God had to intervene to tell Abraham to do what he was already doing; namely, to go to Canaan. Moses' Bible God apparently did not know that Abe was already on his way, if the Bible text is to be believed.

Furthermore, Moses' Bible God said he would make a Saint of Abraham's descendants "a great nation." This prophecy failed completely. The Israelites never were a great nation. They amounted to nothing among the nations of the world, being insignificant in both size and in power.

So after Saint Abraham and his wife Saint Sarah and entourage arrived in Canaan there was one of those frequent Palestinian droughts. Therefore Abe and his party and herds of cattle went south into Egypt to find forage. The grass in Palestine had dried up, but the Egyptian delta was well watered by the river Nile, so there was plenty of green grass for cattle in Egypt.

Moses' Bible story tells us: "And it came to pass, when he (Abraham) was come near to entry into Egypt, that he said unto Sarai his wife, 'Behold now, I know that thou art a fair woman to look upon (she was a real beauty.) Therefore it shall come to pass, when the Egyptians shall see thee, that they shall say, 'This is his wife; and they will kill me, but will save thee alive. Say, I pray thee, thou art my sister (which she was anyhow) that it may be well with me for thy sake, and my soul shall live because of thee.'" (Genesis 12:11-13)

Well, you know that when a woman is beautiful as Sarah was said to be, and seemingly unmarried, a lot of men are going to want to marry her. Abraham knew that, and Sarah knew that. (And this is exactly what happened with Sarah.) But in complete disregard of that, Abraham and Sarah persisted in their improper course, knowing that the man who married her would be committing adultery with her.

Some will attempt to excuse Abraham and Sarah by saying they had no other course they could follow. But this is not true. Was it necessary for Sarah to parade her beauty before the Egyptian nobility? Counld she not have stayed at home near her tent and kept in seclusion for the few months while they were in Egypt? Besides that, Semitic women in those days often wore veils to protect their faces from the searing desert sun. Sarah must have done that too. If she had not worn a veil during all her years in the desert, her face would have been leathery and wrinkled, and she would not have been the beauty that Abraham said she was. If she had worn a veil in Egypt she could have masked her beauty and none would have seen her.

No, Saint Abraham and Saint Sarah deliberately followed a course that led to immorality, as Moses' Bible story shows: "And it came to pass that when Abram was come into Egypt, the Egyptians beheld the woman and she was very fair. The princes also of Pharaoh saw her, and commended her before Pharaoh; and the woman was taken into Pharaoh's house. And he entreated Abram well for her sake; and he (Abraham) had sheep, and oxen, and he asses, and menservants and maidservants (slaves), and she wasses, and camels." (Genesis 12:14-16)

So why did Pharaoh, the ruler of Egypt, take Sarah into his house? She who was so beautiful. Well, for one thing, Pharaoh did not take her into his palace to wash the lavatories. He took this beautiful woman Sarah into his palace to be his wife or mistress, of course.

We must remember also the customs of the ancient Egyptians, which were vastly different from ours. Egypt is situated on the continent of Africa, and the climate is very hot. The pictures carved on ancient Egyptian walls show Pharaoh sitting on his throne completely naked, and he is being waited on by numerous women who are also completely naked. The only thing Pharaoh wore was his high brimless hat which was his badge of rank, such as a crown is in Europe. Under such conditions when Saint Sarah lived in Pharaoh's palace, Sarah too had to be completely naked. It would be very difficult for Sarah to avoid having sexual intercourse with Pharaoh under those conditions. So they did copulate together as the saintly Bible writer reveals in his next statement.

And what was the result? Moses' Bible tells us: "And the Lord plagued Pharaoh and his house with great plagues because of Sarai, Abram's wife." (Genesis 12:17) Or in plain, modern-day language stripped of superstitious nonsense, Pharaoh caught a venereal disease from Sarah, and transmitted this venereal disease to his wife and all his mistresses.

Oh, Pharaoh was angry; He called Abraham to his palace and gave him a tongue lashing. "What is this thou hast done to me?" Pharaoh exclaimed. "Why didst thou not tell me that she was thy wife? Why saidst thou, 'She is my sister?' So I might have taken her to me to wife." (Genesis 12:18, 19) Here Pharaoh implies that he had no sex relations with Sarah in order to spare Sarah and himself from public humiliation. However, today we know that Pharaoh caught this venereal disease from Sarah, probably gonorrhea, and you can't catch a venereal disease by chatting amiably in a palace reception room. You know that, and I know that.

The American Standard Version translation of this Hebrew Bible text is even more clear on this point. It quotes Pharaoh as saying: "Why saidst thou, 'She is my sister?' so that I took her to be my wife?" (Genesis 12:19) Pharaoh here admitted having sexual intercourse with Sarah.

Then Pharaoh ordered Saint Abraham and his company out of Egypt. "And Pharaoh commanded his men concerning him (Abraham); and they sent him away, and his wife (Sarah), and all that he had." (Genesis 12:20) "And Abram went up out of Egypt, he, and his wife, and all that he had, and Lot with him, into the south. And Abram was very rich in cattle, in silver, and in gold." (Genesis 13:1, 2) Abraham's scheme of keeping Pharaoh busy in bed with Sarah while his cattle grazed off all of Pharaoh's pasture paid off bountifully. Anything to make a shekel, as Moses' Bible indicates. Even pimping.

WHO GOT SARAH'S MAID PREGNANT?

Sarah was getting older and had never had any children, although she and Saint Abraham had lived as man and wife for many decades. Undoubtedly the venereal disease she had, which medical men believe was gonorrhea, had prevented her from bearing children. Sarah must have caught the disease early in life. Of course, she may have caught it innocently enough; like while being in bed with her daddy when he was teaching her all about sex. Oh, you don't think they did that back in those days? You have a lot to learn. But anyway, infertility left Abraham and his wife without an heir to their wealth, and it worried them considerably.

Moses' Bible tells us: "Now Sarai, Abram's wife, bare him no children. And she had an handmaid, an Egyptian, whose name was Hagar. And Sarai said unto Abram, 'Behold now, the Lord hath restrained me from bearing. I pray thee, go in unto my maid (have sexual intercourse with her). It may be that I may obtain children by her. And Abram hearkened to the voice of Sarai." (Genesis 16:1,2)

Here is the first instance of surrogate mothering mentioned in the Bible. Surrogate mothering is greatly frowned on by many religious leaders of today, but for Saint Sarah and Saint Abraham it was just a practical commonplace matter. The conduct of the Bible saints differs greatly from the preachments of today's clergy, we note. Many preachers and priests consider Abraham's conduct here highly immoral, and seek to hide it from the public, along with Saint Abraham's other sexual deviations.

"And Sarai, Abram's wife, took Hagar her maid the Egyptian (after Abram had dwelt ten years in the land of Canaan) and gave her to her husband Abram to be his wife. And he went in unto Hagar. (Abraham had sexual intercourse with Hagar.) And she conceived." (Genesis 16:3,4) Abraham was eighty-five years old at that time.

Look at that scripture quoted from the Bible again. It says: "And he went into Hagar. And she conceived." Isn't that graphic? Isn't that explicit in describing the act of sexual intercourse? And this is what the

Bible says. If this statement appeared in any book other than the Bible, the book would be damned by religionists as foully pornographic.

But back to the story. Suppose you had a housemaid, and suppose your wife was infertile and told you to have sex relations with your housemaid so she could produce a child for you. Do you think the pastor of your church would approve? We'll bet not. You'd probably find yourself excommunicated. But Abraham and Sarah, being saints, got away with it. Anyway, they weren't bothered much with clergy at that time. But their course of action produced its own troubles, as we read in Moses' Bible:

"And when (the maid Hagar) saw that she had conceived, her mistress (Sarah) was despised in her eyes." (Genesis 16:4) This enraged Sarah. Imagine having a slave maid turn her nose up at her mistress!

"And Sarai said unto Abram, 'My wrong be upon thee. I have given my maid into thy bosom, and when she saw that she had conceived, I was despised in her eyes. The Lord judge between me and thee.'" (Genesis 16:5)

Well, Abraham had no intention of getting in between his two battling women. He wasn't that big a fool. So he told Sarah: "'Behold, thy maid is in thy hand; do to her as it pleaseth thee.' And when Sarah dealt hardly with her, she (Hagar) fled from her face." (Genesis 16:6)

At any rate, battle or no, eventually Hagar's baby was born. "And Hagar bare Abram a son; and Abram called his son's name which Hagar bare, Ishmael, to Abram. And Abram was fourscore and six years old, when Hagar bare Ishmael to Abram." (Genesis 16:15, 16)

So this saintly case of surrogate mothering worked, with the Biblical Saint Abraham as the father, and his wife's housemaid as the surrogate mother. Regardless of that, Abraham was very proud of his first-born son.

A CASE OF TOO MUCH HASHEESH

The Semites were avid hasheesh users centuries ago as they still are today, and Abraham was no different. He smoked hash frequently, and when he did, of course he heard voices and saw visions. If you wonder why thousands of years ago the saints frequently talked to angels and to God, and the angels and God talked to the saints, now you know. But neither angels nor God talk to people unless people first use a lot of hasheesh. This is apparent, as you notice even today.

So when you read in Moses' bible that God talked to Abraham, you know what Abe was smoking before that. Anyway, the Bible tells us: "And when Abram was ninety years old and nine, the Lord (Jehovah) appeared to Abram, and said unto him, 'I am the Almighty God; walk before me, and be thou perfect . . . . This is my covenant which ye shall keep, between me and you and thy seed after thee; Every man child among you shall be circumcised. And ye shall circumcise the flesh of your foreskin; and it shall be a token of the covenant betwixt me and you.'" (Genesis 17:1, 10, 11)

Can you imagine what Abraham's wife Sarah had to say when Abe told her he was going to circumcise himself? Do you think any wife wants her husband to butcher up his sexual equipment? You can be sure she didn't like it one bit. The Bible doesn't tell us what Sarah said to Abraham when he told her he was going to circumcise himself, but it probably went something like this:

Abraham walked into their tent and said, "Sary, I just talked to God and he told me to cut off the skin on the end of my penis."

"Oh, come on!" Sarah exclaimed. "You've got to be kidding: This's the craziest thing I ever heard!"

"No, honest to God," Abe insisted. "I heard God say it with mine own ears."

"Well, to tell you the truth, I thought you'd already cut the end off," grinned Sarah. "It's so short."

"Aw, Sary," moaned Abe. "You don't mean that."

"I'm telling you, Abe," she said, "If you cut off any of that little teenie weenie of yours, you won't be able to make it any more."

"But Sary," Abe protested, "I heard God tell me I hadda do it yet."

"You been smoking to much hash lately, Abe."

"No I ain't," Abe said. "Just the usual amount."

"Which is way too much," Sarah told him. "Oh Well, if you cut yourself off too short, I'll just bed down with another handsome king like Pharaoh was. Now he was a real stud."

At any rate, the Bible text quoted earlier is why Abraham and most Jewish men after him have circumcised themselves. It shows what hasheesh will do for a man if he isn't careful.

CHAPTER III. A LADY SAINT IN THE KING'S BEDROOM

After awhile Saint Abraham in his peregrinations moved his cattle operation to pasture in the southern end of Palestine near the coast. Here was the city of Gerar and surrounding country over which King Abimelech ruled.

Abraham had not changed his trick of telling local rulers that his wife Sarah was his sister. This had given him good free pasture land in Egypt before that, and Abraham figured the same scheme would work well with the king of Gerar. Moses' Bible tells us that the same thing happened here that had happened in Egypt before this: "And Abraham said of Sarah his wife, 'She is my sister.' And Abimelech, King of Gerar, sent and took Sarah." (Genesis 20:2)

So once again a local ruler caught this venereal disease from Sarah, and it had a devastating effect on King Abimelech's household. His wives and mistresses then caught the same venereal disease from King Abimelech, and as a result were unable to bear children, just as Sarah was unable to have children. This is the exact effect of gonorrhea on men and women. They become sterile. The Bible says: "For the Lord has fast closed up all the wombs of the house of Abimelech because of Sarah, Abraham's wife." (Genesis 20:18)

Of course, King Abimelech was in a towering rage. He called Abraham into his palace. "Then Abimelech called Abraham, and said unto him, 'What hast thou done unto us? And what have I offended thee that thou has brought on me and on my kingdom a great sin? Thou hast done deeds unto me that ought not to be done.' And Abimelech said unto Abraham, 'What sawest thou, that thou hast done this thing?'"

"And Abraham said, 'Because I thought, surely the fear of God is not in this place; and they will slay me for my wife's sake. And yet indeed she is my sister; she is the daughter of my father, but not the daughter of my mother; and she became my wife. And it came to pass, when God caused me to wander from my father's house, that I said unto her, 'This is the kindness which thou shalt show unto me; at every place whither we shall come, say of me, 'He is my brother.'" (Genesis 20:9-13)

Again the Bible story claims that Sarah had no sexual intercourse with King Abimelech, but the facts given in the Bible are to the contrary. We know today that the probability of transmitting gonorrhea or some similar venereal disease is very unlikely without sexual intercourse.

And secondly, note that the effect of this venereal disease was to prevent King Abimelech's wife and mistresses from bearing children, just as Sarah was unable to bear children. How long do you suppose it would take for King Abimelech to determine that his women were unable to bear children? A few days or a week? Well, hardly. It must have been a matter of months without a pregnancy taking place, before King Abimelech would come to such a conclusion. And note that Sarah was in King Abimelech's household all this time after she had transmitted this venereal disease to Abimelech, who in turn transmitted it to his other women.

Now here King Abimelech had taken Saint Sarah into his household for the express purpose of making her his wife of mistress. Sarah was in the King's household for many months, as the above facts show. Is it reasonable to suppose that Abimelech would have Saint Sarah in his house all these months without having intercourse with her? If you were in their place would you have gone months without having sexual intercourse? Of course not. That wouldn't be normal. It wouldn't be human. And it didn't happen that way with Sarah and Abimelech either. Regardless of Moses' Bible alibi to protect the reputations of the saints, the facts stated in the Bible show that Saint Sarah and King Abimelech had sexual intercourse, that is, committed adultery with each other. Saint Sarah's halo came off for sure that time, once more. It was truly scandalous.

Ah, Well! Other hagiographers report only the kneeling posture of the saints, but I as a hagiographer report the reclining posture of the saints. We all have our specialties, you know.

HOW SARAH HAD A CHILD

Well, after King Abimelech gave Sarah back to her husband Abraham, then the Bible states: "So Abraham prayed unto God; and God healed Abimelech, and his wife, and his maid-servants; and they bare children. For the Lord had fast closed up all the wombs of the house of

Abimelech, because of Sarah, Abraham's wife." (Genesis 20:17, 18)

This of course is the religious attitude toward those events. However, the facts undoubtedly were that King Abimelech had a good physician in his court whose medical skill was responsible for the healing. Religious-minded people would attribute the healing to God, even though it would not have taken place without a physician's services.

Proof for this point is the fact that Saint Sarah was healed also, even though Abraham did not pray for her healing. Sarah too was able to bear children after that healing medicine which she received from King Abimelech's physician, because immediately thereafter the Bible tells us: "For Sarah conceived, and bare Abraham a son in his old age." (Genesis 21:2) Abraham had incestuous sexual intercourse with his sister and she bore him a child.

WERE BIBLE SAINTS REALLY INSPIRED?

Not very, if you take the following yarn as a sample. We return to the Bible text, which says: "And Abraham called the name of his son that was born unto him, whom Sarah bare to him, Isaac. And Abraham circumcised his son Isaac being eight days old, as God had commanded him. And Abraham was an hundred years old when his son Isaac was born unto him." (Genesis 21:3-5)

Now this age of Saint Abraham is an important thing to note. When Isaac was born, Abraham was one hundred years of age. But when Ishmael, his first son was born, Abraham was eighty-six years old, as the Bible tell us at Genesis Chapter 16 and Verse 16. So this means that Saint Abraham's first son Ishmael was fourteen years old at the time Isaac was born. You'll see what I'm getting at with this data very shortly.

Moses' Bible then tells us: "And the child (Isaac) grew, and was weaned. And Abraham made a great feast the same day that Isaac was weaned." (Genesis 21:8) Baby Isaac was probably a year old when he was weaned, and Abraham's oldest son Ishmael then would have been fifteen years of age.

"And Sarah saw the son of Hagar the Egyptian, which she had born unto Abraham, mocking. Wherefore she (Sarah) said unto Abraham, 'Cast out this bondwoman and her son, for the son of this bondwoman shall not be heir with my son, even with Isaac." (Genesis 21:9.10)

Well, this was very upsetting to Saint Abraham. He thought a lot of his firstborn son, even though Sarah did not. "And the thing was very grievous in Abraham's sight because of his son." (Genesis 21:11)

However, Abraham realized that there would be nothing but a constant battle between Sarah and Hagar and their respective sons, so he had a rough decision to make. For the sake of Sarah whom he loved, and his son Isaac, he decided to do as Sarah wished. "And Abraham rose up early in the morning, and took bread, and a bottle of water, and gave it unto Hagar, putting it on her shoulder, and the child, and sent her away. And she departed and wandered in the wilderness of Beer-sheba." (Genesis 21:14)

Let's read that Bible text again. Here the Bible says that Saint Abraham put bread and a bottle of water, along with the child (Ishmael) on Hagar's shoulder! Remember: Ishmael was fifteen years old at that time. Do you know how much the average youngster weighs at the age of fifteen? In the United States the average young man at fifteen weighs one hundred and twenty-five pounds. So here the Bible says Abraham put this one hundred and twenty-five pound young man on his mother's shoulder; along with bread and a jug of water yet! Hagar would have had to be a horse, not a woman, to carry all that!

Here we see just how inspired Moses' Bible really is. Some people read this sort of nonsense over and over again and it never dawns on them that the whole thing is completely unreasonable and impossible. Hagar would have fallen flat on her back if her fifteen year old son had been put on her shoulder as Moses' Bible confidently claims!

But the nonsense isn't over yet. Let's read in the Bible further: "And the water was spent in the bottle, and she cast the child under one of the shrubs." (Genesis 21:15) Can you just see Ma Hagar tossing her one hundred and twenty-five pound son under a shrub? That's beyond the flights of normal imagination. Yet the Bible brazenly tells us: "All scripture is given by inspiration of God." (2 Timothy 3:16, K.J.) So the Bible writers shift the blame to God for the irrationality of their scribblings.

We read in the Bible further: "And she (Hagar) went and sat her down over against him a good way off, as it were a bowshot; for she said, 'Let me not see the death of the child.' And she sat over against him and lift up her voice and wept. And God heard the voice of the lad; and the angel of God called to Hagar out of heaven, and said unto her, 'What aileth thee, Hagar? Fear not; for God hath heard the voice of the lad where he is. Arise, lift up the lad, and hold him in thine hand; for I will make him a great nation.'" (Genesis 21:16-18)

So now the Bible writer of this yarn, allegedly Saint Moses, says that the angel of God is silly too. He claims that the angel wants Hagar to lift up a one hundred and twenty-five pound young man and hold him in her hand. How far out in space can a Bible writer get? Quite a way, it seems. We might remember that hasheesh has been a popular recreation drug in the Middle East for thousands of years, and many of the Bible writers apparently were inspired by this drug as they recorded their tales. What else would account for such nonsense?

CHAPTER IV.   THIS SAINT WAS INSPIRED TO
COMMIT MURDER

In the next episode of Saint Abraham's life, the Bible tells us that Abraham heard a voice. Not seeing anyone around, Abraham assumed it was God's voice. In history, we have learned of many people hearing voices. Joan of Arc also heard voices directing her, for example. And under hypnosis people can hear voices or music at the direction of the hypnotist, even though there are no voices or music audible to others. Occultists and hypnotists tell us that the subconscious mind is able to put thoughts on the auditory nerve that are heard by people as "voices". These voices are heard as normal spoken words, but nobody else can hear such voices as they are not produced by sound waves in the air.

So here is what Moses' Bible tells us Saint Abraham heard. The voice said: "Take now thy son, thine only son Isaac, whom thou lovest, and get thee into the land of Moriah; and offer him there for a burnt offering upon one of the mountains which I will tell thee of." (Genesis 22:2)

Immediately, Saint Abraham concluded that this was God's voice. (Genesis 22:1) Is this reasonable? If you heard a voice tell you to kill your son, would you conclude that was God's voice? Or would you think it was the Devil's voice, or something you drank? More civilized people today would never attribute such a vicious and murderous message to God. But Saint Abraham did not hesitate one minute to decide that this was indeed God who spoke.

This shows us the sort of God that Abraham believed in.

God to Saint Abraham was obviously a vicious, murderous monster. Why he should believe that is unclear, except as some have told us, that man has created God in his own image. Abraham's God was a monster and a murderer, and he was vicious. This was normal conduct in Saint Abraham's mind. Otherwise he would not have identified such a bloody message as this with his God.

There is another angle to this hearing of voices by Abraham. As we mentioned earlier, the use of hasheesh as a recreational drug has been common in the Middle Ease for thousands of years. Hasheesh is a drug made from the shrub known as Cannabis Indica, which "produces the most remarkable hallucinations and imaginations" says Dr. William Boericke in his "Homeopathic Materia Medica." It is therefore quite likely that his alleged hearing of God's voice was nothing but a hallucination caused by hasheesh effecting Abraham's mind.

The worship of Molech in Palestine at that time decreed that children should be sacrificed to the God Molech. (2 Kings 23:10) Abraham of course knew of this religion. Under the influence of hasheesh Abraham's mind undoubtedly conjured up thoughts of sacrificing his son Isaac to his God, in imitation of the sacrifices of children to the God Molech.

So after recuperating from his bout with hasheesh, Saint Abraham arose early the next morning to perform the heinous act that his drugged mind (allegedly God) had told him to do. The Bible says: "And Abraham rose up early in the morning, and saddled his ass, and took two of his young men (slaves) with him, and Isaac his son, and clave the wood for a burnt offering, and rose up, and went unto the place of which God had told him." (Genesis 22:3)

No mention is here made of Saint Sarah's involvement in this bloody project. From the story in the Bible she apparently knew nothing about it. Abraham arose early in the morning, apparently .before she was up, and made off with their boy. Otherwise her attitude toward this act would have been given. She was outspoken enough in their dealings with Hagar and Ishmael, Abraham's other son, and we may be sure she would have had plenty to say about this matter too if she had known anything about it. She was Isaac's mother, and mothers are very protective of their offspring.

Moses' Bible story continues: "Then on the third day Abraham lifted up his eyes and saw the place (Mt. Moriah) afar off. And Abraham said unto his young men (slaves), 'Abide ye here with the ass, and I and the lad will go yonder and worship, and come again unto you.'" (Genesis 22:4,5) Note the deceptive statement of Abraham, and his scheming. He didn't want the two slaves present when he murdered his son. He was afraid they might intervene to save the boy Isaac. So he had the slaves stay behind.

"And Abraham took the wood of the burnt offering, and laid in upon Isaac his son. And he took the fire (vessel) in his hand, and a knife; and they went both of them together."

"And Isaac spake unto Abraham his father, and said, 'My father.'"

"And Abraham said, 'Here am I, my son.'" (This is brilliant Biblical dialog.)

"And he (Isaac) said, 'Behold the fire and the wood; but where is the lamb for a burnt offering?'"

"And Abraham said, 'My son, God will provide himself a lamb for a burnt offering.'" (This was not only a lie, but a deliberate trick to prevent his son from escaping. (Genesis 22:7,8)

Then this drug besotted Saint Abraham built an altar of rock and laid the firewood on it. Suddenly he seized his young son, bound his hands and feet, and laid him on top of the altar.

The boy Isaac undoubtedly cried out in terror and begged for his life as his father raised high the huge glittering knife and readied to plunge it into his young son's heart.

Moses' Bible story tells us that Abraham at that instant noticed a wild goat nearby with its horns caught in the bushes and struggling to get loose. Lucky for Isaac, crazy Abe decided this was an omen from God that he should substitute the goat for his son Isaac. So crazy Abe released his son, killed the goat, and offered it on the altar. (Genesis 22:9-13)

Immediately when he was released, young Isaac ran off and returned to his mother for protection.

But Saint Abraham was afraid to return to Sarah, knowing that Isaac would tell her how he had almost been murdered by his lunatic father. Sarah might have had Abraham put in chains as a madman by the local ruler of the land. So Abraham took the two slaves that were with him, and they went to another location to stay for awhile until Sarah's anger might cool off. Saint Moses' Bible says:

"So Abraham returned unto his young men, and they rose up and went together to Beer-sheba: and Abraham dwelt at Beer-sheba." (Genesis 22:19) You notice that there is nothing said of Isaac being with them, or Sarah either. If you read the Bible closely you learn a lot.

Although Moses' Bible says that Saint Abraham was a would-be murderer he is held up as a holy example for Christians to follow. Saint James, another Judeo-Christian chosen by Jesus Christ, writes this in the Bible New Testament: "Was not Abraham our father justified by works when he had offered Isaac his son upon the altar? . . . Abraham believed God, and it was imputed unto him for righteousness; and he was called the Friend of God." (James 2:21,23) Christian fathers are encouraged to murder their children by this "holy" and "saintly" example, and some of them have been known to do it.

Saint Moses' Bible also claims that God said "Abraham obeyed my voice and kept my charge, my commandments, my statutes and my laws." (Genesis 26:5) Yet Moses' Bible says that Abraham indulged in gross immorality, and was also a would-be murderer. Since Moses' Bible approves this kind of conduct as obedience to Gods Law, most people are now looking elsewhere for guidance in proper living.

According to what Moses in his Bible, wrote, Abraham and Sarah were two more scandalous saints.

CHAPTER V. WHAT DID THE SNAKE REALLY DO TO EVE?

The story of Saint Adam and Saint Eve and their encounter with the naughty snake that enticed Eve, begins first with an account of the creation of the world and then of Adam and Eve. So we shall begin there too.

Some religious souls may complain that Adam and Eve were not saints but sinners. Yet, however they may have been alleged to have sinned, they were at one time saints. In fact, as we see herein, many of the Bible saints were sinners if we examine their conduct as given in the Bible. As for Adam, the Bible at Luke Chapter 3 and Verse 38 speaks "of Adam, which was the son of God," So if Adam was God's son, he must certainly have been a saint, and Eve being God's daughter must also have been a saint.

The Bible tells us: "In the beginning God created the heaven and the earth." But Moses' Bible does not tell us who created God. The Bible says, "For every house is builded by some man but he that built all things is God." (Hebrews 3:4) However, the unbeliever can reverse this argument and say, "If everything is built by someone, then someone had to build or make God. Who did it?"

To this, the clergy will answer, "God always existed." But the scientist will replay, "It is more reasonable to believe that nature or matter always existed in some form." The Bible says that, "No man hath seen God at any time." (1 John 4:12) Since this is a self-evident fact, the scientist logically asks the question, "Then how do we know there is a God?" In answer to this question religion gives no proof. We only have the statement of one clergyman supporting another, and this has gone on for thousands of years as the Bible record and secular history shows us. (We might add that a clergyman's testimony on this point is not reliable, since he is in the religion business and makes money from his claim that there is a God.)

Of course, the fact that science has not found proof of God's existence, does not of itself prove that there is no God. However, it strongly weights the argument in that direction.

Yet the saintly Bible writer confidently asserts that: "In the beginning God created the heaven and the earth." (Genesis 1:1) And he does so without proof. Moses' Bible continues: "And the earth was without form and void." As science describes it, the earth was a barren, lifeless, rocky planet with some lifeless seas upon its surface. Many and various gases drifted over the face of the earth, and tremendous storms raged over its surface. Lightening flashed and thunder roared.

The saintly Bible writers did not know that lightening is electricity. Instead, these ancient barbarians thought that lightening was God's sword, and thunder was God's voice. "God thundereth marvelously with his voice." (Thus says the Bible in the book of Saint Job, Chapter 37, Verses 3-5) Today we know that thunder is caused by the expansion of air due to sudden heating from the flash of lightening. It is not the voice of a God. Neither is the lightening flash the sword of a God. But the ancient Jewish savages believed in the existence of a God whose voice they heard as thunder and whose glittering sword they thought they saw. This voice of thunder in the clouds also led to the belief that God lived up in the sky of heavens.

By way of contrast, in 1953, University of Chicago scientists sought to imitate the conditions on earth millions of years ago. Dr. Harold C. Urey and Stanley L. Miller put methane, ammonia and hydrogen gases into a closed vessel and flashed electric sparks like lightening through it. A marvelous thing happened. They created life. From inert chemical gases they created by this means various amino acids, organic substances which are the building blocks of protein out of which our bodies are made. So with this experiment they proved that life could be generated on a lifeless planet by normal routine events of nature without the intervention of any kind of super intelligence or god.

Then when Dr. Sidney W. Fox allowed these amino acids to dry out they formed long chains of little molecules joined end to end. Such chains of molecules are found in ordinary protein cells. So one step more in the naturel evolution of life on earth was solved. Further experiment by Dr. Fox showed how these chains of protein molecules formed tiny microspheres that were the same size as some bacteria.

This was a great shock to those who believed that there had to be a God, a creator, who made everything we see and feel and are. They are still trying to explain away this tremendous proof of the development of life by means of evolution. The fundamentalist clergy fear evolution greatly because it makes a creator God unnecessary.

SOME ENORMOUS ERRORS

The Bible saint's story of the creation begins right at the first Chapter and first Verse: "In the beginning God created the heaven and the earth. And the earth was without form and void, and darkness was upon the fact of the deep. And the Spirit of God moved upon the face of the waters. And God said, 'Let there be light; and there was light. And God saw the light, that it was good. And God divided the light from the darkness. And God called the light Day, and the darkness he called Night. And the evening and the morning were the first day." (Genesis 1:1-5)

Then on the second day God created heaven, or in other words, the firmament, or expanse of the sky, according to the Jewish Bible account: "And God said, Let there be a firmament in the midst of the waters, and let it divide the waters from the waters. And God made the firmament, and divided the waters which were under the firmament from the waters which were above the firmament, and it was so. And God called the firmament Heaven. And the evening and the morning were the second day." (Genesis 1:6-8, in the Bible)

This puzzles many Bible readers. Where are the waters that are supposed to be above the firmament or heavens or sky? There are none. Dr. Werner von Braun, the German scientist, showed American scientists how to make rockets to put men on the moon and send unmanned space probes millions of miles into space, and yet we found no waters out there. So where did these ancient barbarian Bible writers get the notion that there were waters out beyond the expanse of the sky? Actually, their reasoning was simple. The ancient Jewish barbarians looked out at the Mediterranean sea and saw that it was blue. Well, the Mediterranean was water, so the barbarian saints who wrote the Bible thought that beyond the sky there must also be water, because it was blue like the Mediterranean sea. So that was the first mistake.

But their next errors were worse yet. According to these ancient barbarian saints, on the third day God caused the dry land to appear. The saintly Jewish savage wrote in the Bible: "And the earth brought forth grass, and herb yielding seed after his kind, and the tree yielding fruit, whose seed was in itself, after his kind. And God saw that it was good. And the evening and the morning were the third day." (Genesis 1:12,13)

Now finally on the fourth day, what did God create? The saintly Bible writer says: "And God made two great lights: The greater light to rule the day, and the lesser light to rule the night. He made the stars also. And God set them in the firmament of the heaven to give light upon the earth, and to rule over the day and over the night, and to divide the light from the darkness. And God saw that it was good. And the evening and the morning were the fourth day." (Genesis Chapter 1 and Verses 16 through 19.)

But here is the joker in this tale, According to the Bible saints God created the grass and trees first. After that, on the fourth day, he made the sun and moon. What we would like to ask is: Have you ever tried to grow grass and trees in the dark without sunlight? They won't grow, will they? Of course not. But here we are supposed to believe that God was so stupid as to try to grow grass and trees before the created the sun.

In spite of this enormous error, Saint Paul has the unmitigated effrontery to write in the Bible: "All scripture is given by inspiration of God." (See 2 Timothy Chapter 3 and Verse 16, King James Version) So the Bible saints who wrote this idiotic nonsense then want to blame God for their ghastly mistake.

(Note carefully the word "made" here, where Moses' Bible says God "made" the sun or "greater light" on the fourth day. This word "made" is translated from the same Hebrew word "aw-saw" that the Bible uses where it says: "The Lord God made the earth." (Genesis 2:4) "Made" in both cases means exactly the same thing. Don't let anybody fool you.)

But the ignorance and stupidity of the Bible saint who wrote this does not end here. After stating that God created "the fruit trees yielding fruit" on the third day of creation, this saint writes in the Bible that God didn't create bees to pollinate the blossoms on the fruit trees until the sixth day of creation. (Genesis 1:24, 31) And you can't get fruit off trees without insects to pollinate the blossoms. Also Saint Peter wrote in the Bible that "one day is with the Lord as a thousand years, and a thousand years as one day," (2 Peter 3:8) showing that the creative "days" of the bible were believed to be 1000 years long. So here you have trees blossoming and bearing fruit for at lease one thousand years in the dark, with no sun and no bees to pollinate the blossoms, according to the nonsense written in the Bible by this ignorant saint.

And both the apostle Saint Paul and the apostle Saint Peter insist that God inspired these writings in the Bible. This shows that Christian apostles were just as ignorant as the saint who wrote this absurd account twenty centuries before them. It also shows that saintly writing in the Bible was not inspired by God, and that this is nothing but ignorant barbarian nonsense, written by a saint who lived in the desert and knew nothing about trees and fruit.

This reminds one of the American proverb: "If they fool me once, shame on them. But if they fool me twice, then shame on me." We have our brains. Let's use them.

THESE ERRORS APPEAR IN ALL BIBLES

Do not imagine for one moment that your Bible is different from the Bible I quote here. Just take your Bible now, whether it be Protestant, Catholic, Orthodox, or whatever, and in whatever language, and compare the text with the quotations I have given here from the King James Version Bible in English. You will find that your Bible makes the same statements and contains exactly the same errors that I have pointed out here. Why? because all Bibles are translated from the ancient Hebrew text that Moses and the other saints wrote thousands of years ago. Your Bible is not the invention of your church denomination. For example, I also have before me a Bible in the Spanish language, and because I can read Spanish I can assure you that the same errors appear in the Spanish Bible as I have just quoted from the Bible in the English language.

SO GOD CREATES DISEASE GERMS

The Bible continues: "And God created great whales, and every living creature that moveth, which the waters brought fourth abundantly after their kind. And every winged fowl after his king. . . . . And the evening and the morning were the fifth day." (Genesis 1:21, 23)

"And God made the beast of the earth after his kind, and cattle after their kind, and everything that creepeth upon the earth after his kind. And God saw that it was good." (Genesis 1:25) "All things were made by him, and without him was not anything made that was made." (John 1:3) God created the wolves and the lions and the rattlesnakes and scorpions and disease germs. "And God saw that it was good." This Jewish Bible God was some God, don't you think? But he doesn't seem to have our set of values.

The Bible also says "God is love." (1 John 4:8) Is creating poisonous snakes and disease germs your idea of love? I doubt it.

So now, after creating rattlesnakes and disease germs, the Bible

God decides to create mankind and put them into this wonderful paradise he has brought into existence, germs and all. The Bible saint writes: "So God created man in his own image, in the image of God created he him; male and female created he them." (Genesis 1:27)

It is precisely because there are such things as poisonous snakes and disease germs that the majority of educated people have rejected a belief in any God. Instead they have turned to evolution as the only logical explanation for our existence, and the existence of disease germs.

TWO ACCOUNTS OF THE CREATION

The Bible contains two accounts of the creation. The first we have just examined in Chapter One of the book of Genesis in the Bible. However, in Chapter Two, beginning at Verse 4, there is a second tale of creation. How do we know this? Because the first account refers to God by the Hebrew word "Eloheem," meaning "Gods." And the second account calls God "Yahwah Eloheem," or in English, "Jehovah Gods." (In some English translations the name Jehovah is left out and replaced by the word Lord.)

You notice in the above that "Eloheem" is in the plural, and correctly translated "Gods." The singular of this Hebrew word is "elo-ah." So the Jews believed in a plurality of Gods, rather than one god? That's what the Hebrew Bible says, although most rabbis will dispute that. The Christian sect of the Jews does believe in a plurality of Gods in what they call their Godhead, "the Father, Son, and Holy Ghost" trinity.

So in this second Bible account of the creation we find God referred to as Jehovah God, which was a name for God introduced by Moses. This second account of the creation had to be written either by Saint Moses or by someone after Moses' time, since the name Jehovah God was not known before that. The pervious account of the creation in Chapter One of Genesis came from an earlier source.

In this second account we find the creation of Adam and Eve given in detail. The Bible Saint writes: "And (Jehovah) God formed man of the dust of the ground, and breathed into his nostrils the breath of life; and man became a living soul." (Genesis 2:7)

Then the saint tells us how God created a woman for Adam. He writes: "And (Jehovah) God caused a deep sleep to fall upon Adam, and he slept: and he (God) took one of his (Adam's) ribs, and closed up the flesh instead thereof; And the rib, which (Jehovah) God had taken from man, made he a woman, and brought her unto the man." (Genesis 2:21,

22)

Now if God had actually done this, Adam and Eve would have been more closely related than brother and sister, and any sexual intercourse between them would have been incest. Also any children born to them would have been deformed because of the incestuous relationship. This sort of an arrangement would certainly have made God look stupid and lacking in knowledge, whereas the stupidity and ignorance really belonged to the ignorant Jewish barbarian who wrote this nonsense, whether it was Saint Moses or some other Bible saint.

Furthermore, if God had to take a rib from Adam to make a female for him, then God would have had to do the same for every species of animal, bird, fish, and insect life, and for some vegetable life as well. This would have really kept God busy with scalpel and suture, considering all the forms of life in existence. Can you just see God putting the first male mosquito to sleep and removing his rib, if mosquitoes have ribs, and making a female mosquito out of it? If you can, you have a better imagination than most folks. Saint Moses must have been on hasheesh when he composed this yarn.

ENTER THE NASTY SNAKE

There is no account of God taking one of the snake's ribs and making a female snake out of it. However, that would have been more reasonable, because snakes have dozens of ribs and the male snake could easily have spared one and never missed it. Anyway, the snake was there in the Garden of Eden with Adam and his female rib Eve, and up in a fruit tree yet.

The snake spoke to the woman, according to Moses' yarn. (Have you even heard a snake speak? Now surely Saint Moses was on hasheesh when he wrote this.) Moses' Bible says: "Now the serpent was more subtle than any beast of the field which (Jehovah) God had made. And he said unto the woman, 'Yea, hath God said, "Ye shall not eat of every tree in the garden?"

"And the woman said unto the serpent, 'We may eat of the fruit of the trees of the garden. But of the fruit of the tree which is in the midst of the garden, God hath said "Ye shall not eat of it, neither shall ye touch it, lest ye die."'"

"And the serpent said unto the woman, 'Ye shall not surely die. For God doth know that in the day ye eat thereof, then your eyes shall be opened, and ye shall be as Gods, knowing good and evil.'"

"And the woman saw that the tree was good for food, and that it was pleasant to the eyes, and a tree to be desired to make one wise, she took of the fruit thereof and did eat, and gave also unto her husband (Adam) with her, and he did eat." (Genesis 3;1-6)

So according to Moses' Bible, this is why humans die. It's not a very scientific reason, because all other animals die too, and trees and grass and fish and insects die too. Nothing lives forever, even though there is no record that any of them ate of the fruit that Adam and Eve were alleged to have eaten. But this is Moses' story and he's stuck with it.

Moses Bible says that because Adam and Eve filched and ate the fruit from God's tree, God told Adam, "In the sweat of thy face shalt thou eat bread till thou return unto the ground. For out of it wast thou taken. For dust thou art, and unto dust shalt thou return." (Genesis 3:19)

Adam and Eve were God's children, according to Moses' Bible. If you had a couple of kids and they took some apples from your apple tree after you told them not to do it, would you put them to death? No, of course you wouldn't. But when Saint Moses wrote this yarn he thought that was a fair punishment for kids who pilfered fruit out of a tree. Of course, Moses had massacred thousands of men, women and children (Numbers 31) so it isn't surprising that he took this view.

WAS THE SNAKE REAL?

However, when the Bible came into the hands of the more civilized Romans they couldn't swallow this kind of a story. Even though the Romans had carried on many bloody wars of conquest, they couldn't conceive of a father putting his children to death for filching fruit out of a tree. So the Roman branch of the Christian religion groped for a better explanation of this Bible story. And their explanation was this: The tale of Adam and Eve and the snake was an allegory. It really didn't mean what it said.

So what did it mean? It had to be something awfully sinful to warrant a death sentence, so they decided that sin had to be sex. Sexual intercourse was the greatest sin the celibate Roman clergy could conceive of, because they were under vows never to engage in sexual intercourse. But the personal torment the lack of sexual intercourse caused, drove them to the conclusion that Adam and Eve had also been forbidden to engage in sexual intercourse, but had broken this commandment of God. In the allegory presented by Moses, the snake represented -- well, you know what the snake represented. Adam had the snake, and Eve was tempted by it, and they yielded to the temptation and engaged in sexual intercourse. So they were condemned to death by God. This seemed reasonable to the saintly celibate priests.

However, there is no record of Adam and Eve being commanded to live a celibate life. In the Bible at Genesis Chapter one and Verse 28 it says this: "And God blessed them (Adam and Eve), and God said unto them, 'Be fruitful and multiply, and replenish the earth." Adam and Eve could not obey this commandment without engaging in sexual intercourse.

So this seeming conflict of commandments confounded the saintly clergy, but not for long. They will tell you that God gave two conflicting commandments to Adam and Eve, and they had to break one commandment in order to keep the other.

How could God be so unreasonable? And how could any intelligent person believe in an unreasonable God like that? But sex is a big deal with clergymen in spite of the fact they say that God prohibited it on pain of death. Because they say that it is sinful they want everybody who engages in sex relations to keep it quiet and never talk about sex, and hide the human body and especially the sex organs. This is the overwhelming obsession of the saintly clergy of most Christian church denominations. Yet why should the Bible be so coy in talking about sexual intercourse here, so that it had to use an allegory? Elsewhere the Bible is very blunt about sex relations, describing sex graphically by saying: "And he (Abraham) went in unto Hagar, and she conceived." (Genesis 16:4) How could anyone describe sexual intercourse more fully without drawing a picture?

However, now that their original interpretation of the Adam and Eve story is so widely ridiculed, many of the clergy have backed off into a more esoteric and amorphous explanation which also makes no sense to any rational person. Now they claim that Adam and Eve's sin was that they had sexual intercourse when they desired to have sexual intercourse. If they had engaged in sexual intercourse when they didn't desire to have sexual intercourse, say the clergy, they would have committed no sin. (This is like saying that it's sinful to eat when you're hungry.) Meanwhile, some of the other Christian denominations have dropped the allegorical interpretations and have gone back to the literal belief that God killed Adam and Eve because they ate the fruit of the tree contrary to God's command. So now they are back to square one, trying vainly to explain why other animals, birds, insects, fish, trees and vegetation all die too, although they never ate any forbidden fruit. Ain't religion grand? Especially the Jewish Christian Kind.

CHAPTER VI.   DID SAINT NOAH ACTUALLY HAVE A
FLOATING ZOO?

We don't get far into the Bible before we run into the story of
Noah, the holy saint, who with his family escaped destruction in a great
flood that came upon the land.

Moses' Bible tale begins, "And God saw that the wickedness of
man was great in the earth, and that every imagination of the thoughts of
his heart was only evil continuously. And it repented the lord Jehovah that
he had made man on the earth, and it grieved him at his heart. And the
Lord Jehovah said, 'I will destroy man whom I have created from the face
of the earth; both man and beast, and the creeping thing, and the fowls of
the air. For it repenteth me that I have made them." (Genesis 6:5-7)

Now let's stop and analyze this statement a bit. Some folks tend
to read over these things without examining them closely. Let's not be that
foolish and be misled by religious nonsense.

Here in the above Bible quotation it says that God was angry with
mankind on the earth because of their sinfulness. So he decided to kill
them all. But he also said he would kill "both man and beast, and the
creeping things and the fowls of the air." But what had the beasts and
creeping things and fowls done that was wrong? Nothing. There is no
statement that they had done anything to displease God. But God is mad at
mankind, so in his Divine displeasure God is going to destroy innocent
animals and birds too. Does that sound reasonable? According to the Bible
saint who wrote this, God is a monster, an unrighteous unjust demon.
Otherwise he would not slaughter the innocent. So much for the saints
Bible God Jehovah. As we have noted elsewhere, man creates God in his
own image. Here Saint Moses represented God as being another ruthless
murderer like himself. Saint Moses was expert at slaughtering people, as

his massacre and rape of the Midianites shows, and the God he invented was no more righteous than he. (See Chapter XIV herein)

As Thomas Paine, one of the proponents of the United States Declaration of Independence, stated: "Of all the systems of religion that ever were invented, there is none more derogatory to the Almighty, more unedifying to man, more repugnant to reason, and more contradictory in itself, than this thing called Christianity."

The fact of the matter was that in those early days religion was asked to explain all natural phenomena. There was little natural science then, so instead of asking scientists for their interpretations of the facts, this task fell to the religious leaders. Of course, bound up with religion was the idea that man must please the Gods. Hence, if an event such as a flood did great harm, it was assumed that the nation had somehow displeased God. The reason God was displeased, according to Moses, is that "The earth also was corrupt before God, and the earth was filled with violence." (Genesis 6:11) We may well ask, when was the earth not corrupt and filled with violence? Moses himself contributed more than his share to the bloodshed. Yet there is not a great flood every day, which there would be if that were caused by the violence of man against man. So Saint Moses' religious explanation for the flood of Noah's day does not hold up in the light of history.

That a great flood actually took place in Noah's day we cannot deny. Our own Archaeologists have dug down into the earth in the land of Babylonia and found whole cities buried under fifteen feed of alluvial silt, showing that an enormous torrent of waters had covered that area in ancient times. Furthermore, the ancient survivors of that flood had built the Tower of Babel thirty stories high for the express purpose of escaping another like flood, if it should come again. Such was their terror regarding the deluge of Noah's time. And the Tower of Babel stood in Babylon for thousands of years. This cannot be denied.

Ancient historic records of these eastern nations further add to the evidence of Noah's flood. However, Moses' Biblical claim that the flood engulfed the entire planet earth, or that it destroyed the entire human race except for Noah and his family, or that the flood lasted for about a whole year as Moses Bible says: these points and others are in great doubt. Those and similar issues are raised by the accounts of the flood given by other ancient historians and nations existing in the area around Babylon, where archeological evidence of a great flood has been found.

Bishop Alexander Hislop writes in his book, "The Two Babylons:" "In the Babylonian Mysteries, the commemoration of the flood, of the ark, and the grand events in the life of Noah, was mingled with the worship of the Queen of Heaven and her son. Noah, as having lived in two worlds, both before the flood and after it, was called "Diphues,' or 'twice-born,' and was represented as a God with two heads looking in opposite directions, the one old, the other young. Though we have seen that the two-headed Janus in one aspect had reference to Cush and his son Nimrod, viewed as one God in a two-fold capacity, as the Supreme and Father of all the deified 'mighty ones,' yet in order to gain for him the very authority and respect essential to constitute his properly as the head of the great system of idolatry that the apostates inaugurated, it was necessary to represent him as in some way or other identified with the great patriarch who was the Father of all, and who had so miraculous a history. Therefore in the legends of Janus, we find mixed up with other things derived from an entirely different source, statements not only in regard to his being the 'Father of the world,' but also his being 'the inventor of ships,' which plainly have been borrowed from the history of Noah; and therefore the remarkable way in which he is represented in the figure here presented to the reader, may confidently be concluded to have been primarily suggested by the history of the great Diluvian patriarch, whose integrity in his two-fold life is so particularly referred to in the Scripture, where it is said (Genesis 6:9), 'Noah was a just man, and perfect in his generation,' that is, in his life before the flood, and in his life after it. The whole mythology of Greece and Rome, as well as Asia, is full of the history and deeds of Noah, which it is impossible to misunderstand. In India, the god Vishnu, 'the Preserver," who is celebrated as having miraculously preserved one righteous family at the time when the world was drowned, not only had the story of Noah wrought up with this legend, but is called by his very name. Vishnu is just the Sanscript form of the Chaldee 'Ish-nun,' 'the man Noah,' or the 'man of rest.' In the case of Indra, the 'king of the Gods,' and the god of rain, which is evidently only another form of the same God, the name is found in the precise form of Ishnu. Now, the very legend to Vishnu, that pretends to make him no mere creature, but the supreme and 'eternal god,' shows that this interpretation of the name is no mere unfounded imagination. This he is celebrated in the "Matsya Puran:' "The sun, the wind, the earth, and things incorporeal, were absorbed into his Divide essence; and the universe being consumed, the eternal and omnipotent God, having assumed an ancient form, reposed mysteriously upon the surface of that (universal) ocean. But no one is capable of knowing whether that being was then visible or invisible, or what the holy name of that person was, or what the cause of his mysterious slumber. Nor can anyone tell you how long he thus reposed until he conceived the thought of acting; for no one saw him, no one approached him, and none can penetrate the mystery of his real essence." In conformity with this ancient legend, Vishnu is still represented as sleeping four months every year. Now, connect this story with the name of Noah, the man of 'Rest' (Note: The name Noah means 'rest' in the Hebrew language) and with his personal history during the period of the flood, when the world was destroyed, when for forty days and forty nights all was chaos, when neither sun nor moon nor twinkling star appeared, when seas and sky were mingled, and all was one wide universal 'ocean,' on the bosom of which the patriarch floated, when there was no human being to 'approach' him but those who were with him in the ark, and 'the mystery of his real essence is penetrated' at once, 'the holy name of the person' is ascertained, and his 'mysterious slumber' fully accounted for."

Hislop continues: "The most learned explorers of Egyptian antiquities, including Sir Gardiner Wilkinson, admit that the story of Noah was mixed up with the story of Osiris. The ship of Isis and the coffin of Osiris, floating on the waters, point distinctly to that remarkable event. There were different periods, in different places in Egypt, when the fate of Osiris was lamented; and at one time there was more special reference to the personal history of 'the mighty hunter before the Lord,' and at another to the awful catastrophe through which Noah passes. In the great and solemn festival called 'The Disappearance of Osiris,' it is evident that it is Noah himself who was then supposed to have been lost. The time when Osiris was 'shut in his coffin,' and when the coffin was set afloat on the waters, as stated by Plutarch, agrees exactly with the period when Noah entered the ark.

CHAPTER VII. THE NAKED SAINT AND THE JUGS OF VINO

The mere fact that we find ample evidence that a great flood did take place in the area around Babylon does not mean that we should swallow Moses' Biblical tale of Noah hook, line and sinker, and fishing pole as well. Assuredly not. A casual reading of the Bible story raises numerous questions in the mind that makes much of Moses' tale dubious indeed.

First let's look at the Bible account and see what it says: "And God said unto Noah, 'The end of all flesh is come before me for the earth is filled with violence through them; and behold, I will destroy them with the earth." (Genesis 6:13) What does this mean: "I will destroy them with the earth?" Was God intending to destroy the earth too? If so, he did not succeed, for the earth is still here although the flood is long gone. So there may be no misunderstanding, the Hebrew word here translated "earth" is "ehrets:" the same word used in Chapter 7 and Verse 10 where the Bible says: "the waters of the flood were upon the earth." So it must have referred to the mundane sphere. Obviously the Bible God's statement: "I will destroy them with the earth" is simply not true. The earth is still here. That takes care of lie number one.

We go on with the Bible Saint's tale, The Bible God says to Noah: "Make thee an ark of gopher wood; rooms shalt thou make in the ark and shalt pitch it within and without with pitch. And this is the fashion which thou shalt make it of: The length to the ark shall be three hundred cubits, and breadth of it fifty cubits, and the height of it thirty cubits." (Genesis 6:14,15) So the ark was 525 feet long, or nearly a city block in length, 87.5 feet wide, and 52.5 feet high, according to some authorities. Or three stories high as verse 16 tells us. It was a big boat, for sure. But was it big enough for the job? Let's find out.

God further said to Noah: "But with thee will I establish my covenant; and thou shalt come into the ark, thou and thy sons and thy wife, and thy sons' wives with thee. Of every living thing of all flesh, two of every sort shall thou bring into the ark to keep them alive with thee. They shall be male and female. Of fowls after their kind, of every creeping thing of the earth after his kind, two of every sort shall come unto thee to keep them alive." (Genesis 6:18-20) "Of every clean beast thou shalt take to thee by sevens, the male and his female. And of beasts that are not clean by two, the male and his female. Of fowls of the air by sevens, the male and the female; to keep seed alive upon the face of all the earth." (Genesis 7:2,3)

This was a big order when you think of it. Have you ever gone through one of the large zoos near our metropolitan centers? There are only a small number of species of animals represented there, but do you think Noah could have crammed them all into his boat? It is doubtful.

And think of all the tons and tons of food that would have been needed to feed this vast menagerie for a whole year, because Moses Bible story tells us that Noah was aboard this boat for a whole year. (Genesis 7:11 and 8:13-19) One cow requires at least three tons of hay to survive for a year, and Noah had seven head of cattle aboard using a total of 21 tons of hay. Think how much hay the elephants and hippopotamuses required! With all the hay aboard they wouldn't have had room for the animals! And the lions and tigers and wolves, etc., needed fresh meat daily! Where did it all come from? Noah took it aboard, the Bible saint tells us. (Genesis 6:21)

Actually Noah could not have been aboard his ship with all these animals and birds for a whole year or even one month. The ancient Chaldeans wrote on their tablets that the Deluge lasted for only one week, and this is more reasonable. Archaeologists have also found tablets in the remains of the ancient city of Ebla in Haran (Northern Syria) which pre-dated the patriarch Abraham, and these state that Noah's flood lasted six days. This whole Jewish tale by Saint Moses is similar to other wild exaggerations he and other Biblical writers concocted about the ten plagues upon Egypt, etc. The later Jewish Rabbis even enlarged upon Moses' tales and stated that when Adam was first created he was so tall he reached up into heaven and frightened the angels, so God then reduced Adam's size. The Jews were addicted to vast exaggerations far more than to the truth, so Moses' tale of Noah's flood cannot be taken as fact. It was an attempt to make a good story better, but it distorts the facts until it defies rational belief.

The truth is, Saint Noah did not have all the species of animals on his boat, and didn't even come near it. Ask yourself this question: Why are all the kangaroos in Australia, and none in Armenia where Noah's ark is said to have landed? If Noah had kangaroos on his ark there should be more kangaroos in Armenia and surrounding countries than in Australia. Actually, with Australia isolated as it is, there would probably be no kangaroos in Australia today if the story of Noah in the Bible were true. The fact remains that this of itself proves that the flood of Saint Noah's day was not a globe encircling deluge as the saintly Bible writer claims.

Similarly the declaration the God told Noah to build the boat is contrary to reason. Does God ever tell us to build anything nowadays? On the contrary, we don't even have proof that there is an intelligent being such as a God, similar to the God described in the Bible. So it is beyond belief that we should expect a God to tell Noah to build a boat to escape a flood. Such things just don't happen.

Moses blames the flood on rain that fell for forty days and forty nights. Having lived in the desert for so many years, he would naturally think that anytime it rained forty days and forty nights it would produce enough water to cover all the mountains, but we know better. The author has seen it pour down rain for ninety days and ninety nights in the Pacific Northwest, and it produced no flood and covered no mountains, but the water just ran down the rivers to the ocean.

However, Saint Moses writes: "In the six hundredth year of Noah's life, in the second month, the seventeenth day of the month, the same day were all the fountains of the great deep broken up, and the windows of heaven were opened. And the rain was upon the earth forty days and forty nights." (Genesis 7:11, 12) This was hardly reason enough for the flood to cover up the Himalayas and mount Everest, almost six miles high, and engulf the entire surface of the globe.

What probably did happen was that Noah ran a zoo and circus, and had this floating menagerie on his ship going from city to city down the Tigres river. He would stop at each city along the way and give performances until the crowds dwindled, and then he floated downstream to the next city. This is how he made his living, and his family with him. In the course of his travels this great flood struck, probably caused by an enormous earthquake under the Persian Gulf, throwing a tidal wave up over Babylonia. There is the Great Rift Valley running across Northern Africa, and perhaps this valley may have been formed by that earthquake. Some of the ancient historians claim that there were numerous volcanic eruptions at that time, and this would tie in with the possibility of a great earthquake also occurring then.

It was a cataclysmic event that wiped out a whole nation of people, but Saint Noah and his family and his circus animals escaped on their ship. Legend added to this event, until many religious people today believe the flood encompassed the entire earth, and the Revised Standard Version of the Bible supports this view. However, if Saint Noah's flood covered the entire globe, why is it that there is no history of such a flood in ancient Africa or ancient Europe?

Let's suppose for one minute that these religious people are right, and that the flood waters did cover the entire earth. As Moses writes in his Bible: "And the waters prevailed exceedingly upon the earth; and all the high hills that were under the whole heaven were covered. Fifteen cubits upward did the waters prevail, and the mountain were covered." (Genesis 7:19,20, K.J.V.) Fifteen cubits is less than 25 feet. How can you cover mountains with water barely 25 feet deep?

Even so, let's suppose all the mountains were covered. Mount Ararat in Armenia (where Noah is supposed to have landed his boat) is over three miles high. Mt. Everest in India is almost six miles high. This would take a lot of water. The problem is: with flood waters covering the entire earth (including the seas) over six miles deep, where in the Old Harry did all this water go after the flood was over?

In the Dark Ages the clergy told people that the earth is flat and the water just ran off the edge. But nowadays that sort of argument won't convince many people. Moses would have to do better than that. So here Saint Moses is, with water six miles deep all over the globe, and nowhere to siphon it off. A heck of a mess. Worse than no plumber and a big leak in a pipe on Sunday.

Anyway in spite of this dilemma, Moses' Bible says the flood ended. "And in the second month, on the seventh and twentieth day of the month, was the earth dried." (Genesis 8:14) The great flood of waters six miles deep had magically engulfed the earth, and just as magically all this water disappeared. You have to believe in magic to believe the saintly Bible writers.

However, this unscientific Bible tale cost at least one man his life. The Inquisition burned to death at the stake the astronomer Cecco D'Ascoli for saying that the Earth is round, a fact that is undisputed today. The bloody Christian priests knew that with a round Earth the Bible yarn about the great flood would be discredited. Only with a flat Earth could the waters of the deluge run off the edge and disappear. So the saintly Roman Catholic clergy murdered astronomer D'Ascoli to prevent the world from learning the truth that the Earth is round and the Biblical story of the flood is therefore obviously false. Noah's flood of waters most certainly did not cover all the mountains; nor did it engulf the entire Earth. It was strictly a local Babylonian affair.

ST. NOAH LIKES THE SAUCE

So after leaving his boat what did Saint Noah do? The Bible says: "And Noah began to be a husbandman, and he planted a vineyard. And he drank of the wine and was drunken, and he was uncovered within his tent." (Genesis 9:20,21) Noah was a Bible saint, but he was not so saintly as to stay sober. He got himself royally drunk, and you know how drunks are. They slobber and drool, they stagger, they get sick and vomit. It's ghastly. Noah was drunk in his tent, grovelling and vomiting, and the weather was hot in that region so he took off all his clothes. What a sight! What a saint! The Bible says: "Noah walked with God." (Genesis 6:9) Noah didn't walk. He staggered.

In the midst of all this, Saint Noah's son Ham entered the tent. The Bible says: "And Ham, the father of Canaan, saw the nakedness of his father, and told his two brethren without." (Genesis 9:22) You can bet Ham had a big laugh at his father's expense. "And Shem and Japheth (Noah's other sons) took a garment and laid it upon their shoulders, and went backward, and covered the nakedness of their father. And their faces were backward, and they saw not their father's nakedness." (Genesis 9:23) Here is a fine religious display of prudishness, and an improbable tale at that. How could any two persons walk backward into the tent, not seeing their father on the floor and not knowing where he lay in his drunken state, and manage to cover the old man? Not likely. What they probably would have done is trip over the old man and fall on top of him. But this tale is put in here by the prudish Moses for a specific purpose, as we shall soon see.

Prudishness is not a characteristic of the white race, but a big thing among Semites: that is, Jews and Arabs. The only whites who are prudish are many of the British; often for religious reasons.

Eventually old man Noah awoke from his drunken stupor and was in an ugly humor. He was sick, and his head felt three sizes too large, and man, did it ache! The Bible says: "And Noah awoke from his wine, and knew that his younger son had done unto him (seeing his nakedness.) And he said, 'Cursed be Canaan' a servant of servants shall he be unto his brethren.'" (Genesis 9:24,25) Canaan was the son of Ham, and Ham had seen his father's nakedness. So with customary Bible logic, Noah does not curse Ham, but curses Ham's son! Is that justice? It's typical Bible justice, as we have previously seen.

What Moses was driving at is this: The Israelites under Moses and Joshua were invading the land of Canaan, and slaughtering Canaanites or making them slaves. This curse on Canaan; "A servant of servants shall he be," Moses inserts here as justification for the enslavement by the Israelites of whatever Canaanites escaped being slaughtered. The curse was pure fiction, and an opportunistic invention of Moses.

CHAPTER VIII. SHOULD A QUEEN MARRY HER OWN SON?

After the great flood of Noah's day, his grandchildren multiplied and gradually moved down the Tigris river, and also along the Euphrates river. These two great rivers joined in the land we know as Babylonia, and between them a great civilization sprang up as Noah's descendants replaced the people who had died in the flood.

The two rivers supplied much needed irrigation water for that thirsty region. Great canals and dikes carried the irrigation water across the fertile land and made agriculture and cattle raising possible. All sorts of grains and legumes were grown, and dates and other tropical fruits flourished.

Cities were built on the silt that covered earlier cities that had perished in the deluge. The great city of Babylon was built on both sides of the wide Euphrates river. The city was many miles across and was joined together by a large bridge. Cush was the ruler who began to build Babylon, and at the request of his beautiful queen, Semiramis, he surrounded the city with walls 300 feet high and seventy-five feet thick, and huge gates of brass to close the entrances in time of danger.

His blonde Queen Semiramis was homesick for the mountains from whence she had come, so King Cush had the world famous Hanging Gardens built for her in Babylon. It was built in a square including almost four acres, and consisted of terraces rising one above another with each terrace supported on masonry arches. The gardens rose to a height of more than a seven story building, a real man-made mountain for his queen. The Hanging Gardens of Babylon were one of the Seven Wonders of the ancient world.

The inhabitants of Babylon were in fear of another great flood such as Noah experienced, and therefore King Cush began to build an enormous high tower, the Tower of Babel, over thirty stories high. Thus if another flood came, the populace could climb this tower and escape from drowning. History shows that this Tower of Babel remained in Babylon for thousands of years in spite of the false statement of Saint Moses in the Bible that the tower and the city of Babylon were not completed. (Genesis 11:4-8)

Religionists denounced the building of the Tower of Babel. They considered this a defiance of God's will. Their view was that if God saw fit to destroy them with a flood, then the people should meekly submit to such destruction and not try to thwart it. We hear similar pratings by some religionists today, who insanely denounce antibiotics when used to cure venereal disease, as a defiance of God's curse on immoral people. However, venereal disease is caused by micro-organisms and not immorality, and therefore endangers all people, regardless of their moral state, and this fact such stupid religionists ignore.

The Bible gives us the viewpoint of the Israelite saints about the Tower of Babel: "And they (the Babylonians) said, 'Go to, let us build us a city and a tower, whose top may reach unto heaven; and let us make us a name, lest we be scattered abroad upon the face of the whole earth.'"

"And the Lord Jehovah came down to see the city and the tower, which the children of men builded. And the Lord Jehovah said, (How do they know what he said? Were they there?) 'Behold, the people is one, and they have all one language' and this they begin to do; and now nothing will be restrained from them, which they have imagined to do. Go to, let us go down, and there confound their language, that they may not understand one another's speech.'"

"So the Lord Jehovah scattered them abroad from thence upon the face of all the earth: and they left off to build the city." (Genesis 11:4-8) This is a complete saintly Biblical falsehood. The Tower and city of Babylon were finished, and the city still stood even after Jerusalem was destroyed by the Romans over five thousand years later. In Roman times Saint Peter wrote in the Bible about "the church that is at Babylon" (1 Peter 5:13) So this Bible saint contradicts the other Bible saint, although both were supposed to be writing under inspiration of God. (2 Timothy 3:16, K.J.V.)

THE PROBLEM FACING QUEEN SEMIRAMIS

Unfortunately for Queen Semiramis, her husband King Cush suddenly died. What could she do now? She was faced with the task of ruling the whole country of Babylonia by herself. Yes, she was a very beautiful woman, blonde and voluptuous. She could marry almost any man she wanted. But was that the wisest thing to do? If she married, her throne would go to her new husband and be lost to her own son, and she wanted her son to inherit the throne.

Many of the clergy have denounced Queen Semiramis as being highly sexed and immoral, and there may have been something to that. One account insists that she was able to have sex relations with a stallion. She was apparently of generous dimensions in the essential area. However, no data at hand shows that she actually engaged in sexual intercourse with a stallion. Even today there are millions of women whose vaginas are large enough to accommodate a stallion, but that is usually due to stretching from repeated childbirth. So this statement regarding Queen Semiramis indicates nothing unusual about her, nor does it in itself support the allegation that she was immoral. Nor is it immoral to be highly sexed. This is a matter of heredity, and there are scores of millions of highly sexed women in this world today who are entirely decent.

No, the charge of immorality would have to be based on something more than that. Semiramis was also accused of being promiscuous. This, of course, would put her in a class with Saint Abraham and his wife Saint Sarah. But Semiramis was a widow, and being without a husband put a tremendous strain on her highly sexed nature. Yet again, do you know of many major political rulers in the world today who are strictly monogamous, and who have not enjoyed numerous sex partners in their careers? So while the clergy are loud in their condemnation of Queen Semiramis, we today have many rulers of state who have reputations far worse than hers. According to news reports, U.S. President John F. Kennedy was alleged to have bragged that he had enjoyed sex relations with sixteen hundred different women before entering the presidency. And Kennedy was a devout Roman Catholic churchman. We doubt that Queen Semiramis was as promiscuous as he.

There is no claim here that Queen Semiramis was an Israelite saint, yet she was a Babylonian saint. We write about her because her deceased husband Cush and her son Nimrod are discussed in the Bible, which says: "And Cush begat Nimrod: he began to be a mighty one in the earth. He was a mighty hunter before the Lord Jehovah: wherefore it is said, 'Even as Nimrod the mightier hunter before the Lord.' And the beginning of his kingdom was Babel, and Erech, and Accad, and Calneh, in the land of Shinar. From that land he went forth into Assyria and builded Nineveh, and the city Rehoboth, and Calah. And Rezen between Nineveh and Calah: the same is a great city." (Genesis 10:8-12) Cush and Nimrod were also

Babylonian saints above named in the Bible.

The Israelites are linked to Babylon, because they are descended from Saints Abraham and Sarah, who came out of the area around Babylon on the Persian Gulf, and who migrated westward along the Euphrates river until they reached the shores of the Mediterranean Sea and the land of the Canaanites. Much of the religion of the Israelites and the commandments were taken from the Babylonians, although Moses gives no credit to Babylon for that. So we see the close link between the Israelites and the Babylonians, and it is not surprising that Cush and Nimrod and Babylon are discussed in the Bible. Also the sexual morality of the Israelites and the Babylonians is not much different.

Bishop Alexander Hislop, in his book, "The Two Babylons," gives an exhaustive account of affairs in ancient Babylon. Because the bishop supports the religion of the Israelites, he therefore denounces Queen Semiramis and the Babylonian religion. He writes: "The Chaldean Mysteries can be traced up to the days of Semiramis, who lived only a few centuries after the flood, and who is known to have impressed upon them the image of her own depraved and polluted mind. That beautiful but abandoned queen of Babylon was not only herself a paragon on unbridled lust and licentiousness, but in the mysteries which she had a chief hand in forming, she was worshipped as Rhea, the great 'Mother' of the gods." Yet the bishop, like most religionists of the Judeo-Christian superstition, never denounces the licentiousness of Abraham and Sarah and other Israelite saints.

Bishop Hislop continues: "It was from her son, however, that she derived all her glory and her claims to deification. That son, though represented as a child in his mother's arms, was a person of great stature and immense bodily powers, as well as most fascinating manners."

"Now, this Ninus, or 'Son,' borne in the arms of the Babylonian Madonna, is so described as very clearly to identify him with Nimrod. 'Ninus, king of the Assyrians,' says Trogus Pompeius, epitomized by Justin, 'first of all changed the contented moderation of the ancient manners, incited by a new passion, the desire of conquest. He was the first who carried on war against his neighbors, and he conquered all nations from Assyria to Lybia, as they were yet unacquainted with the arts of war.' This account points directly to Nimrod, and can apply to no other. The account of Diodorus Siculus (the historian who wrote in the days of Julius Caesar) entirely agrees with it, and adds another trait that goes still further to determine the identity. That account is as follows; 'Ninus, the most ancient of the Assyrian kings mentioned in history, performed great actions.

Being naturally of a warlike disposition, and ambitious of glory that results from valor, he armed a considerable number of young men that were brave and vigorous like himself, trained them up a long time in laborious exercises and hardships, and by that means accustomed them to bear the fatigues of war, and to face dangers with intrepidity.' As Diodorus makes Ninus 'the most ancient of the Assyrian kings,' and represents him as beginning those wars which raised his power to an extraordinary height by bringing the people of Babylonia under subjection to him."

"In this respect, then, the story of Ninus and of Nimrod exactly harmonize. The way, too, in which Ninus gained his power is the very way in which Nimrod erected his. There can be no doubt that it was by inuring his followers to the toils and dangers of the chase, that he gradually formed them to the use of arms, and so prepared them for aiding him in establishing his dominions; just as Ninus, by training his companions for a long time 'in laborious exercises and hardships,' qualified them for making him the first of the Assyrian kings."

"Thus, then, Nimrod, or Ninus, was the builder of Nineveh; and the origin of the name of that city as 'the habitation of Ninus,' is accounted for, and light is thereby at the same time, cast on the fact that the name of the chief part of the ruins of Ninevah is Nimrod at this day."

"Now, assuming that Ninus is Nimrod, the way in which that assumption explains what is otherwise inexplicable in the statements of ancient history greatly confirms the truth of that assumption itself. Ninus is said to have been the son of Belus or Bel, and Bel is said to have been the founder of Babylon. If Ninus was in reality the first king of Babylon, how could Belus or Bel, his father, be said to be the founder of it? Both might very well be, as will appear if we consider who was Bel, and what we can trace of his doings. If Ninus was Nimrod, who was the historical Bel? He must have been Cush; for 'Cush begat Nimrod.'" (Genesis 10:8)

"This lamented one, exhibited and adored as a little child in his mother's arms, seems, in point of fact, to have been the husband of Semiramis, whose name, Ninus, by which he is commonly known in classical history, literally signified 'the Son.' As Semiramis, the wife, was worshipped as Rhea, whose grand distinguishing character was that of the great goddess 'Mother,' the conjunction with her of her husband, under the name of Ninus, or 'The son,' was sufficient to originate the peculiar worship of the 'Mother and Son,' so extensively diffused among the nations of antiquity; and this, no doubt, is the explanation of the fact which has so much puzzled the inquirers into ancient history, that Ninus is sometimes called the husband, and sometimes the son of Semiramis." So writes

Bishop Hislop.

THE QUEEN DECIDES TO MARRY

Heretofore we noted the problem facing Queen Semiramis. Her husband, King Cush, had suddenly died. Because of her voluptuous blonde beauty she could easily marry, but this caused a problem. She had a tall, handsome son to whom she wanted to leave the throne of Babylonia. If she married, the throne would pass to her new husband, and her son Nimrod would be pushed aside, and might even be killed. She didn't feel able to rule Babylonia by herself. What then should she do?

The answer was obvious. She would have to marry her son Nimrod. And this is exactly what Queen Semiramis did, thus preserving the throne of Babylonia for her son.

The clergy of today rise up in denunciation of Semiramis for this act. Yes, it was incestuous. No, our laws would not permit such incest today. But in those early times incestuous marriages were quite common. We remember the incestuous marriage of Saint Abraham and his sister Saint Sarah, which none of the clergy ever mentions, let alone condemns. We remember that Moses was born of an incestuous marriage. So to be consistent why do not the religious clergy damn Abraham and Sarah, and Moses' parents? The obvious answer is, these are heroes of their Judeo-Christian faith.

However, this event in Babylon explains why the puzzling inscriptions on the monuments of ancient Nineveh refer to Ninus or Nimrod sometimes as the son of Queen Semiramis, and sometimes as her husband. He was both.

After their marriage, Nimrod launched a military campaign to subjugate the surrounding peoples, all the way over to distant Libya and Assyria. But as a result of Nimrod's wars, during which his army killed many people, he made thousands of deadly enemies among his new subjects. No, these conquered peoples did not have the military strength yet to overthrow Nimrod's rule. But Nimrod was only one man. And it only takes a dagger thrust to kill one man.

So it was that a number of Nimrod's enemies ganged together, came to Babylon, and killed Nimrod themselves. In their fury, they literally tore his body to pieces. Nimrod's wife and mother, Semiramis, had to flee from Babylon to save herself. Thus ended the life of one of the earliest politicians and military heroes that oppressed humanity.

Nimrod's object in his military ventures was subjugation, and not annihilation. He was therefore not as vicious a criminal as Saint Moses or Joshua or David, who carried on wars of annihilation and genocide against other peoples in order to steal their lands and houses and wealth; and these holy Jewish saints murdered wholesale millions of men, women and children, and raped all the women that they captured. (We will examine these saintly crimes shortly.)

Therefore in comparing the Babylonian Nimrod with Saint Moses, Saint Joshua, and Saint David, history shows that Nimrod was far more saintly than they.

CHAPTER IX.   WHAT SAINT REUBEN DID TO HIS
                FATHER'S PRETTY MISTRESS

In the previous chapters we digressed temporarily to examine the
saintly tales of Adam and Eve and Noah. Now we return to the time
immediately following the deaths of Abraham and Sarah, which occurred
much later than the days of Noah.

Several generations passed following the deaths of Saint Abraham
and Saint Sarah. Their son Isaac married Rebecca, and they produced two
sons, Esau and Jacob. Esau was the elder, who married native Palestinian
girls and also one girl descended from Ishmael. Saint Jacob stayed closer
to the family line and married two of his mother's nieces, Rachel and Leah.
In time Jacob had twelve sons, who became the heads of the twelve tribes
of Israel. (Israel was Jacob's other name.) The Israelites were thus named
after their father Israel in an eponymous matter of nomenclature, as were
the Hebrews named after their ancestor or eponym Heber.

The oldest of Israel's sons was named Reuben. Now Saint Reuben
should have been given a wife or a least a concubine by his father, but no
such luck. The old man apparently wanted to keep his son single so he
could get more work out of him, as some parents do. But this plan
backfired, to old man Israel's regret.

The fact that Saint Reuben had neither wife nor concubine did not
diminish Reuben's masculinity one bit. So when he became acquainted with
his father's concubine Bilhah, he of course was strongly attracted to her.
She was undoubtedly his father's youngest concubine, and a very nice
looking woman. And Bilhah, in turn, was strongly attracted to Reuben.

Old man Israel no longer had the fire of youth in his blood, and
found it difficult to have frequent sexual intercourse with all his wives and
concubines. This compounded the problem, and naturally his women would

miss such connubial attention to no small degree. They became restless and began looking around, and that is how Bilhah noticed Saint Reuben.

With both Bilhah and Reuben lacking sex partners, it was only to be expected that they would be drawn to each other. Eventually their association led to a climax. Literally. Reuben and Bilhah had sexual intercourse together. It was so pleasant, and such a welcome relief to them both, that they repeated the act more than once. As a result, eventually old man Israel discovered it.

The Bible tells us: "And it came to pass, when Israel dwelt in that land, that Reuben went and lay (sexually) with Bilhah his father's concubine: And Israel heard it." (Genesis 35:22, King James Version) Israel apparently was walking past their tent and heard their desperate cries as the thrills reached a climax. He might even have peeked into the tent and seen them inter-twined.

This made Israel furious, but apparently Bilhah did not get pregnant as a result. At least there is no record of such pregnancy in the Bible, and it undoubtedly would have been reported if there had been such. However, Israel never got over his resentment against Reuben, and even mentioned it on his death bed.

As he lay dying, Israel, also called Jacob, spoke to his sons: "And Jacob called unto his sons, and said, 'Gather yourselves together that I may tell you that which shall befall you in the last days. Gather yourselves together and hear, ye sons of Jacob; and hearken unto Israel your father.'"

"'Reuben, thou are my firstborn, my might, and the beginning of my strength, the excellency of dignity, and the excellency of power. Unstable as water, thou shalt not excel; because thou wentest up to thy father's bed; then defiedst thou it; he went up to my couch." (Genesis 40:1-4)

Even on his death bed Israel could not forget his son Reuben's sexual intercourse with one of his concubines.

And so it goes. Reuben became the father of one of the twelve tribes of Israel and is one of the Biblical saints. However, because of this sexual irregularity he is another scandalous Bible saint.

NOW CONSIDER SAINT JUDAH, BROTHER OF REUBEN

Saint Judah was another son of Jacob who became the head of one of the twelve tribes of the nation of Israel. His career was also marred by various sexual indiscretions. We turn to the most notable of these.

Saint Judah married the daughter of a Canaanite and had three sons. Er was the oldest. Then came Onan, and Shelah was the youngest. The Bible tells us: "And it came to pass at that time, that Judah went down from his brethren and turned in at a certain Adullamite, whose name was Hirah. And Judah saw there a daughter of a certain Canaanite, whose name was Shuah. And he took her, and went in unto her (had sexual intercourse with her). And she conceived and bare a son, and he called his name Er. And she conceived again and bare a son, and she called his name Onan. And she yet again conceived and bare a son, and called his name Shelah. And he was at Chezib when she bare him." (Genesis 38:1-5)

When Saint Judah's oldest son Er grew up, he provided Er with a wife. But the marriage didn't last long. The Bible account says: "And Judah took a wife for Er his firstborn, whose name was Tamar. And Er, Judah's firstborn, was wicked in the sight of the Lord Jehovah, and the Lord slew him." (Genesis 38:6,7)

What Er did that annoyed the Jewish God Jehovah, the Bible doesn't say. It couldn't have been adultery or incest or attempted murder, because Saint Abraham had done all these things before, and they were approved by this God. (Genesis 26;5) Maybe Er paid his bills on time, and this angered his God. Anyhow, Er died.

A WEIRD MARRIAGE LAW

This left his wife Tamar a widow. Now the Jews had a peculiar law among them that required the next of kin to her dead husband, to get the widow pregnant and pay the bills to raise up children in the name of his dead relative. This was a silly law that didn't allow the widow to marry another man she liked. She was required to become the wife of her husband's relative whether she wanted to or not. Her new husband was also an unwilling victim of this law. He already had a wife or two and had all he could do to support them and his own children by them: so he didn't want the job of taking on another family in the name of his dead relative. (The Biblical Saint Moses established polygamy. Only the Roman conquest put an end to this Bible law of plural marriages, and that's why the New Testament prohibits polygamy among church officials. They didn't want to get in trouble with the Roman government.)

Here was the unwelcome situation that Saint Tamar now found herself in, being a widow. But she had to follow their idiotic Bible law of Moses, so she went back to Saint Judah and asked for another husband. The Bible account reads: "And Judah said unto Onan, 'Go in unto thy brother's wife (have sex relations with her) and marry her, and raise up seed to thy brother.'" (Genesis 38:8)

Saint Onan was Judah's second oldest son, so he was the number one candidate for this job. And Onan didn't like it. Moses' Bible says: "And Onan knew that the seed (the children he produced) should not be his; and it came to pass, when he went in unto his brother's wife (has sex relations with her) that he spilled it on the ground, lest he should give seed to his brother." (Genesis 38:9) Or in modern phrase, when their sexual intercourse reached its climax, Onan withdrew.

The Bible tells us that this angered the Israelite God. "And the thing which he did displeased the Lord Jehovah. Wherefore he slew him also." (Genesis 38:10) Here Moses' Bible insists that this crazy law was their God's law, and disobedience to this law was one thing their God Jehovah simply would not tolerate. Their Jehovah didn't object to incest, and adultery meant nothing either, or attempted murder, for Abraham received Jehovah's blessing in spite of all such immorality. But violating the widow-marriage custom was simply outrageous; it was worthy of death in the eyes of this Jewish God, his followers said. So Onan dies.

What actually happened, of course, was that Saint Onan was probably overweight and had a heart condition. So when he engaged in this type of kinky sex it was too much of a shock for his state of health. He just had a heart attack and died. But the Hebrew barbarians knew nothing about heart problems. Whenever a person died in odd circumstances it was their God Jehovah who struck him down in punishment for something or other. And here they decided it was punishment for violating this widow-marriage custom.

We wonder if worshippers of Biblical law and Jehovah, ever consider that this law is binding on them too today? And what they do about it? Of course, we know of some male church members who are always ready to accommodate a newly widowed church lady and see that she misses nothing of connubial comforts and entertainments, regardless of whether they are related or not. Undoubtedly this could bring on a divorce, but if the churchman's wife is devout enough she will not object, and life will be sweet for the churchman and the widow lady from then on.

CHAPTER X. WHY THIS HOLY MAN GOT HIS DAUGHTER-IN-LAW PREGNANT

Well, this is not the end of our story here. We're just getting started. So when Onan toppled over dead of a heart attack during sexual intercourse, what did Saint Tamar do? She just got up, dressed, and went back to Judah for husband number three.

But Saint Judah received a jolt when he heard that his second son also died while having sexual intercourse with Tamar. Maybe Saint Tamar was one of those repeater widows you hear about. They kill one man after another somehow. So Saint Judah was reluctant to give Tamar his last son. Moses' Bible continues:

"Then said Judah to Tamar his daughter-in-law, 'Remain a widow at thy father's house, till Shelah my son be grown:' for he said, 'Lest peradventure he die also as his brethren did.' And Tamar went and dwelt in her father's house." (Genesis 38:11)

"And in the process of time the daughter of Shuah, Judah's wife died, and Judah was comforted, and went up unto his sheepshearer to Timnath; he and his friend Hirah the Adullamite. And it was told Tamar, saying, 'Behold, thy father-in-law goeth up to Timnath to sear sheep." (Genesis 38:12,13)

Now the widow Saint Tamar had not been given Judah's last son Shelah to be her husband, as Saint Judah had promised. Shelah was now grown up and ready to be her husband. So Saint Tamar felt cheated, and decided to take matters in her own hands.

Prostitutes in those days used to sit along isolated country roads and do business with whatever men came by. So Saint Tamar decided she would pose as a prostitute on the road that Saint Judah would walk along to get to Timnath.

Moses' Bible tells us: "And she put her widow's garments off from her, and covered her with a veil, and wrapped herself, and sat in an open place which is by the way to Timnath; for she saw that Shelah was grown, and she was not given unto him to wife."

"When Judah saw her, he thought her to be an harlot; because she had covered her face. And he turned unto her by the way, and said, 'Go to, I pray thee, let me come in unto thee.' (For he knew not that she was his daughter-in-law.)"

"And she said, 'What wilt thou give me, that thou mayest come in unto me?' (Genesis 38:14-16)

Well, Saint Judah had nothing with him wherewith he could pay for her services. But he told Tamar that he would send her a kid from his flock.

That was agreeable to Saint Tamar, but she wanted some security to guarantee that he would send her the young goat. She asked Judah to give her his signet ring, staff, and bracelets a pledge for her to hold until the goat arrived. So Saint Judah gave her these items, and then they had sexual intercourse together.

As Moses' Bible says: "And he gave it to her, and came in unto her, and she conceived by him." (Genesis 38:18)

Saint Tamar had got her wish. Judah was legally obligated to provide her with the services of a husband so she could have a child, and now she had achieved her purpose by having sexual intercourse with her father-in-law. This of course would be considered highly irregular and immoral by civilized people, but this is required by the Bible law of Moses.

So after their sexual encounter, Saint Judah went on his way, not realizing he had sex relations with his daughter-in-law. Sex with a prostitute was all right, you know. Perfectly legitimate for men, according to Saint Moses' law. There is not one Bible law that punishes men for having sexual intercourse with harlots. So you see what immorality Bible saints were permitted to indulge in without condemnation.

Moses' Bible tells us what Saint Tamar did next: "And she arose, and went away, and laid by her veil from her, and put on the garments of her widowhood."

"And Judah sent the kid by the hand of his friend the Adullamite, to receive his pledge from the woman's hand; but he found her not. Then he asked the men of that place, saying, 'Where is the harlot that was openly by the wayside?'"

" And they said, 'There was no harlot in this place.' And he returned to Judah and said, 'I cannot find her; and also the men of that place said that there was no harlot in this place.'"

"And Judah said, 'Let her take it to her, lest we be ashamed; behold, I sent this kid, and thou hast not found her.'" (Genesis 38:19-23)

Note Saint Tamar's clever trick. She was not interested in Judah's goat kid. She wanted Saint Judah's signet ring and bracelets and staff. And why she did so, we will soon find out.

Three months passed and Saint Tamar was obviously pregnant to all who knew anything about pregnancy. She was probably bothered with morning sickness and so forth, and even though her figure was not enlarged yet so others could notice, everyone around her could tell she was pregnant. She may even have called attention to her condition.

The Bible tells us: "And it came to pass about three months later, that it was told Judah, saying, 'Tamar thy daughter-in-law hath played the harlot; and also, behold, she is with child by whoredom.'"

"And Judah said, 'Bring her forth, and let her be burnt.'" (Genesis 38:24)

Note the terrible punishment they laid upon prostitutes. Saint Judah ordered Tamar to be burned to death at the stake because she was pregnant and accused of prostitution. This is also the law of Moses. (Leviticus 21:9)

And worse yet, Saint Judah was a customer of prostitutes as this Bible story shows, but he had the hypocritical arrogance to condemn Tamar to death for prostitution. There is not one word of punishment in the Bible for a man who patronizes prostitutes, but Moses' Bible law requires prostitutes to be put to death by burning. Talk about hypocrisy and double dealing. Anyone can see that the Biblical laws were written by men and not by God. If prostitution is to be considered wrong, then certainly the male customer of a prostitute is just as guilty as she is, and should suffer the same punishment.

Saint Tamar knew beforehand that she would be treated unfairly this way, and was ready for her accusers. "When she was brought forth, she sent to her father-in-law (Judah), saying, 'By the man whose these are, am I with child'. And she said, 'Discern, I pray thee, whose these are, the signet, and bracelets, and staff.'" (Genesis 38:25)

Saint Judah was stunned. Here before his whole family Saint Tamar produced his ring, bracelets, and staff that he Judah had given to Tamar when he had sexual intercourse with her, thinking she was a prostitute. Saint Judah was trapped.

"And Judah acknowledged them, and said, 'She hath been more righteous than I; because I gave her not to Shelah my son.'" (Genesis

38:26)

So Saint Tamar escaped being burned to death at the stake as a prostitute. She was lawfully entitled to get pregnant by Saint Judah, according to Moses' Bible.

But here we have a plain statement of the Bible showing that Judah, the saint, was accustomed to have sex relations with prostitutes. His halo is indeed missing, even though he was the father of one of the twelve tribes of the so-called "chosen people" of their God. How holy and pious and scandalous all this is!

CHAPTER XI.   THE SAINT WHO DALLIED WITH HIS
BOSS'S WIFE

The saintly Reuben and saintly Judah we have just considered had another brother, the Biblical Saint Joseph. (The Bible has two Saint Josephs. This is the first one.) All three of these saintly brothers were also brothers of their nine other brothers by Israel their father. Thus all the brothers numbered twelve.

Among white European families it used to be commonplace for one mother to produce twelve children or more. But this never seemed to happen among the Jews. Their women were unable to do that, so Israel had to have two wives and two concubines in order to produce twelve children. Maybe the Israelite men worked their women too hard. But some blamed it on the masturbation that Israelite women practiced, which caused metritis and infertility. At any rate, the maternal capabilities of Israelite women were quite limited.

So now we come to the story of Saint Joseph in the Bible. This was Israel's youngest son, and he was the favorite of his father because he was the baby. This made Joseph's other brothers envious and angry. So one day when Joseph was about seventeen years old and out with his brothers tending sheep, the brothers decided to do away with Joseph. However, the oldest brother, Reuben, intervened, and instead they dropped Saint Joseph down into a shallow well that was dry at that time. (Genesis 37:13-24)

Moses' Bible story continues: "And they sat down to eat bread. And they lifted up their eyes and looked, and behold, a company of Ishmeelites came from Gilead with their camels bearing spicery and balm and myrrh, going to carry it down to Egypt."

"And Judah said unto his brethren, 'What profit is it if we slay our brother and conceal his blood?   Come, and let us sell him to the Ishmeelites, and let not our hand be upon him; for he is our brother and our flesh.' And his brethren were content."

"Then there passed by Midianites, merchantmen; and they drew and lifted up Joseph out of the pit, and sold Joseph to the Ishmeelites for twenty pieces of silver. And they brought Joseph into Egypt." (Genesis 37:25-28)

Selling people into slavery was a routine form of commerce among the Jews and their neighboring nations. Moses' Bible has no laws against slavery. Saint Moses in fact approved of slavery, and laws governing the slave trade are a part of his "holy" Bible commandments. (Exodus 21:1-11; Leviticus 25:44-46)

So Saint Joseph became a slave. The Bible tale continues: "And Joseph was brought down to Egypt. And Potiphar, an officer of Pharaoh, captain of the guard, an Egyptian, bought him of the hands of the Ishmeelites which had brought him down thither." (Genesis 39:1)

Saint Joseph proved to be a good slave and a capable young man, so over the years Potiphar gradually placed all of his affairs under Joseph's management. Joseph was diligent in his work, and so Potiphar's business affairs prospered.

Because he had complete control of Captain Potiphar's business, Joseph was frequently in Potiphar's home, and there he met the beautiful wife of his boss. While Potiphar was away tending to Pharaoh's business, Saint Joseph was in Potiphar's house taking care of his boss's wife.

Well one thing led to another and their relationship as it usually does when man and woman are involved. Hand holding led to kisses, and kisses to tight embraces, and finally they got down to the basic question. Mrs. Potiphar suggested that she and Joseph should have sex relations together. As Moses' Bible story puts it: "And it came to pass after these things that his master's wife cast her eyes upon Joseph, and she said, 'Lie with me (sexually).'" (Genesis 39:7)

According to Moses' Bible story, Saint Joseph apparently was nobody's fool when it came to sex or anything else. At least not this time. He knew that if he had sexual intercourse with Mrs. Potiphar once, they'd have sex together many times. And it would only be a matter of time before she would get pregnant by him, and she would have a baby with Hebrew features like his own, and then they'd be in real trouble. There was no way Mrs. Potiphar could claim that a baby with Hebrew features, an Israelite bent nose and all, was her Egyptian husband's child. So Joseph tried to persuade Mrs. Potiphar that friendship was one thing, but sex relations together would get them both in trouble.

Yes, the Egyptians had invented condoms made of linen, and they worked most of the time. But contraceptives then as now are never one-hundred percent dependable, and Saint Joseph was not willing to gamble.

But according to the Bible story Mrs. Potiphar wouldn't take no for an answer. Their affair had got beyond the reasoning stage with her, and now was an emotional and sexual one. Her desire had become uncontrollable and she had to have sex relations with Joseph. She begged and pleaded, the Bible says, but Joseph remained adamant. He insisted that sex relations would only result in disaster.

Well, in time her love for Joseph turned to anger. All her beauty and desirability as a sex partner were to no avail in persuading Joseph, so now it became a matter of wounded pride. She had thought her charms to be irresistible, and here was this common foreign slave refusing her beauty. She was enraged, and planned Joseph's destruction. If she couldn't have him, no woman would.

Moses' Bible tale continues: "And it came to pass about this time that Joseph went into the house to do his business, and there was none of the men of the house were within. And she caught him by his garment, saying, 'Lie with me (sexually).'"

"And he left the garment in her hand, and fled, and got him out. And it came to pass, when she saw that he had left his garment in her hand, and was fled forth; that she called unto the men of her house and spake unto them, saying, 'See, he (Potiphar) hath brought in an Hebrew unto us to mock us. He came in unto me to lie (sexually) with me, and I cried with a loud voice. And it came to pass, when he heard that I lifted up my voice and cried, that he left his garment with me and fled, and got him out.' And she laid up his garment by her until his lord (Potiphar) came home." (Genesis 39:11-16)

When Captain Potiphar came home that evening his wife told him the same tale. Of course, Potiphar became angry. "And Joseph's master took him and put him into the prison, a place where the king's prisoners were bound. And he was there in prison." (Genesis 39:20)

At this point we can only guess whose story should be believed. Moses' Bible, which is the Jewish book of history and nationalistic propaganda, accuses Potiphar's wife of making a false accusation against Joseph. However, we have to remember Joseph's own brothers, Reuben and Judah. They were sex offenders too. Under these circumstances we might be justified in believing Mrs. Potiphar's accusation that Joseph had attempted to rape her. Perhaps Saint Joseph was a would-be rapist. Rape was considered lawful by Moses' Bible. Joseph was single and apparently had no outlet for his sex drive. His brother Saint Reuben under such circumstances had seduced his father's mistress. And Saint Judah, after being widowed, was a patron of prostitutes. Might not Saint Joseph also step over the line to satisfy his sexual appetite? He might very well have tried to rape Mrs. Potiphar, and damaged his saintly halo.

In any event, Saint Joseph now lay in a prison cell. While he was there, two of his fellow inmates had dreams, and Joseph undertook to interpret their dreams, as luck would have it, Joseph interpreted their dreams correctly. One of the men was pardoned by Pharaoh, and the other was executed in fulfillment of the interpretation Joseph had given them.

THEN THE PRISON DOORS OPENED

Two years passed and Joseph still lay in prison. Then unexpectedly the prison doors clanged and Saint Joseph was hauled out and taken before Pharaoh. Was he too now to be tried and executed?

But Pharaoh had two dreams which none of his advisors could interpret for him. Then Pharaoh was told of Joseph in prison who had interpreted dreams correctly, so Joseph was called into Pharaoh's presence.

Pharaoh related his dreams to Joseph and Joseph gave him his interpretation. Saint Joseph told Pharaoh that seven prosperous years were coming with good crops, and this would be followed by seven years of dire famine. Joseph therefore advised Pharaoh to lay up grain in the prosperous years, so Egypt could survive the famine.

Thereupon Pharaoh met with his councilors and they decided that it wouldn't hurt to follow Joseph's interpretation of the dreams. Saving grain would hardly damage the nation even if Joseph's interpretation might prove wrong. So a twenty-percent tax was levied on the crops. And just so the blame would fall on the right shoulders if the famine didn't arrive as predicted, Joseph was put in charge of collecting this heavy tax on all the crops. He became prime minister of Egypt, with all the elaborate perquisites pertaining to that position. Moses' Bible tale says:

"And Pharaoh said unto Joseph, 'See, I have set thee over all the land of Egypt.' And Pharaoh took off his ring from his hand, and put it upon Joseph's hand, and arrayed him in vestures of fine linen, and put a gold chain about his neck. And he made him to ride in the second chariot which he had. And they cried before him, "Bow the knee!' And he made him ruler over all the land of Egypt." (Genesis 41;41-43)

Well, you can imagine what all the young single ladies thought of this. Here was Joseph, the new prime minister of Egypt, a young and handsome bachelor. What a catch for some lucky girl! So every eligible lady in the country set out to capture Joseph, with every scheme and artifice known to the female of the species.

Saint Joseph had a marvelous time with all these girls, we may be sure. At the royal grand balls, and in private rendezvous he received the attention every young man hopes and dreams of. But the stratagems of the young ladies were not to be taken lightly. They meant business, and eventually Joseph was caught in their web. Asenath was the young lady who eventually trapped him. She was the daughter of the priest of On.

Moses' Bible doesn't give all the details, but it does say that Pharaoh "gave him (Joseph) to wife Asenath, the daughter of Potipherah, priest of On." (Genesis 41;45) We would imagine that under ordinary circumstances Joseph could have chosen his own wife. However, -- and probably of necessity -- Pharaoh required Joseph to marry this particular young lady. Pharaoh didn't want any scandal to be attached to his capable prime minister. He must have known why Joseph had been in prison. So he ordered Saint Joseph to marry this particular girl, probably on complaint of her father that Joseph had got her pregnant. Otherwise, Joseph would most likely have been permitted to select whatever wife he might choose.

So by royal decree Saint Joseph escaped being involved in another sex scandal, which would have certainly been one too many. However, due to Joseph's entanglement with his former boss's wife, which landed him in prison for attempted rape; and now his forced wedding (shotgun wedding) to Asenath, this leaves Joseph's saintly halo somewhat tarnished and not a little bent, like those of Saint Joseph's other sexy brothers.

CHAPTER XII. THE HOLY SAINT WHO WAS BORN OF INCEST

Now we come to one of the greatest and holiest of saints in the Bible, namely dishonor Moses. Moses is the saint that climbed on top of a mountain in the desert near Egypt, and afterwards told everybody he had talked to God "face to face as a man speaketh unto his friend" (Exodus 33:11) even though just below that on the page God is quoted as saying to Moses: "Thou canst not see my face; for there shall no man see me and live." (Exodus 33:20) Moses was so addled on hasheesh he couldn't keep his stories straight. On the mountain Moses claimed he received a lot of laws from the Almighty, including the Ten Commandments.

Saint Moses' father was named Amram. This Amram married his own aunt, and his aunt bore him two sons: Moses and Aaron. The Bible says: "And Amram took him Jochebed his father's sister to wife; and she bare him Aaron and Moses." (Exodus 6:20) So Saint Moses and Saint Aaron were born of an incestuous relationship. This is quite in line with Moses' later career. Scandalous.

Moses was an Israelite that was born in Egypt after the time of Joseph. Several centuries later, in fact. All these years since Joseph the Jews had lived in Egypt, as they had earlier moved there during the great famine of that time on that part of the Mediterranean coast. Eventually when the Israelites multiplied greatly the Egyptians put them into slavery, and required them to make brick and work in the fields.

Along about this time Saint Moses was born, and was adopted by an Egyptian princess and raised as her son. As he grew older he attended the Egyptian college and was instructed in all the higher learning of the Egyptians, as was befitting a son of the princess. (Acts 7:20-22)

One day while Saint Moses was visiting among the Hebrews, he saw a slave driver whipping one of the Israelite workers. This enraged Moses who struck down the Egyptian and killed him. Immediately a murder warrant was issued for Moses' arrest, so Moses was forced to flee from Egypt. He took refuge in the desert among the Midianites, and married one of their women. (Exodus 2:11-21)

Now committing murder was hardly proper conduct for a saint, but when you learn of all the other things that Moses did you will realize that this was probably the least of his sins. His halo was already absent.

Because he was wanted for murder in Egypt, Moses had to remain in Midian for many years. He had to stay there, in fact, until Pharaoh and his officers had died and Moses' crime was forgotten. Then his brother Aaron met Moses at their secret rendezvous in the desert, and Saint Moses learned that it was safe for him to return to his own people in Egypt. So he took his wife and child and returned to the Israelites.

Out in the desert Moses had brooded about the slavery of the Israelites in Egypt. He sought to find some way to get his people out of their plight. Now, returning to Egypt, he offered himself as spokesman for his people. He was acquainted with the royal court of Egypt due to his early upbringing, and going before Pharaoh to plead for his people held no terror for him.

The Egyptians were worried about the rapid multiplication of the Israelites. There were more Jews then in Egypt than there were Egyptians. Pharaoh told his people, "Behold, the people of the children of Israel are more and mightier than we." (Exodus 1:9) Pharaoh sought to find a way to stop the increase in the numbers of Israelites.

At first the Jews were put to hard work making brick, but still their numbers multiplied. Then Pharaoh ordered the midwives to kill all male children that were born to the Hebrews. This failed as the midwives did not cooperate with the wishes of the Egyptians. Finally, Pharaoh commanded that all male children born to the Israelites must be cast into the Nile river to drown.

Times were tough for the Israelites, so Saint Moses went before Pharaoh with the complaints of his people.

According to the Bible tale, the Egyptians refused to let the Jews leave Egypt. However, this is unreasonable in light of the facts. The Egyptians were afraid of the Jews who out numbered them. Naturally they would have been delighted if the Israelites would leave their country. (Exodus 1:9,10)

What Saint Moses was undoubtedly trying to do was to persuade Pharaoh to ease up on the hard labor he required of the Jews. They were not anxious to leave Egypt. The Nile delta was by far the best cattle grazing land in that part of the world, and the Israelites were unwilling to leave it. Their cattle thrived there, and the Jews multiplied and grew rich. Even after the Hebrews left Egypt later on, they longed to return. (Numbers 14:4)

The only insect in the ointment was the heavy burden of labor required of them by Pharaoh, and the killing of their infant boys. This is therefore what Saint Moses was trying to persuade Pharaoh to ease. If he could do that, all would be well for the Israelites. These heavy tasks had undoubtedly been levied by Pharaoh to encourage the Jews to leave the country.

However, when Pharaoh refused to ease their burdens, what could Moses tell his people? That he was a failure? No political leader wants to do that; and political leader Moses was. He was acting as the head of the Israelite nation. So, rather than admit he was a failure, he turned the story around and claimed that Pharaoh refused to let the Jews leave Egypt.

THE DIME-STORE MAGICIAN WHO BECAME DICTATOR

Next in his bag of tricks, Moses persuaded his people that now he would perform a series of plagues upon the Egyptians which would force Pharaoh to let the Israelites leave Egypt. This setting up a straw man and then knocking him down is an old trick among politicians to divert their followers from seeing the facts. There was a wet winter that year in Egypt, so Saint Moses' so-called miracles were hinged on this weather pattern.

Consider now the so-called "first plague" upon the Egyptians that Saint Moses claimed God performed through him. Moses' Bible tells us: "And he lifted up the rod and smote the waters that were in the river, in the sight of Pharaoh, and in the sight of his servants; and all the waters that were in the river were turned to blood." (Exodus 7:20) Of Course, the water wasn't really blood. It was turned red by the mud that flowed down the river, churned up by the heavy rains of that wet winter. The Colorado River and many other western rivers are likewise "turned to blood" every Spring. But the stupid and ignorant class of people that followed Saint Moses believed it was real blood.

Pharaoh didn't believe the river Nile was turned to blood. His own men also turned the river "to blood." The Bible admits: "And the magicians of Egypt did so with their enchantments." (Exodus 7:22) So Moses' "Miraculous plague" fell flat as far as Pharaoh was concerned, but with the ignorant multitude of Israelites that followed Moses it was accepted as from God.

The next so-called plague Saint Moses pulled was allegedly to bring up hordes of frogs unto the land. "And Aaron stretched out his hand over the waters of Egypt; and the frogs came up and covered the land of Egypt." (Exodus 8:6) Again Aaron acted as Saint Moses' representative by pretending to bring up the frogs. Actually, the frogs would have been there whether Aaron waved his hands or not. Did you ever see a wet Spring that didn't produce a surplus of frogs? There are always plenty of frogs when there are heavy Spring rains, and so it was in this case. But here again Moses took credit for a common natural phenomenon, and his ignorant followers believed it was "God's plague" upon the Egyptians.

Then Moses claimed he brought on a plague of lice, although plenty of lice in Egyptian Africa is hardly a singular occurrence. Moses' Bible says: "Aaron stretched out his hand with his rod, and smote the dust of the earth, and it became lice throughout all the land of Egypt." (Exodus 8:17) Did you ever hear of dust actually turning into lice? Because of this fanciful tale in the Bible, people for centuries believed that dust would become lice. However, in our present day of enlightenment, biologists laugh when the clergy try to persuade them that dust can literally turn into lice. Lice are produced from lice eggs, and not from dust. This is another reason why you never find a scientist believing the "holy" Bible. It is just too much for an educated person to swallow.

Plague number four that Saint Moses is alleged to have brought upon Egypt was swarms of flies. "And there came a grievous swarm of flies into the house of Pharaoh, and into his servants' houses, and into all the land of Egypt. The land was corrupted by reason of the swarm of flies." (Exodus 8:24) However, they had just got through having a horde of frogs in Egypt. Moses' Bible admits: "And the frogs died out of the houses, and out of the villages, and out of the fields. And they gathered them together upon heaps; and the land stank." (Exodus 8:13,14) So this then was the origin of the swarms of flies that covered Egypt. Saint Moses and Saint Aaron had nothing to do with it. You have piles of dead frogs around everywhere and flies will multiply by the millions in short order. But the ignorant boobs that followed Moses knew nothing of this. To them the flies were a plague from God. Of course, anybody would consider that many flies a plague. But Saint Moses revealed himself to be a rascal by claiming he had produced these flies, whereas they were just another natural phenomenon of the circumstances attending a wet Spring.

Next came disease upon the castle as a result of all this pollution in the land, and this was to be expected because of all the rotting dead frogs, and the flies to carry disease germs around. So Moses claimed credit for that too, saying it was another of his plagues.

Plague number six according to Saint Moses was disease attacking people too, and not only cattle. Moses claimed that this was caused by dust he sprinkled in the air. "And they took ashes of the furnace and stood before Pharaoh. And Moses sprinkled it up toward heaven, and it became a boil breaking forth with blains upon man and upon beast." (Exodus 9:10) This is like the plague of lice being created from dust. You tell a doctor of medicine that by tossing a few handfuls of dust in the air you will create boils on a whole nation full of people, and he will probably have you laced up in a straight jacket, a candidate for the funny farm. Again, it is impossible for an educated person to believe all this nonsensical stuff in Moses' Bible. It just doesn't agree with the facts. But the ignorant and superstitious Israelites swallowed Moses' mumbo-jumbo whole. Saint Moses was a great and holy man in their eyes.

And so goes this dreary Biblical recitation of Moses' ten plagues upon Egypt. It's too much to wade through all of it here, but suffice it to say that eventually, at Moses' command, the Hebrews packed up their duds and marched out of Egypt, proudly imagining that their Moses had forced Pharaoh to let them go. In their supposed triumph they forgot that they really didn't want to leave Egypt's lush pasture land, and this is exactly what Moses wanted them to do.

WHOLESALE THEFT

Before the Jews left Egypt Saint Moses told them to borrow jewelry from their Egyptian neighbors. Moses' Bible says: "And the children of Israel did according to the word of Moses. And they borrowed of the Egyptians' jewels of silver, and jewels of gold, and raiment . . . And they spoiled the Egyptians." (Exodus 12:35,36) When the Jews left Egypt they took the Egyptians' jewelry with them and thus robbed the Egyptians.

This of course did not sit well with Pharaoh. When his people complained, he sent the Egyptian army after the Israelites. However, the millions of Hebrews and their cattle had already crossed the marshy ground north of the pasture land of Goshen where they lived. Thus when Pharaoh's army attempted to follow them over the muddy ground their chariots of iron sank in the mire and lost their wheels, and they were unable to overtake the Israelites.

Saint Moses then boasted of this as another great miracle of God, even though it was quite routine and commonplace. Did you ever hear of a car getting stuck in the mud? Of course you have. And we'll bet you didn't think it was a miracle of God either. The marshy ground in Moses' case was at the end of a slough leading to the Red Sea. The water in the shallow slough had diminished so the Israelites could walk through what Moses called the Red Sea. Some sea!

But Moses said it was a miracle. Moses' Bible says: "Then sang Moses and the children of Israel this song unto the Lord Jehovah . . . .Pharaoh's chariots and his host (army) hath he cast into the sea; his chosen captains were also drowned in the Red Sea." (Exodus 15:1,4) Of course, to call this marshy slough the Red Sea is an exaggeration, but it does make the story sound more miraculous, doesn't it?

So by this means the Jews were able to escape from Egypt with the jewelry they had stolen.

But once the Israelites got out into the desert North of Egypt, they began to realize they had left the finest pasture land in that part of the world. Moses' Bible admits: "And the whole congregation of the children of Israel murmured against Moses and Aaron in the wilderness. And the children of Israel said unto them, 'Would to God we had died by the hand of the Lord Jehovah in the land of Egypt, when we sat by the flesh pots, and we did eat bread to the full. For ye have brought us forth into this wilderness to kill this whole assembly with hunger.'" (Exodus 16:2,3) So the life of a politician is not always a bed of roses. Even though Moses had freed the Israelites from rigorous slavery they didn't appreciate it.

However, Saint Moses was capable as a politician so he still had some tricks in his bag. He had lived in this desert before. In fact, he had spent many years there, and he knew how to get along in the desert. A shrub grows there called the Tamarisk, and when bugs bite into the bark of its branches, the sap from the Tamarisk drips down onto the ground to form globes or dried wafers. The sap is full of sugar, and that makes these wafers nourishing food to eat, for both man and beast. So Moses told the Israelites to gather these wafers daily and use them for food. Of course Saint Moses told them this was a miracle of God, thus making the Israelites think that Moses was a holy man. Moses' Bible says: "And when the dew that lay was gone up, behold, upon the face of the wilderness there lay a small round thing, as small as hoar frost on the ground. And when the children of Israel saw it they said one to another, 'It is manna.' For they wist not what it was. And Moses said unto them, 'This is the bread which the Lord Jehovah hath given you to eat.'" (Exodus 16:14,15)

Saint Moses also claimed that the multitude of quail living in the desert were a miraculous supply of food for them. The Bible says: "And it came to pass, that even the quails came up and covered the camp." All these quail lived on the manna too. And so the Israelites had plenty to eat, both of quail and manna. But miracle it most certainly was not.

By these various lies that Saint Moses told the people he managed to gain a solid hold on his job as dictator of the Israelites. He was obviously a capable politician. However, he was not the holy man he claimed to be. But he had been educated in Pharaoh's college and learned the tricks of gaining control of and maintaining rule over the common people. These tricks he used very effectively.

CHAPTER XIII.   THIS SAINT FILCHED THE TEN
                 COMMANDMENTS.

Next Moses decided that he had to issue laws to govern the nation
of Israelites. After all, there were probably over three million people there,
and strife would arise if they had no laws to go by. (Exodus 12:37,38) A
mountain stood in the desert, and Saint Moses led his people to this
mountain. Moses' scheme was to tell the Jews he would climb to the top
of the mountain to talk with God, and God would give him laws to govern
people. (Exodus 19:1-3) This mountain was erupting somewhat at the time
and that made the event even more awesome to the superstitious Hebrews.
Moses' Bible says: "And mount Sinai was altogether on smoke, because
the Lord Jehovah descended upon it in fire; and the smoke thereof ascended
as the smoke of a furnace, and the whole mount guaked greatly." (Exodus
19:18) The Israelites were ignorant of volcanic action and so believed that
God was surely up on top of the mountain making all the smoke and fire.
And laws that Saint Moses would bring down to them they would now obey
diligently since they certainly must be God's laws.

The Bible tells us: "And Moses rose up early in the morning, and
went up unto mount Sinai, as the Lord Jehovah had commanded him, and
took in his hand the two tables of stone. And the Lord Jehovah descended
in the cloud, and stood with him there, and proclaimed the name of the
Lord Jehovah." (Exodus 34:4,5) How do we know that God was on the
mountain with Moses? Because Moses tells us so in the Bible book of
Exodus which he wrote. Nobody else was up on the mountain top with
him. Saint Moses was his own witness, and when Moses the dictator said
that God was up there talking with him, nobody had better disagree. It
would cost him his head.

Just suppose now that the president of the United States would climb up on a mountain, and later come down, claiming that God had spoken to him and given him laws that the people of the United States had to obey. Would you believe him? Would anybody believe him? No. People today aren't that stupid. Instead, the president would be led away quietly to a padded cell in a mental institution while the vice president took over his duties.

But back in Moses' day most of the Jews believed what Saint Moses told them, and those who didn't believe that God was on the mountain with Moses were smart enough to keep their mouths shut. They valued their necks. However, today there are still millions of religious people who devoutly believe Moses' claim that God spoke with him up on the mountain, even though they only have Moses' words in proof of that, and what's more it is said to have happened four thousand years ago making it all the more difficult to prove. How gullible can people be?

We are always told about the Ten Commandments and how God-like and wonderful such laws of Moses are. However, the commandments were not original with Moses. He copied them from the laws of the Babylonians. When Moses was in Pharaoh's college he and his classmates studied Babylonian laws and religion to give them a broad knowledge of what was going on in the world. (Acts 7:21,22) In that college Saint Moses learned the commandments that King Hummarapi of Babylon had inscribed on his great stone monuments three centuries earlier. This sounded like good law to Moses, who copied it and claimed he had received these laws from God on Mount Sinai.

In 1901 the law code of King Hummarapi of Babylonia was discovered carved on a block of black diorite stone nearly eight feet long, lying on the acropolis of Susa in Babylonia. In addition to prohibiting murder and theft and false testimony such as Saint Moses copied onto his rock slab, the Babylonian law gave instructions for proper legal procedure, laws concerning property rights, loans, deposits, debts, and family rights. King Hummarapi's law sought to protect the weak from the powerful. Women as well as men could own and dispose of property, and both had the right to divorce their mates on sufficient grounds. This was different from the law of Moses which allowed only men to obtain a divorce. Monogamy alone was legal in Babylonia, and this also differed from Moses' law, which allowed polygamy. However, Babylonian law did allow concubines under certain restrictions. No religious worship was required by law in Babylonia. This was far superior to the fanaticism and bigotry of Saint Moses and the Jews.

King Hammurapi's inscribed law contained 282 paragraphs. At the top of the monument is a sculpture showing the king receiving this code of Laws from the sun god. This gave Saint Moses the idea of telling the Israelites he had received his laws form the Jewish tribal God Jehovah, even though Moses had copied many of his commandments from Babylonian law.

These facts prove the claim false that civilized laws came only from God through Saint Moses on Mount Sinai. The Babylonian civilization existed for thousands of years before Moses, and was governed by laws superior to those of Israel, as we shall show in later examination of Saint Moses' laws.

Moses also copies his Jewish temple religious ceremonies from rituals carried on in the world-renown Temple of Bel-Meradach in Babylon. In that temple the Babylonians had ceremonies such as the daily morning and evening sacrifice, the sin offering, and meat and drink offerings, the free-will offerings, and the show bread. These were all copied in the religious ceremonies held in Moses' Tabernacle. (Compare Leviticus Chapters 1 through 7 and Chapter 24:5-9; also Exodus 39:36, etc., in the Bible.) But the ignorant Israelite rabble knew nothing of Babylonian laws or religion, and actually believed that all this was given to Moses by God atop Mount Sinai. So it was that Moses the clever politician fooled his followers, and is even highly esteemed by religionists to this day. However, educated people know that Saint Moses' religion was basically nothing but a crude copy of the Babylonian religion which is called pagan.

SAINT MOSES MURDERS RELIGIOUS COMPETITORS

Moses was up on top of the mountain desperately trying to engrave the Ten Commandments on small slabs of stone. But the slabs frequently broke under the blows of his chisel, and it seemed as though he never would get the engraving done. He couldn't carve these commandments on huge stone monuments as King Hammurapi of Babylonia had done, but Saint Moses did the best he could to carve these laws on small tablets of stone. Eventually he was successful, and then descended from the mountain top.

Meanwhile, Saint Moses' long stay on the mountain stirred up rebellion among the Israelites. The Bible tells us: "And when the people saw that Moses delayed to come down out of the mount, the people gathered themselves together under Aaron and said unto him, 'Up, make us gods which shall go before us. For as for this Moses the man that brought us up out of the land of Egypt, we wot not want has become of him.'" (Exodus 32:1)

Well, Aaron hesitated a bit, but he too was not sure what had happened to his bother Moses. Meanwhile, he didn't want to lose control of rulership over the Israelites, so he consented to their request. "And Aaron said unto them, 'Break off the golden earrings which are in the ears of your wives, your sons, and your daughters, and bring them unto me.'"

"And he received them at their hand, and fashioned it with a graving tool, after he had made it a molten calf. And they said, 'These be thy gods, O Israel, which brought thee up out of the land of Egypt.'"

"And when Aaron saw it, he built an altar before it, and Aaron made a proclamation and said, 'Tomorrow is a feast to the Lord Jehovah'"

"And they rose up early on the morrow and offered burnt offerings and brought peace offerings. And the people sat down to eat and to drink, and rose up to play." (Exodus 21:1,2,4-6)

Some have said that the above scripture means that the people indulged in immorality. This is not true. The word "play" in the above text is a translation of the Hebrew word "Tsaw-Khak", which means "to laugh outright in merriment or scorn." In other words they were having fun as at a picnic. People do not "laugh outright" when they are engaging in sexual intercourse, illicit or otherwise. Furthermore, the Bible says they: "rose up to play." People rarely 'rise up' to engage in sexual intercourse either. There is nothing here to imply that the people were doing anything immoral at all.

In the midst of all the celebration Saint Moses came down off the mountain, and when he saw what was going on he was enraged. They set up a new religion of golden calf worship. (Exodus 32:19,20)

Then Moses ordered all the calf worshipers to be killed because they were not following the religion he had set up. This was religious intolerance in the extreme, but this is what Saint Moses teaches in his Bible. In Europe for over 1,000 years the same bloody religious intolerance flourished as Roman Christian followers of Saint Moses persecuted and made war on all who disagreed with them in religious matters. Great numbers of people were burned to death at the stake by the Roman Christian clergy. An army was sent to Germany by the Pope to destroy the followers of the Teutonic God Thor, and later huge armies were sent against the Christian followers of John Huss and Martin Luther, and the Huguenots and others. Judeo-Christian religious persecution and slaughter flourished in Europe for centuries, but finally was overcome by force of arms, bringing freedom of religion and freedom from religion to us today. So now the majority of people reject Christianity, and are not followers at all of the Jewish-Christian religion.

But in Moses' day there were none who could withstand his orders to kill, and three thousand followers of the calf religion were slaughtered. Religious bigotry and intolerance reigned supreme in the name of Jehovah, Moses' God. It was nothing but a holocaust. It was a massacre.

The Bible related: "And he (Moses) said unto them, 'Thus saith the Lord Jehovah God of Israel, "Put every man his sword by his side, and go in and out from gate to gate throughout the camp and slay every man his brother, and every man his companion, and every man his neighbor. And the children of Levi (Moses' tribe) did according to the word of Moses. And there fell of the people that day about three thousand men." (Exodus 32:27,28)

Religious bigotry and murderous religious intolerance are taught by Moses in his Bible. This is contrary to the laws of all civilized nations today. Religious murders are not permitted by today's civilized governments.

There are those who attempt to alibi for Moses' action here in killing those of differing religious belief. These say that the people he killed were indulging in immorality. However, there is not one word in the Bible indicating that they engaged in any immoral acts whatsoever. It is true that the Bible states that the worshippers of the calf were naked, but this is because Aaron had ordered them to be naked. It was not their desire to be naked. Note the Bible words: "And . . . Moses saw that the people were naked (for Aaron had made them naked)." (Exodus 32:25) Aaron was responsible for their nakedness. However, nakedness per se is not immoral, or we'd all be jailed at birth. There is not one word about immorality mentioned in the Bible account of this event. So the claim that Saint Moses was stamping out immorality by killing all these thousands of people is a complete lie, made for the purpose of justifying religious intolerance and murder.

Note also that even though Saint Aaron was guilty of making the golden calf for the Israelites, and Aaron was also responsible for causing them to be naked, Saint Moses did not order Aaron killed. Why? Aaron was Moses' brother, so he was let off scot-free even though he was a chief promoter of the calf religion. This shows the complete dishonesty of Saint Moses. If Moses had indeed been evenhanded he would have put his brother Aaron to death with the other calf worshippers; for he would certainly have held Aaron guilty also.

MOSES ENFORCES RELIGIOUS INTOLERANCE

Saint Moses wrote in the Bible: "He that sacrificeth to any God, save unto the Lord Jehovah only, he shall be utterly destroyed." (Exodus 22:20) Saint Moses ordered people to be put to death if they followed any religion but his Bible religion. This is part of the much vaunted "Judeo-Christian ethic." It is the height of blood bigotry. If Moses were in the United States today and attempted to enforce his Bible law, he would be executed for murder.

The 3,000 calf worshippers that Saint Moses murdered at Mt. Sinai were Israelites. But Moses was just as intolerant of the religions of foreigners. The Bible says: "But thus shall ye deal with them (the non-Jews); ye shall destroy their altars and break down their images, and cut down their groves, and burn their graven images with fire." (Deuteronomy 7:5)

But Saint Moses didn't stop there. He not only wanted to destroy the images of other people's religions, but to destroy the worshippers themselves. His Bible commands: "And thou shalt destroy all the people which the Lord Jehovah thy God shall deliver thee; thine eye shall have no pity upon them; neither shalt thou serve their Gods for that will be a snare unto thee." (Deuteronomy 7:16)

Those who follow the Bible teachings of Saint Moses have learned such bigotry well. The history of European Christian religious wars shows over sixty millions of people were slaughtered or burned to death at the stake as a result of this Bible teaching of Moses.

The European religious wars started with an attack on the Christian followers of John Huss, a Roman Catholic priest and rector of the Prague, Czechoslovakia, university. Huss disagreed with the Roman Catholic Pope on matters of Christian doctrine. The Pope insisted that he conform to the teachings of the Roman church. Huss refused, and so was burned to death at the stake in 1415 A.D.

Then Huss's Christian followers, including many of the nobility, broke with Rome. At this, the Christian Roman Pope sent the Austrian army against them. For many years the Christian followers of Huss were successful in their war with the papal army, but in the end they were defeated. Multitudes of Christian saints died on both sides.

In all this the Pope of Rome claimed to be the head of the church, and also the government. Moses, the founder of the Bible religion, was both head of the state, and also the head of their religion. As such Saint Moses had put to death all who disagreed with him on matters of religion; the Christian Roman Pope followed the Biblical Moses' example and did likewise. It was Moses' fault that Roman Catholicism was led into such bloody bigotry.

On the other hand, the Christian followers of Huss, and the other Protestants, rejected the claim that the Pope was the head of the church. The protestants said that the only head of the church was Jesus Christ, and quoted the words of Jesus: "for one is your Master, even Christ; and all ye are brethren." (Matthew 23:8) And so the battle was joined, with each side claiming Gods authority.

The defeat of the Czechoslovakin followers of John Huss was not the end of the rebellion against the Christian Roman Pope. Some 130 years later the Huguenots, a group of Christians in France who had disagreed with the Christian Roman Pope on religious matters, were attacked by the Pope's Christian followers. A series of wars followed in France, and thousands of Christians were killed on both sides.

In the year 1517 a Roman Catholic priest in Germany named Martin Luther broke with the Catholic Pope of Rome over various religious doctrines and practices. Luther was particularly outraged at the Pope's sale of indulgences to commit sin. The Pope had entrusted the sale of these indulgences for forgiveness to John Tetzel, a German Dominican, in order to raise money for building the church of St. Peter's at Rome. Luther also attacked not only the abuses of the papacy, but its claim of supremacy. This pleased many German princes who were tired of papal meddling in German affairs.

Multitudes of Christians were killed on both sides. The land of Germany was devastated by the battles which raged back and forth over that unfortunate country. Then the king of Spain sent an army to assist the Pope's Austrian army, but the Swedish army joined the French in defeating Spain. This conflict, known as the Thirty Years War, ended in 1648 as a victory for the Protestant Lutheran Christians, who won the right to practice their form of Christianity without interference by the Roman Catholic Christians. Thus in a sea of blood they earned the right to freedom of religion, speech, and press which we all enjoy to this day.

When Martin Luther broke with the Pope of Rome over Christian doctrinal differences, King Henry VIII of Britain rushed to the Pope's defense. Henry fancied himself to be a great Bible scholar and theologian, and wrote a book on the sacraments in an attempt to refute Luther's statement. For this effort the Pope rewarded Henry with his title, "Defender of the Faith," I.E. the Roman Catholic faith. Oddly enough, British rulers still cling to this title although they are no longer Catholic.

Meanwhile, King Henry VIII, married six different women, all of whom he divorced except two whom he beheaded on the pretext of infidelity, and his last wife who fortunately for her, outlived him. Anne Boleyn, the wife whose head King Henry VIII chopped off with an axe first, was accused of having sexual intercourse with her brother and four other gentlemen, but did she become pregnant and bear a child that was obviously not Henry's? Either they had better contraceptives in those days then we have now, or the whole accusation was a lie and fraud. No, Anne was not sterile. She was the mother of a daughter who later became Queen Elizabeth I. Her daughter was two years old when Mama Anne's head was chopped off by the great King Henry VIII.

Incidentally, Anne Boleyn had six fingers on one hand, (and for this reason some said she was a witch), and six toes on one foot, and an extra nipple on her chest. And her daughter, Queen Elizabeth I of Britain, had deformed genitalia and so could never marry, but became England's "Virgin Queen" after whom the U.S. state of Virginia was named. (Were these deformities the real reason for the execution of Anne Boleyn by her husband King Henry VIII?) Certainly Henry should have noticed the six fingers on Anne's hand before he married her. Or did Henry also have six fingers on each hand and thought this was normal?

The next wife whose head was chopped off by King Henry was Catherine Howard. She was accused of having sex relations with two men prior to her marriage with King Henry. (Oh, come on! That doesn't count!) But King Henry VIII chopped her head off with an axe anyway, since he was looking for an excuse to do just that.

Here was this big, brave and saintly King Henry VIII of England killing women right and left. Some men are like that. They're such cowards they don't dare to fight men; they fight women instead. And Henry spent his lifetime fighting with women. This reminds one of Saint Moses, another queer duck, who ordered his Jewish army to fight and murder thousands of women and children. How brave, how manly, how saintly all this was! King Henry VIII followed Moses' Bible religion which is heavily biased against women.

The Roman Pope opposed Henry's scandalous behavior, so the king broke off relations with the Pope and set himself up as the head of the Church of England. Thus Britain joined the revolt against Rome, not because of honest differences in religious interpretations, but because of the immorality of King Henry VIII.

Later, during the reign of Henry's daughter, Queen Elizabeth I, the Spanish king sent his huge armada of ships to attack Britain at the behest of the Roman Christian Pope. This Spanish armada was made up of 132 ships carrying 20,000 soldiers, and 8,000 sailors, which were to be followed by an additional 100,000 more soldiers.

In all its history England had not been able to defeat any invading force. In the days before Christ, Julius Caesar had invaded and conquered Britain with his Roman army. The Romans ruled England for 465 years. Then the Roman army was suddenly withdrawn because the German army under Aleric was sacking Rome but the Romans had invaded Germany earlier, so turnabout was fair play.

Nest the Saxons and Jutes conquered Britain and put their kings on the British throne. After that the Danes of little Denmark invaded and ruled Britain. They were followed by the Norman French, whose kings ruled Britain after their invasion victory at the Battle of Hastings.

Now came this mighty Spanish armada with its landing force of soldiers, and the English would certainly have been invaded and defeated again, since they had always been one of the weaker nations in Europe militarily. Every nation that had ever attempted to invade England had succeeded. However, luckily for the British, a tremendous hurricane struck and destroyed the Spanish armada. So England was saved from being conquered by Spain and remained independent of Papal Rome.

All these countries that separated from Roman Christianity caused a great financial loss to Rome. It is no wonder that the papacy fought so hard to hold back from tide of rebellion.

Then in France came the final blow. At the time of the American Revolution against Britain, France also had its own revolution. Neither of these revolutions were conflicts between Christian sects. Instead, the French revolution was basically an economic struggle of the impoverished people against a wealthy and unsympathetic royalty and nobility. Unlike the American revolution which had to draft men into the army to force them to fight, the French people rose up en masse and slaughtered supporters of the royalty with picks and shovels. As multitudes of royalty and nobility died on the guillotines, so also large numbers of Christian Roman Catholic priests died the same way.

At this time Napoleon Bonaparte, a French general, came to the fore. Napoleon was not interested in Christian religious differences. He was, instead, a manifestation of the anti-clerical, anti-pope thinking of the French revolutionists who blamed the clergy and Pope for not speaking out against the misconduct of the king of France. Napoleon marched his armies all over Europe, conquering country after country. However when he invaded Germany with his French army he laid the groundwork for future wars in Europe. Napoleon had committed aggression against his neighbor Germany, and this aggression France would many times regret in the future years.

At the same time Napoleon removed kings who had been placed on their thrones by the Christian Roman Pope, as a part of the Pope's "Holy Roman Empire." By Napoleon's action the Holy Roman Empire came to an end. Then to top it off, Napoleon took the Christian Roman Pope Pous VI, captive and hauled him back to France as a prisoner, where the Christian Pope died at Valence in 1799.

Thus all the world learned that neither the Christian Roman Pope nor the Judeo-Christianity are supported by an almighty god, and that Jewish-Christianity is merely another religion, no better than other religions, but infinitely worse than most.

Finally Napoleon was defeated by the German Army of 121,000 men under General Gerhard von Blucher, a German prince, assisted by a smaller international army under British General Wellington of 94,000 Germans, Belgians, Dutch and British. In some American school books the British under Wellington are credited with defeating Napoleon, but this is pure fiction. The final battle took place at Waterloo village, near Brussels, Belgium. After Napoleon's defeat the German army pursued the fleeing French all night, and the Germans under General von Blucher occupied Paris soon afterward. If Napoleon had not made the mistake of invading Germany he would have lasted longer. France again attacked Germany in 1870, which cemented hatred between the two nations.

CHRISTIANITY A DISASTER TO EUROPE

Most of the wars mentioned above were the largest of the military conflicts caused by strife between Christian sects. In addition there were numerous smaller wars and battles between Christians. The murderous bloody religious bigotry taught by Saint Moses in his Bible brought centuries of suffering and disaster to the people of Europe, and over sixty million violent deaths.

Unfortunately these religious wars caused unbelievers to suffer along with the Christians. Religious political leaders drafted many men into their armies who were not in the least interested in religious quarrels. Multitudes of non-religious people died in these wars. Millions upon millions of people today who reject the Jewish-Christian religion do so because of the bloody nature of this savage and barbaric and heathenish form of worship.

However, after these wars were over and people won freedom of religion, they also won freedom of speech and press. Scientists no longer had to fear being burned to death at the stake by Roman papal priests if they announced new scientific discoveries. Since the end of the Thirty Years War when the Germans, Swedes and Danes crushed the Pope's army almost all of our scientific discoveries and inventions have been made. The Jewish-Christian religion could no longer hold back human progress. However, Christianity is responsible for delaying the development of modern science and invention for centuries. We are more than 1,000 years behind where we would have been if the Jewish-Christian religion had not infested Europe.

Remarkably enough, the Jews were also widely persecuted by followers of Moses. After they were driven out of Palestine because of their rebellion against the Romans in 70 A.D., the Jews migrated into Europe and there they were persecuted by the Christian clergy who had learned to practice bloody bigotry from the Jewish Bible. So vicious bigotry made the full circle from Saint Moses and the Israelites slaughtering non-Jews in Palestine, to the non-Jews persecuting the Jews in Europe because of the bigotry they had learned from Saint Moses' Bible. So unless the Jews repudiated their own Bible, how could they justifiably complain?

The bigotry and religious intolerance and religious warfare continues on a smaller scale to this day. Even now in Northern Ireland the Christian followers of the Roman Catholic Church and the Christian Protestants are fighting with guns and bombs. It is a bloody religious war inspired by the biblical example of Saint Moses and the Israelites. As Jesus himself warned his followers: "I came not to send peace, but a sword." (Matthew 10:34)

This bloody bigotry is not limited to Northern Ireland, however. Everywhere the Bible is taught, there vicious religious bigotry exists. The author is well acquainted with the case of an ordained minister of one of the leading religious denominations who frequently threatened the life of his son by pointing a loaded gun at his head while screaming curses in a rage. The preacher did this because the son stopped going to his father's church denomination. This preacher was a highly respected man among his church members and in his community, but at home he was a raving religious fanatic imitating Moses. In a recent similar case a Christian preacher actually shot and killed his own son.

In another case a woman married a preacher who was highly regarded by his church members. But at home it was another story. This preacher beat his wife so badly she was confined to a hospital for eight weeks, and as a result lost her baby by a miscarriage. Her preacher husband was another fine religionist fully instructed in the brutality condoned and praised by Saint Moses in his Bible.

As Col. Robert Ingersoll, the former attorney general of Illinois put it: "The real oppressor, enslaver and corrupter of the people is the Bible. That book is the chain that binds, the dungeon that holds the clergy . . . That book fills the world with bigotry, hypocrisy and fear."

President James Madison, fourth president of the United States, also had a negative view of the Bible. President Madison said that Christianity had brought in arrogance and bigotry and persecution of the people by the clergy. Madison was a graduate of Princeton University, a student of theology, a member of the Continental Congress, and one of the founders of the United States of America. He was obviously an infidel.

CHAPTER XIV. A HOLY MAN'S MANY UNHOLY LAWS

Eventually Saint Moses brought the laws down to the Israelites that he said he was going to get from God on top of the mountain. We often hear about the Ten Commandments, but we never hear about the other laws that Moses gave to the Jews. So now we are going to examine these other laws that Saint Moses put out and see how corrupt or senseless they really are.

Let's consider Saint Moses' laws about incest first, since Moses himself was the product of an incestuous marriage. Saint Moses had learned from the Egyptians of the unfortunate results that incestuous marriages often cause when children are born defective. So he wanted to prohibit incest among the Isrealites.

However, he was up against a problem in the case of Saint Abraham and Sarah. All the Isrealites knew that Abraham had married his own sister, and Abraham had been held up before the Israelites as being a righteous man, as the Bible states. (Genesis 26:5; 20:12) So how could Saint Moses condemn such incestuous brother and sister marriages without condemning Abraham and Sarah as immoral?

To overcome this problem, here is what Saint Moses wrote in his laws: "And if a man shall take his sister, his father's daughter or his mother's daughter, and see her nakedness, and she see his nakedness, it is a wicked thing. And they shall be cut off." (Leviticus 20;17) Here we see a typical shyster lawyer's trick. The law here is so worded that it does not directly condemn brother-sister incest. It merely condemns the seeing of each other's nakedness. Therefore this actually does not condemn Abraham for marrying his sister Sarah, because under this law, if they had sexual intercourse in the dark without seeing each other's nakedness, they would be excused from condemnation. Clever, isn't it? Too clever for honest people.

However, numerous churchgoers to this day hide their nakedness from their wives and husbands because of the wording of Moses' law. It is laughable to intelligent people. And for the same reason we see frequent Judeo-Christian crusades against public nudity in theaters and night clubs by fussy religionists.

The case of "righteous Lot," another Biblical saint, presented a difficult problem for Moses. You will remember how "righteous Lot" had sexual intercourse with his two nubile daughters and had children by them, as discussed in a previous chapter of this book. That tale is given in the Bible at Genesis 19:30-38, This also gave Moses a headache, because Lot was considered to be "righteous" by the Jews (see 2 Peter 2:7). How could Moses get around the problem of fathers like Saint Lot having sexual intercourse with their daughters, without condemning Saint Lot as being unrighteous?

The answer is simple. There is no place in the entire Bible where it says: "A father shall not lie(sexually) with any of his daughters." Read it and see. Father and daughter sexual intercourse is not mentioned at all. Seemingly this was too common a practice among the Jews, and Saint Moses was afraid to condemn it lest the Israelite sheiks toss him out of his job as Dictator. But the Bible forbids a mother to copulate her son. (Leviticus 20:11) That's different!

So when the old man jumped into the sheets with one of his daughters and taught her how, that was all right. But when mommy wanted to take off her dress and frolic with one of her boys, that was strictly O-U-T out, according to Moses' Bible. Only men were allowed to entertain themselves with hanky-panky. Women were just there to do the laundry.

ADULTERY AND POLYGAMY

Among the Ten Commandments that Moses gave to the Isrealites he had this commandment: "Thou shalt not commit adultery." (Exodus 20:14) A lot of religious people assume that this condemns all sorts of sexual relationships aside from marriage, but not so. This law against adultery does not prohibit single people from copulating without being married. It solely prohibits married women from having sexual intercourse with anyone but their legal husbands.

"What do you mean?" some religionists will ask. "This commandment also prohibits married men from having sexual intercourse with any woman other than their wives. Not so. Let's remember that polygamy was the Bible law given by Saint Moses to the Israelites. A man could have as many wives as he wished without condemnation. Therefore a married man could have sexual intercourse with as many women other than his wife as he wished, on the grounds of polygamy. He was not restricted in the number of women he might take as wives or as mistresses (concubines). But with women it was a different matter. Polygamy did not permit a woman to have as many husbands as she wished. Therefore a woman was limited by this law on adultery to having sexual intercourse only with her legal husband.

"But that's sexist; that's not fair to women," some will complain. Of course it isn't fair or reasonable. However, the Bible is strictly a sexist book. Men wrote it, and men saw to it that the laws in the Bible favored men and allowed them many opportunities not given to women. A man could copulate with as many women as he might want and not be condemned for adultery, provided the women he had sexual intercourse with were legally unmarried or divorced. Such was the state of affairs under the administration of the Biblical saints.

Polygamy caused great sexual distress among married Israelite women. A woman was permitted to have sexual intercourse solely with her legal husband, even though her husband had many wives. However, a man's ability to have sexual intercourse is limited. According to the findings of many sexual investigations in the United States, the average man is able to have sex relations only three or four times per week as a regular thing. Consequently, when a man had many wives under the Bible law of polygamy, he could not possibly have intercourse with all these wives on a frequent basis. The Israelite saint, King David, had dozens of wives, for example. And his saintly son, King Solomon, had seven hundred wives and three hundred mistresses. It would be years before he could have sex relations even once with each of those women.

At the same time the average woman requires sexual intercourse two or three times per week to keep her from suffering sexual distress, irritation and aggravation. What was she to do when her husband had many wives under the Bible law of polygamy, and therefore she could have sexual intercourse with him only once a month or once a year? She would be in a state of continual sexual distress. As a result, Jewish married women were always looking around for men other than their husbands to satisfy their sexual needs for additional intercourse. The law of polygamy ordained by Moses in his Bible caused a complete sexual and moral disaster.

For this reason one of the Ten Commandments prohibits adultery on pain of death. (Exodus 20:14) Israelite women were desperate, and adultery was commonplace. Therefore saintly King Solomon inveighs against adultery again and again in his book of Proverbs in the Bible. He should. His thousand wives and concubines must have committed adultery against him time and time again, due to lack of sexual intercourse with their excessively married husband saint.

Saint Solomon writes in Proverbs Chapter 5 and Verses 1,3, and 4: "My son, attend unto my wisdom, and bow thine ear to my understanding: For the lips of a strange woman drop as an honeycomb, and her mouth is smoother than oil: But her end is bitter as wormwood." He describes the Israelite women's tactics thus: "So she caught him and kissed him, and with an impudent face said unto him, 'I have peace offerings with me; this day have I paid my vows. Therefore came I forth to meet thee, diligently to seek thy face, and I have found thee. I have decked my bed with coverings of tapestry, with carved works, with fine linen of Egypt. I have perfumed my bed with myrrh, aloes, and cinnamon. Come, let us take our fill of love until the morning: let us solace ourselves with loves. For the goodman is not at home, he is gone a long journey.'" (Proverbs 7:13-19) Solomon, with so many sexually unsatisfied wives, had plenty to worry about when it came to adultery. And polygamy put him in this position.

Another disaster caused by polygamy was the vast number of in-laws a man would have, insulting him and trying to boss him around. Not to mention the numerous wives a man would have, all telling him what to do and precisely how to do it. This may be the source of a lot of jokes, but actually this alone would be enough to cause intelligent men to avoid polygamy.

With polygamy a law put forth by Saint Moses and represented as a law come down from the Jewish tribal God Jehovah, how can anyone believe that this law is really of divine origin? What civilized, intelligent person would want to follow such a precept?

SEX BETWEEN HUMANS AND BEASTS

While forbidding seeing nakedness, Moses also prohibited men and women from having sexual intercourse with beasts. He apparently thought is was possible for human and other species of animals to cross-breed. This is evident from his requirement that beasts that had sex relations with humans should be put to death, along with the man or women involved. He writes: "If a man lie (sexually) with a beast, he shall surely be put to death: and ye shall slay the beast. And if a woman approach unto any

beast, and lie down thereto, thou shalt kill the woman, and the beast."
(Leviticus 20:15, 16)

Here a question arises. Suppose the woman does not "lie down"
to the beast, but bends over so the beast can perform in typical beastly
fashion? Is she free from condemnation? A smart lawyer should be able
to get her acquitted because the law is so loosely written. This law of
Moses was based on ignorance, and punished people with death for an act
that was of no consequence.

So when a girl has sex relations with the family dog (as many girls
do) she can be glad this law of Moses is not in force here. She can also
take comfort in the knowledge that science has no record of a dog ever
getting a girl pregnant.

MOSES' LAWS ABOUT MENSTRUATION

Moses had laws about almost everything, including menstruation.
No, he didn't try to prohibit it, but he did write this: "If a man shall lie
(sexually) with a women having her sickness (menstruation), and shall
uncover her nakedness; he hath discovered her fountain, and she hath
uncovered the fountain of her blood; and both of them shall be cut off from
among their people." (Leviticus 20:18) They were exiled.

So everybody asks, why the big fuss? Well, for one thing, the
menstrual flow does flush out the uterus and vagina, and if a woman has a
venereal disease it flushes out the pus and disease germs. Therefore a man
was much more likely to contract her disease during her menstrual period
than at other times. So far so good.

However, what Moses apparently did not know was the fact that
if a woman has no venereal disease, copulation during menstruation causes
no problem, so as long as she is comfortable with it. Many women
particularly enjoy copulation during menstruation because they feel more
sexually aroused at that time. So here again is a Bible law harshly
punishing people for nothing.

BURN PROSTITUTES TO DEATH

In an earlier chapter we learned how Saint Judah (who was a
customer of prostitutes) -- how he ordered an alleged prostitute to be put to
death at the stake. (Genesis 38:24) Now Moses continued that Hebrew law
by writing in his Bible at Leviticus Chapter 21 and Verse 9: "If she
profane herself by playing the whore . . . she shall be burnt with fire."

This is part of the highly praised "Judeo-Christian ethic."

Every civilized person will agree that this is a vicious and barbaric law. Only a malicious religionist would burn a human to death. When a person has committed a crime worthy of death, the punishment is never brought about by burning people to death by civilized governments. But religionists like Saint Moses see this with hate, and seek to inflict as much suffering on people as possible. Saint Moses of course was a murderer and worse, so it was nothing for him to burn people to death at the stake. This was perfectly right in his corrupt mind.

In view of the vicious and malicious punishment inflicted on prostitutes, what was the punishment levied against the men who were their customers? None. Absolutely no punishment at all. And not only Moses' laws in the Bible prescribed no such punishment, but the Christian New Testament prescribes no punishment for the men who patronize prostitutes. Bible law does not even excommunicate them from the church.

Again this shows that such laws are unjust and man-made, and not from God at all. Surely if a prostitute is a sinner, then the man who patronizes her must also be a sinner and worthy of punishment. But according to Saint Moses, his Jehovah God did not look at things that way. Men who patronized prostitutes were to be completely exonerated, even though prostitutes could not be prostitutes without the men who are their customers. The men were responsible for the women becoming prostitutes, and therefore if anything, the men were more to be condemned than the women.

What is actually revealed here is that this law was not dictated by God at all, but is entirely man-made. We could hardly expect the saintly men who wrote the Bible to condemn themselves, and so the men who were the customers of prostitutes were not punished. It is as simple as that. We must remember that no women wrote so much as one page in the Bible, and that's why Bible laws are so biased against women.

The Bible tells us how Saint Judah sought to patronize harlots: "When Judah saw her, he thought her to be an harlot: because she covered her face. And he turned unto her by the way, and said, 'Go to, I pray thee, let me come in unto thee:' (for he knew not that she was his daughter-in-law.) And she said, 'What wilt thou give me, that thou mayest come in unto me?' And he said, 'I will send thee a kid from the flock.' And she said, 'Wilt thou give me a pledge, till thou send it?' And he said, 'What pledge shall I give thee?' And she said, 'Thy signet, and thy bracelets, and thy staff that is in thine hand.' And he gave it to her and came in unto her, and she conceived by him." (Genesis 38:15-18) How pure and saintly all this was!

Again Saint Samson, the famous strong man, was a patron of prostitutes. The Bible tells us bluntly: "Then went Samson to Gaza, and saw there an harlot, and went in unto her." (Judges 16:1) Isn't that Bible statement pornographically descriptive of coition? Religious people are very proud of Saint Samson and his exploits. But they never mention his exploits with whores. Nor were any of the Bible saints punished for visiting and patronizing prostitutes. Their Jehovah God apparently just shrugged and looked the other way, muttering, "Boys will be boys."

Saint Jephthah was even the son of a harlot. The very holy Bible tells us: "Now Jephthah the Gileadite was a mighty man of valor, and he was the son of a harlot: and Gilead begat Jephthah." (Judges 11:1) Saint Gilead, in other words, had sexual intercourse with a prostitute, who then became pregnant and bore him a son named Jephthah. How saintly can the Bible be when it has saints like these? The great Christian missionary, Saint Paul, knew that neither Moses nor Jesus Christ had ever declared that for a man to have sexual intercourse with a whore was a sin or a crime. Therefore when Saint Paul found some male members of a Christian congregation were patronizing women prostitutes, he could not even excommunicate them for what they were doing. All he could do was scold them with an argument that was theological rather than practical. Therefore, instead of telling them that they could very likely catch a vicious or deadly disease, he said, "Know ye not that your bodies are the members of Christ? Shall I then take the members of Christ, and make them members of a harlot? God forbid." (1 Corinthians 6:15)

Since neither Moses nor Jesus made it a sin for men to have sexual intercourse with whores, this inescapably renders suspect the personal morality of these two revered leaders of Israel, and makes one wonder how many whores they patronized.

RAPE NOT FORBIDDEN BY THE BIBLE

Nowhere in the Bible is rape made a sin or a crime such as adultery or homosexuality, for example. Neither Moses nor Jesus Christ gave any law forbidding rape. According to the Bible, any Jew or Christian could rape a different woman or girl every week of his adult life and still go sailing off into heaven to spend eternity in bliss with Moses' and Jesus' blessings. Does religion really make people better as they claim? Better rapists, perhaps.

Even girls as young as three years of age could be raped with no condemnation. Nowhere in the Bible is child marriage forbidden, and among the Jews child brides as young as three years of age had sexual intercourse with their adult husbands. So rape of three year old girls would be considered normal.

The only recourse in Bible law for rape was a civil suit for damages. A father whose unmarried daughter was raped could bring suit against the rapist, who was then required to pay the father fifty shekels of silver, but the raped woman got nothing. She didn't count.

The Bible says at Deuteronomy Chapter 22 and Versus 28 and 29: "If a man find a damsel that is a virgin which is not betrothed and lay hold on her and lie with her (sexually) and they be found. Then the man that lay with her shall give unto the damsel's father fifty shekels of silver, and she shall be his wife." This kind of law was worse than nothing. Can you imagine what kind of a marriage this would produce, with the poor girl married to the rapist for the rest of her life?

Saint Moses' Bible law here continues: "Because he hath humbled her, he may not put her away all his days." This is more outrageous than ever. This is the only case in which Saint Moses forbids divorce. In all other cases, a man under Moses' law could divorce his wife merely by handing her a written note stating that she was divorced, and push her out the door. (Deuteronomy Chapter 24 and Verse 1) This did not require a court trial, but was merely up to the Husband's decision entirely, and thus divorces occurred on the slightest pretext, or for no valid reason whatsoever. But in the case of marriage because of rape, the holy Saint Moses completely prohibits divorce, so the poor woman victim must remain married to the repulsive rapist for the rest of her life. The justice in Moses' laws, allegedly received from his God, is difficult to discover.

Of course, it is true that rape is one of the most difficult crimes to prove, but so is adultery. Adultery is the more difficult of the two crimes to prove, because with adultery you have a man and a woman, both of whom favor the act, and neither will file a complaint against the other. With rape, the victim is often willing to file a complaint, but the charge is difficult to prove if normal rules of evidence are followed.

But in the modern court system often the usual rules of evidence are ignored, and the woman's word is taken as truth, while the man's testimony is automatically considered false. It is nothing but trial by accusation. As a result many innocent men have been convicted of a rape they did not commit. Three such cases come to mind. In one case a man served six years of a fifty year sentence, and was then released because the young woman admitted she had falsely accused him in order to cover up the fact she had been having sexual intercourse with her boy friend. Teenage girls often accuse innocent men of rape in such cases, when their parents discover they have been sexually active.

In another case a young man was accused of raping a divorced woman, whereas her testimony showed she had been earning money as a prostitute, and had accused this young fellow because he failed to pay her fee. This also is quite common. However, in spite of the young man's insistence he was innocent of rape, he spent several years in prison. Also in another case, after a woman was raped the police picked up a man in that neighborhood who was on parole from another type of crime. They brought the man to the woman's hospital bedside and she positively declared that he was the guilty man. However, this man escaped prison by being able to prove absolutely that he was elsewhere at the time the crime was committed. He had been falsely accused by the vengeful woman.

In such cases Bible law is superior to modern law, in that the Bible requires that all complaints must be proved by two or three witnesses. The Bible says: "One witness shall not rise up against a man for any iniquity, or for any sin, in any sin that he sinneth. At the mouth of two witnesses, or at the mouth of three witnesses, shall the matter be established." (Deuteronomy 19:15) In other words, in a rape case the victim's testimony alone could not convict anyone. The victim must have other witnesses as well. In this way, the Bible law protects the innocent, which modern law does not.

However, it's one thing to believe in God, but how anyone can believe in the Jewish God who approves rape is beyond reason and common sense.

NO AGE LIMIT ON MARRIAGE

Nowhere in the Jewish Christian Bible is there given any age limit on marriage. Neither Moses nor Jesus Christ ever mentioned such a thing. As a result, among the Jews adult men sometimes married girls as young as three years of age. This was a form of birth control, giving the man sexual intercourse with the girl for a number of years without a pregnancy occurring, in most cases. All the man needed was the usual price for the bride, which he gave to her father.

LOAN SHARKING

Another favorite method of robbing foreigners is Saint Moses' instruction to the Jews regarding excessive interest rates. Here is a method Moses told them to follow in order to plunder those who are not Hebrews, and they would not need a conquering army to do it.

Saint Moses told the Israelites to lend money to foreigners, to anyone who wasn't a Jew, and charge them any interest rate they could possibly get. The higher the interest rate, the better. Then when the Non-Jews could not pay the excessive interest rate, the Jews could seize their property which was security for the loan.

Saint Moses writes in his Bible at Deuteronomy Chapter 23 and Verse 20: "Unto a stranger (a foreigner) thou mayest lend upon usury, but unto thy brother (Israelite) thou shalt not lend upon usury." This kept the Jews from robbing each other through their excessive interest rates. But foreigners were dirt. They didn't count. If the Jews could rob non-Jews of their possessions through excessive interest rates, so much the better, according to Moses' "Holy" Bible. This is part of the wonderful "Judeo-Christian ethic" that religionists like to brag about.

Today we call it loan sharking, and people who try to follow this Biblical criminal practice are thrown into prison. This scheme was followed not only by the ancient Israelites. In the year 1290 A.D. the Jews were all driven out of England because of their practice of charging excessive interest rates on their loans. Furthermore, they are not allowed back into England for three centuries afterward. This would not have happened if they had not been followers of Saint Moses' criminal Bible teachings.

MOSES AND CIRCUMCISION

We can't blame Saint Moses for instituting the erotic practice of circumcision. This was begun by Saint Abraham, long centuries before Moses. Abraham had been down into Egypt and had seen men having the foreskin cut off of their penises in the religious rite of circumcision. So later on, while Saint Abraham was in a drugged stupor from his Semitic practice of using hasheesh, he imagined that he heard God telling him to circumcise himself and all males in his household, which he did. And thereafter this practice was followed by all of his descendants. (Leviticus 12:1-3) So when Saint Moses came on the scene he had no choice but to endorse the practice of circumcision, which was an established sexual religious rite among the Jews.

In Africa where circumcision originated, circumcision was and is associated to this day with fertility rites, and worship of the God of fertility.

And so, by adoption of this erotic rite of circumcision, the Israelites incorporated fertility worship into their religion.

Some claim that circumcision was practiced for alleged health benefits, but medical men today scoff at this pretext, stating that circumcision is of no benefit to the health whatsoever. Indeed, if circumcision were beneficial to the health, we would wonder why millions of years of evolution would not long ago have removed the foreskin from men's penises and from the penises of other male animals as well.

The rite of circumcision is nothing but a barbaric erotic ritual of fertility worship followed by the black African tribes for many centuries before Abraham and the Jews ever heard of it. In fact, if circumcision is the mark of the chosen people of the tribal God Jehovah, then the black African tribes were the chosen people of Jehovah God long centuries before Abraham and the Jews came into existence. The Jews were only second-rate pretenders, encroaching on the honor that from the first belonged to the black African people.

It is undoubtedly for this reason that Moses married a black African woman, an Ethiopian. (Number 12:1)

Here also is revealed the reason why Moses' Bible is so biased against women. Moses very much disliked Jewish women. He never married a Jewish woman, choosing instead first a Midianites woman and then a black Ethiopian woman.

THE BIBLE APPROVES SLAVERY

Religionists today like to cover up the fact that the Bible approves the institution of slavery. The truth, however, is that Saint Moses set up laws to perpetuate slavery. Moses even allowed Jews to be sold into slavery. The Bible states: "If thou buy an Hebrew servant, six years he shall serve; and in the seventh he shall go out free for nothing. If he came in (as a slave) by himself, he shall go out by himself; if he were married, then his wife shall go out with him. If his master have given him a wife, and she have born him sons or daughters; the wife and her children shall be her master's, and he shall go out by himself." (Exodus 21:2-4)

This is a fine and holy Biblical law, isn't it, not only establishing slavery, but separating a slave from his wife and children. Very godlike, indeed.

At least the Hebrew slave would be automatically freed from slavery the seventh year, but there was no such luck for the non-Jew, the foreigner that became a slave of the Jews. He or she would never be freed from slavery. As the "holy" Bible states: "They shall be your bondmen forever." (Leviticus 25:44-46) This too is part of the lovable "Judeo-Christian ethic."

Talk about racism; the Bible is full of it.

Furthermore this approval of slavery cannot be ascribed only to Saint Moses. The Christian New Testament in the Bible upholds slavery. It is written at Colossians Chapter 3 and Verse 22; "Slaves obey in all things your masters." This same admonition is given many times in the Christian New Testament part of the Bible. See also Ephesians 6:5; 1 Timothy 6:1,; Titus 2:9; and 1 Peter 2:18. Slavery is a part and parcel in the Bible religion, including Christianity.

OTHERS BURNED TO DEATH TOO

But Saint Moses did not only burn prostitutes to death. He had other pet peeves of his own. For example, Moses writes in the Bible at Leviticus 20:14: "And if a man take a wife and her mother (as a wife too) it is wickedness. They shall be burnt with fire, both he and they."

Polygamy was a lawful practice among the Israelites, so what harm could come from a man marrying a woman and her mother? It wasn't incest. Why should they be punished? And why should they be punished so harshly as by burning the three participants to death in fire? Nowadays people scratch their heads in puzzlement over this Bible law, unable to find a reason for it.

Outright incest, which is admittedly detrimental, is not punished by Moses' Bible with such harsh punishment as burning to death in fire. But this act which is not incest at all, is condemned in the most barbaric fashion by Moses. Moses really had his mental problems, didn't he?

SELL YOUR SICK COWS FOR FOOD

Here is a law that demonstrates fully Saint Moses' crafty and unscrupulous nature, and the unscrupulous conduct taught in his bible.

Suppose you were a Jew and had a cow that was sick with hoof-and-mouth disease, of cancer, or tuberculosis, and it died. You had a substantial potential money loss there. What could you do to avoid this loss?

Saint Moses told the Israelites they should sell their sick and dead cows to anybody that was not a Jew who might be living around them. Moses couldn't care less if non-Jews became sick or died as a result of eating such diseased meat; and according to Saint Moses, his Bible God Jehovah ordains such a vicious and malicious law to be followed by the Jews.

At Deuteronomy Chapter 14 and Verse 21 Moses' Bible says: "Ye shall not eat of anything that dieth of itself. Thou shalt give it unto the stranger that is in thy gates that he may eat it; or thou mayest sell it unto an alien." This is part of the delightful "Judeo-Christian ethic" we constantly hear about.

If you are not a Jew or Judeo-Christian, how would you like to have Moses or one of his followers as your jolly neighborhood butcher?

We hear a lot about racism today. If this law isn't racist, what is? Moses' Bible is absolutely vicious against all who are not Israelites.

Here the Bible is running a worse crime school than Fagin did in Charles Dickens' novel, "Oliver Twist." But laws of civilized governments today make it rough for Bible followers and their evil ways. Prison awaits such Judeo-Christian religionists.

Religious Jews who follow the Jewish Bible likewise show contempt for people of other races to this day. For example, after United States politicians gave billions of American taxpayers' dollars to Israel, then in 1967 the Jewish Israeli Government sent its bombing planes and torpedo boats to viciously attack the U.S. Navy ship "Liberty." For many hours the hateful Israelis bombarded the "Liberty," killing 34 fine American men and wounding 75 others, even though the "Liberty" had its American flags flying through the bombardment. But the vicious Israeli Jews could not sink the "Liberty."

This was an act of war. However, U.S. President Lyndon Johnson issued an order forbidding other U.S. Navy ships and planes nearby to go to the defense of the "Liberty," according to news reports. Johnson thereby gave assistance to the enemy. (What is the definition of "Treason"? We ask you.) Whose side was Johnson on, anyway?

To this day the U.S. Congress and President continue to give to the Israeli Jews over $5,000,000.000. every year with no strings attached. This give-away of the American people's money is clearly un-constitutional, since the U.S. Constitution in Section 8, Paragraph 1, limits collection of taxes for solely "the general welfare of the United States." There is no possible way to show that giving the Israeli Jews $5,000,000,000. and more per year provides for the general welfare of these United States of America. However, it does provide for the welfare of those foreign Israeli Jews who make war on the United States. Whose side is Congress and the President on, anyway?

And at the same time the Congress and religious President Reagan raised the income taxes of all older Americans over the age of 65 by up to 60 percent more than others pay. They give billions of our dollars away to Israeli Jew foreigners and grind the faces of older Americans in the dirt with outrageous enormous income taxes.

SAINT MOSES APPROVES HUMAN SACRIFICE

After damning the native Canaanites because some of them sacrificed their children to the God Molech, Saint Moses then instituted the practice of sacrificing humans among the Jews. Moses' system of sacrifices was even worse than the worship of Molech, because Saint Moses approved not only the sacrificing of children, but also of sacrificing adult humans to his tribal God Jehovah.

In Chapter 27 of the book of Leviticus in the Bible, Moses wrote about all kinds of sacrifices. Then toward the end of this chapter Moses gave instructions regarding human sacrifices in these words: "No devoted thing that a man shall devote unto the Lord Jehovah of all that he hath, both of man and beasts and of the field of his possession, shall be sold or redeemed; every devoted thing is most holy unto the Lord Jehovah. None devoted, which shall be devoted of men, shall be redeemed; but shall surely be put to death." (Leviticus Chapter 27, and Versus 28 and 29 in the Bible, K.J.V.) The American Standard version translation is even more clear. It says: "No one devoted, that shall be devoted from among men, shall be redeemed; he shall surely be put to death."

Humans so devoted or sacrificed were put on an altar, killed and offered up to Moses' tribal God as a burnt offering. I will show you exactly how such human sacrifices were performed among the Jews by quoting directly from the Bible's own description of such a human sacrifice in Chapter XIX of this book. (Please remember that the saints' Bible is what some people call "the inspired word of God.") Human sacrifice is part of the abominable "Judeo-Christian ethic" that we hear about ad nauseam, and human sacrifice is still a part of the Moses Bible religion to this day.

KILL PEOPLE WHO FOLLOW OTHER RELIGIONS

Moses would not last long if he lived in any civilized nation in the world today. The reason is, Saint Moses killed everybody who disagreed with him on religious matters, and taught his followers to do likewise.

In his "holy" bible Saint Moses wrote: "He that sacrificeth to any god, save unto the Lord Jehovah only, he shall be utterly destroyed." You can read this in the Bible at Exodus Chapter 22 and Verse 20.

Moses and his Jewish followers murdered millions of people as a result of this commandment. All other nations of people that they encountered, they killed if they could. On the other hand, when great and powerful nations conquered the Israelites, they allowed the Jews to continue in their own religion. This shows the bloody bigotry of Saint Moses and the Jews, in contrast to the generosity of the great nations that conquered them. There was no freedom of religion or free speech among the Jews.

In Europe the Judeo-Christian Roman Catholic pope and his followers attempted to continue in Moses' footsteps by burning to death at the stake or slaughtering all who disagreed with their religious views, and they terrorized Europe for centuries. However, when the Pope sent his Austrian army against them, the German, Swedish and Danish Lutherans won the Thirty Years War in 1648, and since then we have had freedom of religion, speech and press among the civilized nations of Europe and elsewhere, and the murderous religious bigotry taught in the Jewish Christian Bible and followed by the Roman Catholic Pope has ended. The world is infinitely indebted to the non-Catholic Germans, Swedes, and Danes for giving us freedom of and from religion, freedom of speech, and freedom of the press, which has in turn given us our wonderful development in science and inventions that we enjoy today. No longer are scientists burned to death at the stake when their discoveries disagree with the colossal barbaric ignorance taught by the Jewish Christian Bible.

And it was one lone man, the German Roman Catholic priest Martin Luther, whose courage and daring led him to challenge the supremacy of the Pope, who then ruled Europe. This brave man, Martin Luther, lit the fuse that destroyed the Pope's tyrannical rule of Europe forever. Here we must remember the vast difference between Martin Luther and his followers and the Roman Catholic church. The Lutherans never persecuted anyone who disagreed with their beliefs. Thus their victory gave freedom of religion, speech and press to every one of us. Martin Luther is widely regarded as one of the greatest men this world has ever seen.

So here we have reviewed some of the outrageous and scandalous laws that Moses gave to his followers, which laws are still a part of the vaunted "Judeo-Christian ethic" to this day.

CHAPTER XV.   WHICH SAINT RAPED 32,000 GIRLS?
(WITH SOME HELP, OF COURSE)

Naturally no man was stud enough to rape 32,000 girls all by himself. But this saint had a lot of help in committing this heinous crime. Just stick around and you'll learn how he did it, right from the Bible record of this foul event.

The Bible says: "And when the Lord Jehovah thy God shall deliver them before thee; thou shalt smite them and utterly destroy them. Thou shalt make no covenant with them nor show mercy unto them."

The Bible continues: "And thou shalt destroy all the people which the lord Jehovah thy god shall deliver thee. Thine eye shall have no pity upon them." (Deuteronomy 7, Verses 2 and 16.)

The Jews under Saint Moses and Saint Joshua left Egypt and invaded the land of Palestine, murdering its inhabitants, men, women, and children, and stealing their land and all their property. (Read the book of Joshua in the Bible.) This was alright and proper for them to do according to Saint Moses and the "holy" Bible.

GENOCIDE?

Genocide is a word we frequently hear nowadays, but this is one word the Bible never mentions. According to the Bible, genocide is right and proper as long as the Jews are committing genocide against other people. But the Israelites screamed bloody murder whenever they thought genocide might be directed against them. (See the book of Esther in the Bible.)

Through the native men, women and children they slaughtered, the Jews became wealthy by seizing the lands, houses, vineyards, gold and silver of their dead victims. Today we call this sort of thing murder and robbery, but Saint Moses the murderer thought this was quite all right, and his Bible sets it forth as holy conduct.

The Jews were God's chosen people, the Bible says, and they could do anything they wished to other nations. (Deuteronomy 7:6)

The millions of Israelites that left Egypt gave Moses a huge army which none of the surrounding nations could withstand. The Bible tells us that Saint Moses had an army of over six hundred thousand men. (Numbers 1:45,46) With this army Moses slaughtered and plundered the smaller nations nearby.

In his war of conquest against the Midianites we have a fine example of Moses' saintly conduct. The Midianites were a peaceful people minding their own business when attacked by the Jews. The Bible tells us: "And they warred against the Midianites, as the Lord Jehovah commanded Moses, and they slew all the males. And the children of Israel took all the woman of Midian captives, and their little ones, and took the spoil of all their cattle, and all their flocks, and all their goods." (Numbers Chapter 31 and Versus 7 and 9) This war of aggression was just gangsterism: armed robbery and murder by a gang of Israelite thugs under the command of Saint Moses, the holy man of his tribal God Jehovah.

Saint Moses of course said that God had told him to commit this heinous crime. This justified the Jews, the "chosen people" of Jehovah God, in doing it. It was actually a holocaust, a massacre.

The Bible record continues: "And Moses said unto them, 'Have ye saved all the women alive? . . . Now therefore kill every male among the little ones (the children and infants), and kill every woman that hath known a man by lying with him." (Numbers 31:15,17) Mothers with infants in arms were hacked to death with swords, and the aged were run through with spears. The bellies of the pregnant non-Jewish women were ripped up, so that their unborn infants gushed forth. Blood flowed in torrents and drenched the earth as the thousands of Midianites mothers, children and elderly were slain by the vicious Israelites. It was a massacre. The Jews committed genocide.

Then a tally was made of the plunder that the thieving Israelites had seized. Moses' holy Bible boasts: "And the booty, being the rest of the prey which the men of war had caught, was six hundred thousand and seventy thousand and five thousand sheep. (675,000 sheep). And threescore and twelve thousand beeves (72,000 cattle). And threescore and one thousand asses (61,000 donkeys)." (Numbers 31:32-24) At the announcement of the total plunder, vicious grins wreathed the faces of the

Israelites, and their eyes glittered with greed and avarice. Besides the livestock, they had also seized the houses and lands of the Midianites, and all their gold and jewels. War was indeed profitable, and easier than honest work!

AND NOW WHOLESALE RAPE!

Saint Moses wanted to reward his soldiers and himself for their efficiency in robbery and murder. So he saved alive thousands of Midianites girls for himself and his soldiers to rape. The Bible again quotes Saint Moses' words: "But all the women children that have not known a man by lying with him (have not previously had sexual intercourse) keep alive for yourselves." (In the Bible see the book of Numbers Chapter 31 and Verse 18.) This was no small number of girls handed over to the soldiers for their sexual entertainment. The "holy" Bible says there were 32,000 girls that they raped. "And thirty and two thousand persons in all, of women that had not known a man by lying with him." (Numbers 31:35) Can you imagine the scene of horror when these 32,000 girls were dragged to the ground and raped: forced to engage in sexual intercourse with the vicious conquering Jews? And this Saint Moses commanded them to do. That's what the Bible says: "Keep them alive for yourselves." Today many people are shoving their bibles into their garbage disposals. If you do this, just put in a few pages at a time so you don't jam the mechanism.

Some people excuse the Israelites for all this slaughter by saying that the Midianites were wicked. However, if the Midianites were so wicked they deserved to die, how is it that Saint Moses saved alive 32,000 Midianites girls?

Remember here, that this condemnation applies to Christianity too. The Christian New Testament in the Bible praises Saint Moses for this fiendish crime. The Christian New Testament says: "And Moses verily was faithful." (See Hebrews Chapter 3, Verse 5) So the Christian New Testament and Christianity approves the rapes and massacre Moses committed. This is part of the "Judeo-Christian ethic" we hear about.

Concerning such vicious tales of rape and murder in the Bible, Col. Robert Ingersoll had this to say: "The believers in the Bible are loud in their denunciation of what they are pleased to call the immoral literature of the world; and yet few books have been published containing more moral filth than this inspired word of God." Col. Robert Ingersoll was a former attorney general of the state of Illinois.

However, the Bible is not merely "immoral filth." Here Moses says his Jehovah God commanded him to slaughter and commit genocide against this nation of people and then to rape 32,000 girls! (Number 21:7) Here the Jewish-Christian Bible teaches people to commit genocide and wholesale rape; the vilest of criminality! It is an outrage against civilization. Moses was indeed a criminally scandalous saint.

If Moses and his army of Jews were to commit such war crimes today, he and his entire army would be executed according to the principles laid down in the Nuremberg war crimes trials and since. It has been ruled that a soldier must disobey his commanding officer if he is ordered to commit such criminal acts as ripping up the bellies of pregnant women, butchering children, rape, genocide and other crimes that Moses and the Jewish army committed.

However, no explanation has been given as to what the soldier can do if the commanding officer orders him shot for disobeying orders in wartime.

GOD'S CHOSEN PEOPLE?

Moses justified his murderous, rapist conduct by telling the Jews they were better than anybody else and so were entitled to rob and rape and murder people of other races. The Bible says at Deuteronomy Chapter 7 Verse 8, "For thou art an holy people unto the Lord Jehovah thy God. The Lord Jehovah thy God hath chosen thee to be a special people unto himself above all people that are upon the fact of the earth." This "chosen people" propaganda was used by Moses and Joshua to justify any kind of heinous crimes the Jews chose to perpetrate. It was nothing but war propaganda to encourage the Israelites to kill.

Wouldn't you suppose that if the Israelites were indeed the "chosen people" of God that they would do something better than murder and rob and rape people who are not Jews? Compare the activities of the white race of Europe with the Jews. The white race has provided all people of the world with practically every invention known to humankind. The white race has invented the airplane, the automobile, steamboats, the printing press, railroad trains, computers, typewriters, tractors, plows, mowers, harvesters, threshers, harrows, steel mills, flour mills, electric lights, radio, moving pictures, phonographs, tape recorders, video discs and tape, television, electric motors, electric generators. They discovered disease germs and sanitation, and antibiotics to cure even syphilis and leprosy, and they even put men on the moon. And more, to benefit all mankind. Yet they do not brag that they are God's chosen people.

In contrast to this, Saint Moses and Saint Joshua invented genocide. Moses and Saint Joshua and the Jews slaughtered whole nations of people, wiping them out completely: men, women, children, old and young. None were spared. All were butchered. Other nations just fought to win wars, but the Israelites killed everyone. They gloried in genocide. (See the book of Joshua in the Bible.)

Thomas Jefferson, third president of the United States of America and author of the Declaration of Independence, did not believe that the Jews were the chosen people of God. He wrote "Those who labor in the earth are the chosen people of God, if ever he had a chosen people."

MOSES' MYSTERIOUS FUNERAL

The books of Genesis, Exodus, Leviticus, Numbers and Deuteronomy are commonly said to have been written in the Bible mostly by Saint Moses, but obviously much of Deuteronomy was not because it gives an account of the death of Moses, so surely Saint Moses could not have written that.

The Bible at Chapter 34 of Deuteronomy tells us: "And Moses went up from the plains of Moab unto the mountain of Nebo, to the top of Posgah, that is over against Jericho . . . . So Moses the servant of the Lord Jehovah God died there in the land of Moab, according to the word of the Lord. And he buried him in a valley in the land of Moab, over against Beth-poer, but no man knoweth of his sepulchre unto this day." (Deuteronomy 34 1,5,6)

Thomas Paint humorously comments on Saint Moses' burial in his book, "The Age of Reason," as follows: "The writer of this book of Deuteronomy, whoever he was, (for it is an anonymous work), is obscure, and also in contradiction with himself, in the account he has given of Moses."

"After telling that Moses went to the top of Pisgah (and it does not appear from any account that he ever came down again), he tells us that Moses died there in the land of Moab, and that he buried him in a valley in the land of Moab; but as there is no antecedent to the pronoun he, there is no knowing who he was that did bury him. If the writer meant that he (God) buried him, how should he (the writer) know it? Or why should we (the readers) believe him? Since we know not who the writer was that tells us so, for certainly Moses could not himself tell where he was buried."

"The writer also tells us, that no man knoweth where the sepulchre of Moses is unto this day, meaning the time in which this writer lived; how then should he know that Moses was buried in a valley in the land of Moab? For as the writer lived long after the time of Moses, as is evident from his using the expression "unto this day", meaning a great length of time after the death of Moses, he certainly was not at his funeral; and on the other hand, it is impossible that Moses himself could say that no man knoweth where the sepulchre is unto this day. To make Moses the speaker, would be an improvement on the play of a child that hides himself and cries 'nobody can find me' nobody can find Moses!"

"This writer has nowhere told us how he came by the speeches which he has put into the mouth of Moses to speak, and therefore we have a right to conclude, that he either composed them himself, or wrote them from oral tradition. One or the other of these is the more probably, since he has given in the fifth Chapter a table of commandments, in which that called the fourth commandment is different from the fourth commandment in the twentieth Chapter of Exodus. In that of Exodus, the reason given for keeping the seventh day, 'because (says the commandment) God made the heavens and the earth in six days, and rested on the seventh; but in that of Deuteronomy, the reason given is that it was the day on which the children of Israel came out of Egypt, and therefore, says this commandment, 'the Lord thy God commanded thee to keep the Sabbath day.' This makes no mention of the creation, nor that of the coming out of Egypt. There are also many things given as laws of Moses in this book that are not to be found in any of the other books; among which is that inhuman and brutal law, Chapter XXI., Verses 18, 19, 20, 21, which authorizes parents, the father and the mother, to bring their own children to have them stoned to death, for what it is pleased to call stubbornness. But priests have always been fond of preaching up Deuteronomy, for Deuteronomy preaches up tithes; and it is from this book, Chapter XXV, Verse 4, that they have taken the phrase, and applied it to tithing, that 'thou shalt not muzzle the ox when he treadeth out the corn;' and that this might not escape observation, they have noted it in the table of contents at the head of the Chapter, though it is only a single verse of less than two lines. Oh, priests! Priests! Ye are willing to be compared to an ox, for the sake of tithes. Though it is impossible for us to know identically who the writer of Deuteronomy was, it is not difficult to discover him professionally, that he was some Jewish priest, who lived, as I shall show in the course of this work, at least three hundred and fifty years after the time of Moses."

So wrote Thomas Paine in his book, "The Age of Reason." Thomas Paine was a friend of Thomas Jefferson, third president of the United States of America.

Scandalous Saints

CHAPTER XVI. THE SAINT WHO PRACTICED GENOCIDE

After Saint Moses died, Saint Joshua became dictator of Israel in Moses' place. Joshua had been Moses' right hand man for many years and during this time had been groomed to lead the Israelites following Moses' death.

Saint Joshua continued the plan that Moses had initiated. He marched the huge army of over 600,000 Israelites, together with their wives and children and cattle, ever onward toward the land of Canaan, which is now called Palestine. Since the Jews had been driven out of Egypt, Moses decided they had nowhere else to go except back to the land of Canaan from whence their ancestors had come in the time of Jacob, who was also called Israel. Abraham, Jacob's grandfather had come to Palestine from the vicinity of Babylon some time before that.

The fact that the original inhabitants of Canaan already lived there meant only one thing to Moses. The native Canaanites all had to be destroyed to make room for the Jewish hordes. He had no plan to buy land and live honestly among the other people. Moses had of course claimed that the Canaanites were "wicked", and that this justified the Israelites in killing them. This is what a politician always says when he hurls his army against another nation. This has been going on for thousands of years. Almost four thousand years ago Moses learned this war propaganda technique when he studied in Pharaoh's college in Egypt, and he used it effectively in inciting the Israelites to fight and conquer the Palestinians. (Acts 7:22)

The pity is that today some people still think the Palestinians of Moses' day were actually wicked, instead of seeing from Bible history that the Israelites and their leaders did exactly the same things they condemned other people for doing. For example, Moses denounced the Canaanite worshippers of Molech for sacrificing their children to their God, and yet Abraham tried to sacrifice his son to the Jewish God. So who was the most righteous? And why should any Jew call Palestinians wicked, when Moses himself had instructed human sacrifice to his own religion? It was just war propaganda used by Moses and Joshua to justify their aggression, and murder, rape and robbery of the native inhabitants of Canaan.

As soon as Saint Joshua took command of the Jewish nation he pursued the conquest of Palestine. The Israelites approached Canaan from the east. There apparently had been a drought, so the Hebrews were able to cross the Jordan River dry shod.

The fact that slaughtering the native inhabitants of Canaan was murder, robbery and genocide meant nothing to Saint Joshua. He marched his army toward the first Canaanite city near where he crossed the Jordan river. The city was Jericho, which was a prosperous place that had high walls around it as protection against marauders.

First Saint Joshua sent two spies into Jericho to look over its defense. These spies stayed with a prostitute all night while there. And while they enjoyed her feminine charms. They also learned no doubt that she was disgruntled by interference with her business in Jericho. This prostitute Rehab was therefore cooperative in helping the Jewish spies escape the Jericho military who had discovered their presence in the city.

With the information provided by his spies, Joshua set up battering rams against the city walls of Jericho, while he marched the Israelite round and round the city just out of reach of the arrows of the Jericho army. While the army of Jericho tried to shoot the marching Israelites, the battering rams worked under shields and finally managed to knock large holes in the city walls. Then the enormous Jewish army rushed through the openings and slaughtered the far smaller army of defenders.

But Saint Joshua was not satisfied to kill just the soldiers of Jericho. He wanted everybody in the city of Jericho killed: men, women, children, young and old. Otherwise how could the Jews steal the land and its wealth if any of its rightful owners remained alive? So all the inhabitants of Jericho were killed, as Moses' "holy" Bible tells us at Joshua 6:21 and 25: "And thy utterly destroyed all that was in the city, both men and women, young and old . . . .and Joshua saved Rehab the harlot alive and her father's household, and all that she had . . . . because she hid the messengers which Joshua sent to spy out Jericho." Then Joshua burned the city, but saved out the silver and gold. It was a bloody holocaust. (Joshua 6:24)

This was a fine occupation for a saint: Slaughtering men, women and children, young and old. It was genocide, a practice the Jews feared greatly ever since Moses and Joshua invented the art centuries ago. It is one thing to practice genocide on others; and entirely another thing to have genocide practiced on themselves. By his practice of murder, robbery and genocide, Saint Joshua forever lost his halo if he ever had one.

A SETBACK AT THE CITY OF AI

Flushed with an easy victory by his huge army of over 600,000 men at Jericho, Saint Joshua then tackled the nearby walled city of Ai, also occupied by its peaceful Canaanite inhabitants. Joshua sent spies to Ai. The Bible says: "And they returned to Joshua and said unto him, 'Let not all the people (in the army) go up; but let about two or three thousand men go up and smite Ai; and make not all the people to labor thither; for they are but few." (Joshua 7:3)

So Saint Joshua sent only three thousand men. But then they ran into trouble. It's one thing for a huge army of 600,000 men to run like a steam roller over the defenders of a small city, but when Joshua sent a force only slightly superior to the defending army, the Jews were defeated. "And they (the Israelites) fled before the men of Ai. And the men of Ai smote of them about thirty and six men; for they chased them from before the gate even unto Shebarim and smote them in the going down: wherefore the hearts of the (Hebrew) people melted and became as water. And Joshua rent his clothes and fell to the earth upon his face before the ark of the Lord Jehovah until the eventide, he and the elders of Israel, and put dust upon their heads. And Joshua said, 'Alas, o Lord Jehovah God, wherefore has thou at all brought this people over Jordan, to deliver us into the hands of the Amorites, to destroy us? Would to God he had been content and dwelt on the other side of Jordan!" (Joshua 7:4-7)

The Amorites that Joshua now feared, were a blond haired, blue eyed European people. Man for man they had proved to be superior soldiers to the Israelites, set against them, and Joshua now quaked in fear. The fierce soldiers of the blond Amorites and Ai had Joshua shaking in his boots, and his Israelite army trembling with him.

Saint Joshua thought it great to slaughter other people, but when his own army was slaughtered it was so open after all. Joshua's account in the Bible claims that only 36 of his soldiers had been killed, but obviously it must have been a very substantial number that fell. Otherwise Joshua would not have been ready to quit and flee back across the Jordan river. But then a second thought popped into his mind. He had been stupid to send so few soldiers against Ai when he had so many at his command. Even if they weren't as good, man for man, as the blond, blue-eyed Amorites, still their very numbers would give them victory, as they had done at Jericho. Well, he'd do better next time. He'd throw his entire huge army at the few defenders of little Ai, and then he'd defeat them and slaughter everyone.

SAINT JOSHUA'S ALIBI

But how was he going to alibi for his big military blunder of sending only three thousand men against Ai? Somebody would have to be blamed for this debacle. Then a happy thought struck him. He had an enemy among the Israelites who always spoke against him when the Israelite sheiks gathered together. Achan was his name. Joshua decided he'd blame the whole defeat on Achan and have Achan put to death as a traitor, and that would bag two birds with one arrow.

So the scheme took form. Joshua had some silver and gold from Jericho buried under Achan's tent while none of his family was around. Then in a great religious ceremony in which lots were drawn, Achan was accused of having brought God's wrath on Israel and their resultant defeat in war by stealing this gold. Moses' Bible tells us: "So Joshua sent messengers, and they ran unto the tent; and behold, it was hid in his tent, and the silver under it . . . .and Joshua and all Israel with him took Achan the son of Zerah, and the silver and the garment, and the wedge of gold, and his sons, and his daughters, and his oxen, and his asses, and his sheep, and his tent, and all that he had. And they brought them unto the valley of Ahcor . . . . And all Israel stoned them with stones." (Joshua 7:22,24,25) So Saint Joshua not only killed of his enemy, Achan, but slaughtered all his children too so none would be left to rise up against him at a later date. Killing a man's children because their father was accused, was the Israelite version of Justice fairly executed. How great was Saint Joshua's sense of justice!

You note that this analysis of Achan's experience differs from the superstitious tale Joshua wrote in the Bible by taking into consideration the usual motivations that effect humans. Politicians often look for a scapegoat when they blunder, and it is obvious that Joshua was no different in this regard than many other politicians. We have to carefully scrutinize these nationalistic patriotic tales and supply the missing modifications; for Moses' Bible is basically a Jingoistic history of the Israelite people.

As proof that we have the proper analysis of Saint Joshua's motivation, look now at how Joshua attacked Ai the second time. This time he didn't send just another three thousand soldiers as he had done the first time. He sent his whole mighty army of over 600,000 men against the tiny town of Ai. In other words, Joshua knew very well that his defeat at Ai had nothing to do with Achan, but had everything to do with the number of men he sent against the town. Achan was merely a cover-up for Joshua's military bungling. As Moses' Bible tells us of this second attack on Ai: "So Joshua arose, and all the people of war (all 600,000) to go up against Ai." (Joshua 8:3) Yes, friends, we've got Saint Joshua's number. He was just another crook.

We may marvel at the gullibility of the Israelites in accepting Joshua's alibi for his defeat at Ai. Yet even today big politicians and their chief backers lead the people into accepting government actions that are vastly injurious to the average citizen. It helps one to recognize the slowness in evolutionary development of the human mentality.

Of course Saint Joshua's second assault on the town of Ai was successful due to his use of his entire army of 600,000 men. With only 2,000 blond Amorite soldiers defending Ai, Joshua's army thus had a 300 to one advantage. The tiny army of defenders could not possible win. The "holy" Bible tells us: "And so it was that all that fell that day, both of men and women, were twelve thousand, even all the men of Ai. Only the cattle and the spoil of that city Israel took for a prey unto themselves." (Joshua 8:25-27) Again the non-Jewish men, women, and children were cut to pieces by the swords of the Jews, and the bellies of the pregnant non-Jewish women were ripped up so that their unborn infants gushed forth. Also the young women were raped and then murdered by these Israelite chosen people of their tribal God Jehovah. (2 Kings 15:16) What a holy bloody massacre and holocaust these Bible saints were performing! It was genocide, more murder of peaceful people, more wholesale robbery, all by Saint Joshua and his Jewish gangsters.

So then Saint Joshua had a great religious celebration of their lopsided victory over the poor people of the little town of Ai. The Jews thanked their bloody tribal God Jehovah for the victory, and sacrificed on an altar that Saint Joshua built. The Bible says: "And afterward he read all the words of the law, the blessings and the cursings, according to all that is written in the book of the law. There was not a word of all that Moses commanded, which Joshua read not before all the congregation of Israel." (Joshua 8:34,35) So the slaughter of innocent people ended with an overdose of Biblical religious fervor in an attempt to wash the innocent blood from the hands of the Jewish murderers. A typical saintly procedure.

We note that at this religious celebration Joshua read aloud "all the words of the law" that Moses had given them. We defy any modern politician to read aloud all the words of the laws that the people of the United States are supposed to obey. No one could read aloud all the laws we are supposed to obey here, in a whole year. We have hundreds of thousands of laws here so that neither the politicians nor the lawyers know even a small fraction of them. And citizens are never given a copy of these laws they are required to obey. It was estimated a while back that the lawmakers here pass some 6,000 new laws every year to add to the confusion. Compared to the simplicity of Moses' laws, we live in a legal madhouse today in the United States of America. And this is supposed to be "the land of the free" as our national anthem jokingly tells us.

CHAPTER XVII.   WHY THE SUN STOOD STILL FOR SAINT JOSHUA

After that an alliance of five kings of the native Amorites in Palestine fought against Joshua with their armies at Gibeon. But even so, the size of their armies was far less than Joshua's huge army, so the victorious outcome for the Israelites was a foregone conclusion.

But in the account of this battle we read one of the most ridiculous tales found in the entire Bible. The Bible says: "Then spake Joshua to the Lord Jehovah in the day when the Lord Jehovah delivered up the Amorites before the children of Israel, and he said in the sight of Israel, 'Sun, stand thou still upon Gibeon; and thou, moon, in the valley of Ajalon. And the sun stood still, and the moon stayed, until the people had avenged themselves upon their enemies. Is it not written in the book of Joshua? So the sun stood still in the midst of heaven, and hasted not to go down about a whole day. And there was no day like that before it or ever after it." (Joshua 10:12-14)

Can you imagine such unscientific nonsense? Anyone who knows about the rotation of the earth and movement of the planets knows that stopping the earth's rotation so the sun would seem to stop would also be impossible. But religious people even today devoutly believe that it actually happened. In addition to this, if the sun and moon had actually seemed to stop in their tracks for a whole day, you may be sure that in every nation under the sun there would be a historic record of this singular event. However, nothing of the sort is ever mentioned by anyone except Joshua in Israel. Note, too, that in such nations as Egypt and Babylon the study of astronomy was highly advanced at the time this event was supposed to have occurred, and certainly it would have been noted in their records if the sun and moon had stood still for a whole day. They never once mentioned such an event.

Of course, the Bible is way off scientifically, because the sun does not move around the earth at all. The earth moves around the sun. And since the Bible was supposed to be dictated by God, it sounds as though God doesn't know how the earth and sun operate. The Bible here teaches that the sun moves around the earth, whereas Copernicus the astronomer pointed out that the opposite is true. About a century later, around 1600 A.D., Galileo supported the views of Copernicus. This was a direct challenge to the authority of the Bible, so the priests had the aged Galileo dragged before the Inquisition and tried for his "heretical beliefs." As a result, Galileo was forced to withdraw his teaching that the earth moves around the sun in order to avoid being burned to death at the stake. And to this day, in spite of the facts, that large Roman Christian sect has not rescinded its condemnation of Galileo, and therefore officially still insists that the sun moves around the earth!

On this subject, President Thomas Jefferson had this to say: "In the book of Joshua, we are told, the sun stood still several hours. Were we to read that fact in Levy or Tacitus, we should class it with their showers of blood, speaking of statutes, beasts, etc. But it is said that the writer of that book was inspired. Examine, therefore, candidly what evidence there is of his having been inspired. The pretension is entitled to your inquiry, because millions believe it. On the other hand, you are astronomer enough to know how contrary it is to the law of nature that a body revolving on its axis, as the earth does, should have stopped, should not, by that sudden stoppage, have prostrated animals, trees, buildings, and that without a second general prostration . . . . do not be frightened from this inquiry by any fear of its consequences. If it ends in a belief that there is no God, you will find incitements to virtue in the comfort and pleasantness you feel in its exercise, and love of others which it will procure you." so wrote Thomas Jefferson, third president of the United States, and author of the Declaration of Independence. Jefferson was obviously himself an atheist, and made so by the untruthfulness of the Bible.

So what actually happened at the battle of Gibeon that made Joshua say that the sun and moon stood still? We should remember that the use of hasheesh was quite common among the Semites of that day, as it is now. This is their favorite recreational drug. Saint Joshua was undoubtedly under the influence of hasheesh when he claimed that the sun and moon stood still. Dr. William Boericke, in his "Homeopathic Materia Medica," tells us about the effects of the shrub, Cannabis Indica, which is used in making hasheesh. Dr. Boericke writes that it "produces most remarkable hallucinations and imaginations, exaggeration of the duration of time, and extent of space being the most characteristic. Conception of time, space and place is gone." So here is the answer to Joshua's wild tale of the sun and moon standing still. Saint Joshua was using hasheesh, and as a result he was unable to tell how long the sun and moon were in the sky a whole extra day. In fact, he so much believed that he wrote this in his annals of this war. At this point we can only wonder how many so-called Bible miracles were based on the warped observation of Semite hasheesh users.

Of course, using hasheesh or cannabis or opium is different from using alcohol. With alcohol, a person can be drunk as a sailor at night and be sober the next day, assuming he only goes on an occasional spree. This is because the body can metabolize alcohol, which is really a food. However, cannabis and hasheesh and opium and cocaine or similar drugs are actually nerve poisons. They are not foods, and so cannot metabolized by the body. Consequently after even occasional use the drug remains in the body and affects the nerves and the brain for weeks afterward, distorting the mind and physical reaction. This happens among cannabis and hasheesh users today who cannot judge time and distance and so become involved in numerous automobile traffic accidents, and railroad and airplane crashes. In addition, cannabis produces mental dullness and lethargy that also causes accidents in this high speed age. Cannabis is popularly called pot, grass, marijuana, or hemp.

The name cannabis indica signifies that cannabis originated in India, from whence it has been exported for thousands of years, as it was in Joshua's time. Opium also has been exported from India for centuries. This reminds us that the Christian British Government under Queen Victoria fought the Opium War against China in 1840 to force the Chinese Government to allow British dope peddlers to sell opium to the Chinese people. After two years of fighting, China was defeated by the Judeo-Christian British whose opium peddlers then began to bring tons of opium from India to sell to the Chinese. This was a vicious outrage against humanity, perpetrated by a nation whose queen was also the head of the Church of England. Queen Victoria, by hurling her army and navy against China, is now known as the most powerful drug peddler the world has ever seen. At the same time, the saintly British Queen Victoria took Hong Kong away from China, and Hong Kong remains a British colony to this day, and a monument to Christian Queen Victoria's Opium War. And the saintly British were selling opium in China as late as World War I.

The United States also became addicted to drugs as the result of a war. U.S. President John F. Kennedy put the first United States Combat soldiers into the Vietnam War, which finally included over 3,000,000 men. In Vietnam these men were exposed to cheap opium and other recreational drugs and hundreds of thousands of them became addicts and brought their addiction home. This resulted in a great wave of drug addiction in the United States. Even President John Kennedy was reported in the news media to be using recreational drugs, and newsmen speculated whether Kennedy would be conscious and able to handle a war crises if one arose.

When the Russians put nuclear missiles in Cuba, President Kennedy ran to ex-president Eisenhower, to ex-president Truman, and to ex-president Hoover, asking them, "What must I do?" Seeing this, newsmen wondered if Kennedy's use of recreational drugs had so muddled and weakened his mind that he was unable to make his own decisions.

Incidentally, President Kennedy was a devout Roman Catholic churchman who followed Bible morals, such as they are.

THE SLAUGHTERING CONTINUES

From Gibeon the Jews under Saint Joshua moved on to the city of Makkedah. "And that day Joshua took Makkedah, and smote it with the edge of the sword, and the king thereof he utterly destroyed, them and all the souls that were therein; he let none remain; and he did to the king of Makkedah as he did unto the king of Jericho." (Joshua 10:28) All the men, women and children were murdered. And their goods were stolen by the Israelites. It was genocide. Another bloody holocaust.

Then Saint Joshua marched his army to the city of Libnah. "And the Lord Jehovah delivered it also, and the king thereof, into the hand of Israel; and he smote it with the edge of the sword, and all the souls that were therein; he let none remain in it." (Joshua 10:29,30) Again all the men, women and children in the city were murdered and their property stolen. More genocide. Another massacre drenched in human blood.

Next Saint Joshua and his enormous army of Jews attached the city of Lachish, and the same thing happened. Joshua and his arm slaughtered all the men, women and children in the city and stole their property. (Joshua 10:31, 32) The Bible says: "Then Horam king of Gezer came up to help Lachish; and Joshua smote him and his people, until he had left him none remaining." (Joshua 10:33)

"And from Lechish Joshua passed unto Eglon, and all Israel with him; and they encamped against it, and fought against it. And they took it on that day, and smote it with the edge of the sword, and all the souls that were therein he utterly destroyed that day." (Joshua 10:34,35) All the men, women and children, young and old were murdered by Joshua's gang of Jewish cut-throats. More genocide. Another holocaust.

"So Joshua smote all the country of the hills, and of the south, and of the vale, and of the springs, and all their kings; he left none remaining, but utterly destroyed all that breathed, as the Lord Jehovah God of Israel commanded." (Joshua 10:40) If Jehovah the God if Israel commanded such atrocities, he would not have been a God, but a demon, by common religious definition. Of course, there is no proof that there is either a god or a demon. Such entities are merely imaginary religious assumptions, like angels, elves and fairies.

And so this dreary tale of murder, bloodshed, and robbery goes on and on in the Bible. If you want to read it all, turn to the book of Joshua in the Bible and you will get your fill. City after city of the native inhabitants of Palestine fell under the smashing blows of Joshua's enormous army of 600,000 Jews. None had an army large enough to withstand him, so the native Canaanites were murdered wholesale, one city after another. It was genocide, which the Israelites under Moses invented. Other conquering nations took captives, but the only captives the Jews ever took were young women, for the purpose of rape. In most cases the Israelites completely slaughtered everyone they met. They revelled in bloodshed and genocide. It was an enormous holocaust and massacre by the Jews, leaving bloody corpses of small children, beautiful women, and valiant men.

Under Saint Joshua and Saint Moses the Israelites slaughtered thirty-three kings together with their millions of people: men, women and children. All this murder was carried on for the purpose of stealing the land, houses, vineyards and other possessions that these murdered people once owned. These Palestinian people were living peacefully in their land, and were ruthlessly attached by the Jewish hordes and murdered in the name of the Israelite tribal God Jehovah. The non-Jewish men, women and children were cut to pieces by the swords of the Jews, and the bellies of the pregnant non-Jewish women were ripped up so that their unborn infants gushed forth. (2 Kings 15:16) Also the young women and girls were raped and then murdered by these Israelite "chosen people" of their tribal God Jehovah. What a holy bloody massacre and holocaust these Bible saints were performing! It was genocide, more murder of peaceful people, more wholesale robbery, all by Saint Joshua and his Jewish gangsters.

No decent civilized person can read this bloody record in the Bible and have anything but revulsion and contempt for the saintly Bible religion which sanctifies it and glorifies it.

Saint Moses and Saint Joshua were indeed both bloody, murderous, scandalous saints. As the prophet Isaiah truly says: "Instead of sweet smell there shall be stink." (Isaiah 3:24, K.J.V.)

Meanwhile the Bible is held forth as the guide to all righteousness. Even young children are herded into Sunday Schools and synagogues to be exposed to its influence. Mark Twain, the famous American author, had this to say about the Bible: "The mind that becomes soiled in youth can never be washed clean. I know this by my own experience, and to this day I cherish an unappeasable bitterness against the unfaithful guardians of my young life, who not only permitted but compelled me to read an unexpurgated Bible through before I was fifteen years old. None can do that and ever draw a sweet breath again."

BUT GOD WAS DEFEATED BY IRON CHARIOTS

That's what the Bible says. Almighty God was powerless when faced with chariots of iron. Of course, no Israelite called God "almighty" since the time of Moses. Only Abraham had called God almighty. Moses changed the Israelites' name for their tribal God to Jehovah. So obviously they no longer expected their god to be almighty. And they were right, according to Biblical history.

Proof of this came soon after Saint Joshua's death. The tribes of Israel continued to slaughter the Canaanites in their conquest of Palestine, but then they ran into trouble. They met Palestinians who had chariots of iron and the Israelite God was unable to give them victory.

The Bible tells us: "And the Lord Jehovah was with Judah; and he drave out the inhabitants of the mountain; but could not drive out the inhabitants of the valley, because they had chariots of iron. (Judges Chapter 1 and Verse 19) Can you imagine that? Their god was powerless before horse-drawn chariots of iron! We wonder what the Israelite God Jehovah would do if he were around today and had to face motor driven iron army tanks with rapid firing cannon and machine guns. Not to mention nuclear missiles.

CHAPTER XVIII.   THE SAINT WHO ROASTED HIS OWN DAUGHTER

When Saint Moses was leading the Israelites to attack the native people of Canaan to slaughter them, Moses damned these people up and down for sacrificing their sons and daughters to their God Molech. Saint Moses said: "For every abomination to the Lord (Jehovah), which he hateth, have they (the Canaanites) done unto their gods; for even their sons and their daughters they have burnt in the fire to their gods." (Deuteronomy 12:31) Moses used that justification to incite the Jews to kill all these people.

However, Saint Moses taught the Israelites to do even worse. Saint Moses taught them in his Bible to sacrifice not only children, but adult humans also as burnt offerings. In the last Chapter of Leviticus in the Bible, where Moses gives the laws concerning sacrificial offerings to his God Jehovah, Moses writes: Notwithstanding no devoted thing, that a man shall devote unto the Lord (Jehovah) of all that he hath, both of man and beast, and of the field of his possession, shall be sold or redeemed: every devoted thing is most holy unto the Lord (Jehovah). No one devoted, which shall be devoted of men, shall be redeemed; but shall surely be put to death." (See the Bible at Leviticus Chapter 27 and Verses 28 and 29, K.J.F.) This emphasized that the Bible is here talking about human sacrifices as offerings to the God Jehovah, by speaking "both of man and beast." The American Standard Version translation is even clearer. It says: "No one devoted, that shall be devoted from among men, shall be ransomed; he shall surely be put to death."

Ant this is exactly what the followers of Saint Moses understood. The "holy" Bible gives us an account of one such human sacrifice. The Bible says: "Now Jephthah the Gileadite was a mighty man of valor, and he was the son of an harlot: and Gilead begat Jephthah." He had to have sexual intercourse with a prostitute and got her pregnant. Then she bore this son, Jephthah. However, this was all righteous and holy according to Moses. Saint Moses gave no law punishing men for having sexual intercourse with whores.

The Bible tale continues: "And Gilead's wife bare him sons; and his wife's sons grew up, and thrust out Jephthah, and said unto him, 'Thou shalt not inherit in our father's house; for thou art the son of a strange woman.' Then Jephthah fled from his brethren and dwelt in the land of Tob." (Judges 11:1-3)

As time went on, the Israelites got into a quarrel with the Ammonites who were their distant relatives, and the quarrel finally led to warfare. Then the Gileadites suddenly remembered Jephthah who was a mighty swordsman, and they sent to get him to lead the forces of Israel.

But Saint Jephthah was reluctant to take over the job. "And Jephthah said unto the elders of Gilead, 'Did not ye hate me, and expel me out of my father's house? and why are ye come unto me now when ye are in distress?'" (Judges 11:7)

Well, the Gileadites told Jephthah that if he would lead the army they would make him the head of all the Gileadites, not only during the war, but afterwards as well. This pleased Jephthah, who felt that if he could become their head, he could then be lord over those who had driven him out of his father's house.

Jephthah first attempted negotiations to bring about peace with the Ammonites, but when the talks failed, Jephthah gathered together his army and advanced upon the Ammonites.

Now even though Saint Jephthah was the son of a prostitute, he was a very religious man. He devoutly worshipped the Israelite tribal God Jehovah, and as he began the attack on the Ammonites he made a vow to his God. Moses' Bible tells us: "And Jephthah vowed a vow unto the Lord Jehovah and said, 'If thou shalt without fail deliver the children of Ammon into mine hands, then it shall be that whatsoever cometh forth of the doors of my house to meet me when I return in peace from the children of Ammon, shall surely be the Lord's and I will offer it up for a burnt offering." (Judges Chapter 11 and Verses 30 and 31) Note the words of this vow carefully and see how it was fulfilled according to Bible law.

Then Moses' Bible tells us: "So Jephthah passed over unto the children of Ammon to fight against them; and the Lord delivered them into his hands." (Judges 11:32) Saint Jephthah and his army won the war, and he returned home a hero.

But then something happened that he had not expected. Moses' Bible continues: "And Jephthah came to Mizpeh unto his house and behold, his daughter came out to meet him with timbrels and with dances. And she was his only child; beside her he had neither son nor daughter."

"And it came to pass when he saw her, that he rent his clothes and said, 'Alas, my daughter! Thou has brought me very low.'" (Judges 11:34, 35) He had vowed that "Whatsoever cometh forth of the doors of my house . . . . shall surely be the Lord's and I will offer it up for a burnt offering." It was his only daughter that had come through the doors of his house, and now she was doomed to be his burnt offering to his tribal God!

Saint Jephthah must have known that whoever would come through the doors of his house would be human. Perhaps he had been quarreling with his wife and he had thought that she would be the first to come through the doors of his house, and this would be a dandy excuse to get rid of her by using her as a burnt offering. Instead it was his daughter that was now to be the burnt offering. His plans had gone awry!

"Alas!" Saint Jephthah cried, as he saw his daughter come out of the house. Then he told her of the vow he had made, and that she would have to be offered up as a burnt sacrifice on the altar to their barbaric tribal God Jehovah, as Bible law required.

But Saint Jephthah's daughter was also a follower of their tribal God. She did not object to being used as a burnt offering to Jehovah God. But she had one request to make. She said, "Let this thing be done for me, let alone two months, that I may go up and down upon the mountains and bewail my virginity." (Judges 11:37) She wanted two months to reconcile herself to her fate.

Or maybe she wanted two months to make her escape to a far distant territory where she would be safe from Moses' insane law approving human sacrifices, and her stupid religious father. If she fled northwestward, it was only about seventy-five miles to Sidon in Phoenicia, where she would be completely out of Israel and free from Israel's lunatic religious laws. And maybe her father Jephthah hoped she would do just that. Maybe he hoped she would run off and thus he would be free of his Biblical obligation to sacrifice her on an altar.

In any event, Saint Jephthah told her to go. "And he said, 'Go' and he sent her away for two months." (Judges 11:38)

One would expect any normal teenage girl to run away under these circumstances, and save her life from religious fanaticism. But Saint Jephthah's daughter was not a normal teenage girl. She had been raised by her religious father, and had absorbed her father's religious idea that the

Bible is the word of God, and must be obeyed. Children are like that even today. It takes long years of study oftentimes for offspring to break away from their parents' beliefs, in spite of the fact that there is no proof whatsoever that the Bible is the inspired word of God.

The Bible tells us what happened next: "And it came to pass at the end of two months that she returned unto her father, who did with her according to his vow which he had vowed." (Judges 11:39) And what had he vowed? We return to the Bible statement at Judges Chapter 11 and Verses 30 and 31 which say: "And Jephthah vowed a vow unto the Lord Jehovah and said, 'If thou shalt without fail deliver the children of Ammon into mine hands, then it shall be that whatsoever cometh forth of the doors of my house to meet me, when I return in peace from the children of Ammon, shall surely be the Lord's, and I will offer it up for a burnt offering!'"

So Saint Jephthah built an altar of rock and laid his daughter upon it, and piled firewood all around her. Then he raised high his dagger and plunged it again and again into her young body until she stopped struggling and screaming in pain and was dead. When she ceased breathing Saint Jephthah lit the firewood around her bleeding body, and roasted his daughter as a sacrifice to the barbaric Jewish Bible God Jehovah, as the Bible commands. Now do you really think that such saintly Bible teachings are uplifting to humanity? These human sacrifices reveal the Jewish Christian Bible religion to be one of the most degrading religions of the world.

CHAPTER XIX. THE SAINT WHO CUT HIS WIFE IN PIECES

Many years after the barbaric human sacrifice we just examined, another savage event took place among the Israelites. There was a saintly Levite whose concubine ran away from him and went back to her father's house at Bethlehem. This, of course, is nothing unusual. Newlywed brides of today sometimes go home to mother when they get into an argument with their husbands.

This Levite's concubine, however, stayed away for four months, so the man decided he would have to go to his father-in-law's house to see if he could persuade his concubine to return and live with him. Concubines in Israel were not mere mistresses. They were actually second class wives. The chief difference between concubines and wives was that the offspring of concubines could not inherit from their fathers. Instead they depended upon their fathers to give them gifts in lieu of inheritances.

So the saintly Levite took his young man slave with him, and they rode to Bethlehem on a couple of burros. When the Levite's concubine saw him arrive, she took him into her father's house. There the Levite's father-in-law wined and dined him with much feasting for quite a few days. Finally, however, the Levite and his concubine and the young man slave began their journey back home.

Toward evening as the sun went down, the travelers stopped at the city of Gibeah, in the territory of the Israelite tribe of Benjamin. There were no inns or hotels where they could find lodging, so they waited in the street to see if some of the local people would give them a place to stay for the night. The Bible says: "And behold, there came an old man from his work out of the field at even, which was also of mount Ephraim." (Judges 19:16) Mount Ephraim was the place where the saintly Levite had his home, so he and the old man struck up a conversation together. Then the old man invited them all to come with him to his house to stay for the night, which they did. "So he brought him into his house, and gave provender unto the asses: And they washed their feet, and did eat and drink." (Judges 19:21)

Then, the Bible tells us, trouble erupted, "Now as they were making their hearts merry, behold, the men of the city, certain sons of Belial, (a Bible name for the devil) beset the house round about and beat at the door, and spake to the master of the house, the old man, saying, 'Bring forth the man that came into thine house, that we may know him." (Judges 19:27) The men in this mob wanted to have homosexual sex relations with the saintly Levite man. Homosexuality seems to have been quite common among the Jews even though Moses' law forbade it. Moses' Bible says: "And the man, the master of the house, went out unto them and said unto them, "nay, my brethren, nay, I pray you, do not so wickedly; seeing that this man is come into mine house, do not this folly. Behold, here is my daughter, a maiden, and his concubine. Them I will bring out now, and humble ye them, and do to them what seemeth good unto you. But unto this man do not so vile a thing." (Judges 19:23,24) This is another tale like the Biblical story of Saint Lot, that shows how little the saintly Israelite men cared for their wives and daughters. Here they were quite willing to throw the young women out into the hands of the mob, which was invited to "do to them what seemeth good unto you." In other words, if the men in the mob were not satisfied with normal sex relations, they were invited to engage in anal sex or oral sex relations as homosexuals usually do. This was quite all right with the old man and the saintly Levite man.

Again, when men are more interested in other men than in women, we are correct in assuming that they are homosexuals. So here, with the old man and the Levite man offering the women to the mob, it must be assumed that these two men were interested in each other for the same reason that the mob was interested in the Levite man. What else can we conclude?

Moses' Bible continues: "But the men (of the mob) would not harken to him: so the man (the saintly Levite) took his concubine and brought her forth unto them. And they knew her (they had sexual intercourse with her, in plain words) and abused her all the night until the morning; and when the day began to spring they let her go. Then came the woman in the dawning of the day, and fell down at the door of the man's house where her lord was, till it was light." (Judges 19:25, 26) The saintly Levite's concubine was in a state of collapse after being sexually mistreated all night. Anal sexual intercourse causes great pain and bleeding, and this poor woman was gang raped in this matter by the entire mob.

In the morning the Levite arose and found his concubine dead on the doorstep. You can imagine how the saintly man felt. He was enraged at the mob that had killed his wife with their sexual assault. And yet he must have felt guilt over having thrust her out the door into the hands of the rapist mob. Why hadn't he stood his ground like a man and fought to defend his wife against these vicious rapists? Remorse may have seized him. Yet Jewish Bible religion placed little value on women. There was always another one to be had somewhere at a nominal price.

Still anger against the mob seethed in his bosom. As the sun rose in the sky the saint loaded his concubine's body onto one of his burros. Then he and his man slave set out on their journey home.

By the time the saintly Levite reached his own house a plan for vengeance had formed in his mind, and he was determined to execute it. The Bible tells us: "And when he (the Levite) was come into his house, he took a knife, and laid hold on his concubine, and divided her, together with her bones, into twelve pieces, and sent her unto all the coasts of Israel. And it was so, that all that saw it said, There was no such deed done nor seen from the day that the children of Israel came up out of the land of Egypt unto this day. Consider of it, take advice, and speak your minds." (Judges 19:29, 30) So said the Israelites who saw the pieces of the woman's body and heard the story of her death.

To their credit, the Israelites were all outraged by the vicious murder that had been committed, and the adultery involved. Raping a woman was not unlawful in Israel, according to their Bible. But when she belonged to a man, she was his property and other men must leave her alone. If they raped her then it was adultery, and Moses' law called for the death penalty on the men who dared to do so vile an act.

The Bible says: "Then all the children of Israel went out, and the congregation was gathered together as one man, from Dan even to Beer-Sheba, with the land of Gilead, unto the Lord in Mizpeh. And the chief of all the people, even of all the tribes of Israel, presented themselves in the assembly." (Judges 20:1,2) Among them were four hundred thousand infantrymen who drew the sword. And the Benjamites, where the crime had happened, heard about it.

Then the Israelites asked the saintly Levite to tell them what had happened. "And the Levite, the husband of the woman that was slain, answered and said, 'I came into Gibeah that belongeth to (the tribe of) Benjamin, I and my concubine, to lodge. And the men of Gibeah rose against me, and beset the house round about upon me by night, and thought to have slain me. And my concubine have they forced, that she is dead."

"And I took my concubine and cut her in pieces, and sent her throughout all the country of the inheritance of Israel; for they have committed lewdness and folly in Israel."

"Behold, ye are all children of Israel. Give here your advice and counsel." (Judges 20:4-7)

After hearing the Levite's story the saintly Israelites were even more enraged. They determined to punish the guilty. Moses' Bible says: "So all the men of Israel were gathered together against the city, knit together as one man. And the tribes of Israel sent men through all the tribe of Benjamin (where this crime occurred) saying, 'What wickedness is this that is done among you? Now therefore, deliver us the men, the children of Belial which are in Gibeah, that we may put them to death, and put away evil from Israel.'" (Judges 20:11-13)

However, the tribe of Benjamin flatly refused to deliver up the criminals who had raped and murdered the woman. Instead, they gathered together at Gibeah, where the crime occurred, to protect Gibeah from the other Israelites.

Now if the eleven tribes of Israel had quietly sent a delegation to the chiefs of the tribe of Benjamin, perhaps the issue could have been settled peacefully. But when the eleven tribes massed an army on Benjamin's border, that riled the hotheads in the tribe to resist by massing their own army.

So the Bible says: "And the children of Israel arose, and went up to the house of God, and asked counsel of God, and said, 'Which of us shall go up first to the battle against the children of Benjamin?' And the Lord Jehovah said, 'Judah shall go up first.'" (Judges 20:18) Now from this text some may assume that God spoke with his voice out of the clouds and told them what to do, but that is not the case. The way the Israelites found out what their tribal God Jehovah wanted, was to go to the high priest and ask their question. Then to get the answer, the high priest would cast lots with the "Urim and Thummim," which were two sacred stones. (Exodus 38:30) In other words, they found out their God's will by doing something equivalent to rolling dice. If the priest rolled something like "lucky seven" then he said their God favored the project. However, if he rolled something like "snake eyes" the deal was off. This was nothing but a saintly crap-shoot, with their game imported from Egypt. (At the same time Moses' Bible condemns those who use divination, apparently because they didn't want anyone to compete with the high priest's fortune-telling business.)

Well, the lot fell upon the tribe of Judah to fight with the tribe of Benjamin first. So the saintly soldiers of Israel attacked the Benjamites and were thoroughly defeated on the first day. Then they attacked the Benjamites again the second day and were defeated again. But the third day the attacking Israelites were more cleaver, and while they attacked the Benjamites again as before, the Israelites fell back and pretended to flee from them. Meanwhile the saintly Israelites had set an ambush against the city of Gibeah, and when the Benjamites were drawn away from Gibeah by chasing the fleeing Israelites, the ambushing soldiers attacked the city, killed all the inhabitants, and set the city of fire.

Moses' Bible tells us: "So that all which fell that day of Benjamin were twenty and five thousand men that drew the sword. All these were men of valor. But six hundred men turned and fled to the wilderness unto the rock Rimmon, and abode in the rock Rimmon four months."

"And the men of Israel turned again upon the children of Benjamin, and smote them with the edge of the sword, as well the men of every city, as the beast, and all that came to hand: also they set on fire all the cities (of Benjamin) that they came to." (Judges 20:46-48) Not only the soldiers of the tribe of Benjamin were killed, but also the women and children were all slaughtered.

This was rather drastic vengeance for the rape death of one woman.

MORE RAPE TO SET THINGS RIGHT

The Bible continues: "Now the men of Israel had sworn in Mizpeh, saying, 'There shall not any of us give his daughter unto Benjamin to wife.'" (Judges 21:1) But a problem arose here. They had slaughtered almost all the tribe of Benjamin in their war of vengeance. Only six hundred men of Benjamin survived, and they had no wives since all the women and children of their tribe had been annihilated. (Judges 21:16) The tribe of Benjamin would perish out of the nation of Israel unless something was done. "And the children of Israel repented them for Benjamin their brother, and said, 'There is one tribe cut off from Israel this day.'" (Judges 21:6) The Israelites had learned this type of genocidal warfare from Saint Moses and Saint Joshua, and even practiced it on themselves. Their "holy" Bible teaches genocide well, even to this day.

Because they had sworn that they would not give wives to any of the men of the tribe of Benjamin, they were in a quandary as to where women could be found for the surviving Benjamites. Then they hit on a plan. The Bible says, "They had made a great oath concerning him that came not up to the Lord to Mizpeh, saying, He shall surely be put to death." (Judges 21:5) The Jewish saints were great at making oaths and killing people. Moses' Bible tells us: "And behold, there came not to the camp from Jabesh-gilead to the assembly." (Judges 21:8) So according to their oath, the people of Jabesh-gilead must be put to death. The Bible says: "And the congregation sent thither twelve thousand men of the valiantest, and commanded them, saying, 'Go and smite the inhabitants of Jabesh-gilead with the edge of the sword, with the women and the children. And this is the thing that ye shall do, ye shall utterly destroy every male, and every woman that hath lain by man. And they found among the inhabitants of Jabesh-gilead four hundred young virgins, that had known no man by lying with any male." (Judges 21:10-12)

So the saintly soldiers seized these four hundred girls and brought them to the six hundred surviving soldiers of the tribe of Benjamin, and they gave the girls to them to be their wives. Of course, the consent of the girls was never asked, and therefore the procedure was nothing but wholesale rape.

But the rape wasn't over yet. Four hundred girls, some of them only three years of age, were not enough for six hundred men, so more girls must be found. Yes, there is no age limit for marriage in the Bible, and a girl of three can be married to an adult man and have sexual intercourse, according to Bible law.

Then the saintly Israelites remembered there was to be a dance at a religious festival in Shiloh soon. So they commanded the soldiers of the tribe of Benjamin who had not yet obtained wives, saying: "Go and lie in wait in the vineyards. And see, and behold, if the daughters of Shiloh come out to dance in dances, then come ye out of the vineyards, and catch you every man his wife of the daughters of Shiloh, and go to the land of Benjamin." So this is exactly what the soldiers did. They seized the girls they wanted, and ran off with them, and forced them to engage in sexual intercourse.

This was nothing but rape. However, there is no law against rape anywhere in the Bible, neither under Saint Moses' teachings or under Jesus' teachings, so nobody could be punished for it. And when the girls' fathers and brothers complained, then they were told: "Be favorable unto them for our sakes, because we reserved not to each man his wife in the war. For ye did not give unto them (the girls) at this time, that ye should be guilty." (Judges 21:22) They had not voluntarily given their daughters to the

Benjamites, and therefore they were not guilty of violating their oath.

So to avenge the rape of one woman, and her murder, the saintly Israelites killed thousands of men, women and children and caused the rape of hundreds of girls. This is a typical example of the wild and irrational kind of justice that appears in the Bible time after time. They must have been out in the hot desert sun too long with their turbans off. Too much sunshine can cause people to be overly excitable and mentally unbalanced.

Of course, some will say that even today wars are fought over the killing of one person, and point to the assassination of Archduke Ferdinand as the cause of World War I. However this is an over-simplification of the cause of that war. It is known that Britain had been arming her merchant ships in preparation for war against Germany for a year and a half before the Archduke was murdered and World War I began. Commercial rivalry was one of the major causes of that war.

If the United Stated had not intervened in World War I and saved Britain from being conquered by the Germans, Kaiser Wilhelm would undoubtedly have left King George V on the British throne because he was a German.

As an interesting sidelight, when Britain fought Germany in World War I, the royal family of Britain, which is German, quietly changed its name from the German name of Wettin to Windsor. This reminds one how thousands of Germans in the United States suddenly claimed to be Dutch because of the war. If all of the counterfeit Dutch in America had been real, there wouldn't have been one person left in the Netherlands. Actually, U.S. immigration statistics show that the largest number of white immigrants to the U.S. were German. If the people of German ancestry in the United States ever voted as an ethnic bloc it would change the future of the world.

Since the English boast of being Anglo-Saxon, it seems very peculiar that their royal family should want to hide the fact that they are German. Where do some people think the Saxons came from? Jerusalem? Saxony is one of the largest states in Germany, and was formerly ruled over by an ancestor of the English royal family who was also named Wettin. And the Anglo-Saxon English are similarly of German ancestry.

Also those English of Danish or Norwegian ancestry should remember that all Scandinavians are also Teutonic or Germanic. And those of French ancestry should know that the Franks of France are likewise a Teutonic or Germanic people. So what's the problem?

But all the deception was not in Britain. In the United States Woodrow Wilson was elected president in 1916 on his promise to keep the

United States out of the war in Europe. Once elected, Wilson immediately broke his promise and plunged America into World War I. After all, with the new income tax law just passed there were billions of dollars that could be drained from the taxpayers' pockets and given to those merchants and manufacturers who profited immensely by selling supplies to the military. Hordes of new millionaires were made at the U.S. taxpayers' expense. More money was spent by the U.S. Government in World War I than in all the previous wars combined. This made Wilson a hero in the minds of his dupes and the war profiteers.

Wilson used the sinking of the <u>Lucitania</u> as a pretext to put the United States into World War I. However, the <u>Lucitania</u> was a British ship carrying a cargo of guns and ammunition for the British military, as well as passengers. With Britain and Germany at war, of course German submarines would sink this ship when it tried to run the German naval blockade of Britain. This was no reason at all to put the United States into the war.

Then the Judeo-Christian British Government manufactured a false document supposed to be a German offer to give to Mexico the southwestern states of the U.S. if little Mexico would attack the United States. However, the United States was not at that time at war with Germany, so this document was obviously false since Germany had no reason to promote such an attack. But the British were desperate to enlist the U.S. on their side as Britain and France were then losing the war with Germany. President Woodrow Wilson was pro-British and quickly seized on this fraudulent document as another excuse to make war on Germany. It was an outrage against the American people.

So if you think that Woodrow Wilson was a liar, a scoundrel and a traitor you are in agreement with most Americans of that time. Most people were angry that Wilson, a Democrat, had lied and put the United States into the war in Europe. So the Democrats were thrown out of the presidency with the election of Warren Harding, a Republican, to be president of the United States.

Incidentally, Woodrow Wilson was the Christian son of a presbyterian preacher. So much for the so-called beneficial influence of the Christian church on its members. An even greater expose' of the Christian religion is the fact that American, British, French and Russian Christians were killing German Christians, and German Christians were killing Allied Christians, all in the name of Christianity; with Christian preachers accompanying the soldiers, telling them why it was a holy thing to kill the Christians on the other side.

CHAPTER XX. THE STRONGMAN WHOSE WEAKNESS WAS WOMEN

Most men have a weakness for women, but here we have a man who let his women get the best of him. And we come to the tale of a saint who was so strong he carried off the gates of a walled city. The story begins in typical fabulous fashion with an angel coming down and announcing to a woman that she was pregnant. This happened to Sarah and Abraham too, accoridng to the saintly Bible writers, and was the sort of thing that made a story more saintly and more religious. And if you're trying to peddle religion, why not make these Bible stories as religious as possible? So the more angels, the better.

It seems that this woman was so ignorant and so much of a dim bulb she didn't know that if she skipped a couple of months she was pregnant. So an angel had to be dispatched from heaven by the Almighty to tell her what any of her neighbor women cound have told her, or what she would have found out in nine months anyhow willy-nilly.

Eventually, the saintly Bbile writer tells us, "The woman bore a son, and called his name Samson." (Judges 13:24) So Samson grew into a man, and not only that, a holy man who was consecrated to be a Nazarite, that is, a special kind of holy man who never cut his hair, like the hippies, and who never took a drink of wine, but who may have used hasheesh instead, like most Semites and some hippies.

The Bible writer tells us: "And Samson went down to Timnath, and saw a woman in Timnath of the daughters of the Philistines. And he came up, and told his father and his mother, and said, 'I have seen a woman in Timnath of the daughters of the Philistines: now therefore get her for me to wife.' Then his father and his mother sent unto him, 'Is there never a woman among the daughters of thy (Jewish) brethren or among all my people, that thou goest to take a wife of the uncircumcised Philistines?'

And Samson said unto his father, 'Get her for me; for she pleaseth me well.'" (Judges 14:1-3)

At that time the Philistines had conquered Israel. The Jews had never been able to destroy the Philistines, who dwelt on the Mediterranean coast of Palestine. But now, after the Jews had moved into the highlands of Palestine, killing all the native inhabitants, now the Philistines had attacked the Jews and conquered them, so that the Jews were subjects of the Philistines. What a come-down from the days of Moses and Joshua!

In those days Samson was born, and grew up to be a huge muscleman. He was the kind of guy who today would be a champion boxer or wrestler, or a football lineman. Of course, the religious idiots among the Jews attributed Samson's great strength to the fact that he was a Nazarite who never had a haircut. They never stopped to think that there were numerous other Nazarite holy men who never had a haircut, but who were no stronger than the average guy you'd meet on the street. Religion sure fogs people's brains up, doesn't it?

On his way down to visit his girl friend, Samson was roared at by a young lion. So he grabbed this lion and broke its neck, Saint Samson was so strong. Then he continued on to see his date. "And he (Samson) went down, and talked with the woman; and she pleased Samson well. And after a time he returned to take her (to be his wife), and he turned aside to see the carcass of the lion; and, behold, there was a swarm of bees and honey in the carcass of the loan. And he took thereof in his hands, and went on eating (the honey), and came to his father and mother . . . . So his father went down unto the woman: and Samson made there a feast; for so used the young men to do." (Judges 14:7-10)

So at this wedding feast Samson proposed a riddle to his Philistine guests. "And Samson said unto them, 'I will now put forth a riddle unto you; if ye can certainly declare it to me within the seven days of the feast, and find it out, then I will give you thirty sheets and thirty changes of garments: but if ye cannot declare it to me, then shall ye give me thirty sheets and thirty changes of garments.' And they said unto him, 'Put forth thy riddle, that we may hear it.' And he said unto them, 'Out of the eater came forth meat, and out of the strong came forth sweetness.' And they could not in three days expound the riddle. On the seventh day they said to Samson's wife, 'Entice thy husband, that he may declare unto us the riddle, lest we burn thee and thy father's house with fire: have ye called us to take that we have? Is it not so?" (Judges 14;12-15)

Samson's wife was frightened, and went to Saint Samson and wept and pleaded that he tell her the riddle. She said, "You hate me; you don't love me because you put forth this riddle, but never told me the solution."

But Samson replied that he hadn't even told his parents that, so why should he tell her? But she wept and begged all the more. Well, Samson was one of those men who is an easy mark for a woman's tears, so he finally gave in and told her. Then she ran and told the Philistines.

The Bible tells us: "And the men of the city said unto him (Samson) on the seventh day (of the feast) before the sun went down, 'What is sweeter than honey? and what is stronger than a lion?'

"And he (Samson) said unto them, 'If ye had not plowed with my heifer, ye had not found out my riddle.'" (Judges 14:18) He knew that his wife had told them the solution.

But this mightily angered Samson, and when a very strong man is angry, look out! So Samson went to the Philistine city of Ashkelon and killed thirty men, took off their garments, and gave this raiment to those who had told the riddle. Then still boiling with rage, he went back to his father's house. And Samson's wife was given to his companion, who had been his best man at the wedding.

Why Samson was not charged and tried for murder after killing the thirty men we are not told in the Bible. But the tale of Saint Samson, like many other tales in the Bible, is similar to some of the mystery novels we read today. Logic and fact are often ignored to make the story better. Yes, of course they had laws against murder in those days. Moses had been charged with murder in Egypt long before that, and centuries before Moses they had laws against murder in Babylon, as we know. But how could they tell the rest of this story if the hero was convicted and executed for murder in the first episode? So an arrest and trial for murder is not even mentioned.

TOO MANY FOXES

Next the saintly writer of this tale tells us that Samson finally cooled off enough to go back and visit his wife again, and he brought a kid of the goats for her to eat. But when he got to her house, and wanted to go into her bedroom with her (for some reason), then her father would not let him go in.

The Bible tells us: "And her father said, 'I verily thought that thou hadst utterly hated her; therefore I gave her to thy companion (to be his wife.) Is not her younger sister fairer than she? Take her, I pray thee, instead of her." (Judges 15:2)

This enraged Samson again. The Bible continues: "And Samson

went and caught three hundred foxes, and took firebrands, and turned tail to tail, and put a firebrand in the midst between two tails." (Judges 15:4) Have you ever tried to catch foxes? If a trapper catches three foxes he's happy. But to catch three hundred foxes is impossible. We told you these Jewish writers of the Bible liked to exaggerate, and any fox trapper will tell you that this in one of their wildest exaggerations and egregious mistakes.

But just suppose Samson really caught three hundred foxes. What did he do with them? He'd have to put them in cages to keep them from running off, and with three hundred foxes he would have had three big wagon loads of cages to hall them in. But the Jews had no wagons then, and had little in the way of real roads to run them on.

So here Samson was with three hundred fighting, biting, snarling foxes and no cages to put them in. On top of that, can you see these wild foxes standing still and allowing Samson to tie their tails together? These wild foxes would have slashed and torn Saint Samson to bloody shreds with their teeth. Samson could in no way tie the tails of wild foxes together. This story is obviously pure fiction invented by some Jewish saint who never saw a wild fox in his life. And this is supposed to be the infallible inspired word of God, the holy Bible, and every word of it true. Only a religious fanatic could believe that.

At any rate, Samson is supposed to have caught three hundred foxes, and tied their tails together two by two, and tied a firebrand to the tails of each pair of foxes, lit the firebrands, and turned the foxes loose in the grain fields of the Philistines. The fields of course caught fire and were destroyed. In this way Saint Samson took vengeance on them for losing his wife, although the Philistines in general were not responsible for his losing his wife. Only his father-in-law was responsible for that.

Then the Philistines became angry and wanted to know who had done this. When they found out that Samson did it because his father-in-law, a Philistine, had given Samson's wife to somebody else, they burned down his father-in-law's house, killing his father-in-law and his ex-wife. Talk about the Wild West! This was the Wild East!

Now Samson used this fire as a further excuse to attack the Philistines. The Bible tale says: "And he smote them hip and thigh with a great slaughter: and he went down and dwelt in the tip of the rock Elam." (Judges 15:8)

THIS SAINT LIKED WHORES TOO

So the Philistines sent their army up into Judah to capture Saint Samson and punish him. But the Jews told the Philistines they would catch Samson themselves and deliver him to them. So the Jews sent three thousand men of their own to get Saint Samson.

But before Samson allowed them to tie him up he made the Jews promise they would not themselves injure him. This they did, and the Jews tied Samson up with new ropes and then took him down to the Philistines, who gave a big cheer as Samson was delivered to them.

According to the saintly Bible story, that shout by the Philistines was Samson's signal to go into action. Samson snapped the ropes that bound him, grabbed the bony jaw of a dead donkey that was lying on the ground, and knocked the Philistines flying with the bony weapon. As the Bible states: "And he found a new jawbone of an ass, and put forth his hand and took it, and slew a thousand men therewith." (Judges 15:15)

Now wait a minute. Let's look at this story carefully. There must have been more than a thousand Philistines there to fight Samson. What were these men of the Philistine army doing while Samson busily knocked the brains out of one thousand of their men? You and I know that some soldier in their army must have had a spear, and with that spear could easily have killed Samson no matter how strong he was. Or even without a spear, any of the soldiers could have picked up a rock the size of an orange and thrown it and knocked Samson's brains out, or a bowman could easily have shot and killed Samson with an arrow. So why didn't it happen? Again, do you want to spoil a good story by having the hero killed before the story is over? So we go on to the next episode.

The saintly Bible writer tells us: "Then went Samson to Gaza, and he saw there an harlot, and went in unto her." (Judges 16:1) She was undoubtedly not the first whore that Saint Samson "went in unto." (The Bible is very graphic in its description of sexual intercourse.) Yes, Samson was another holy saint who enjoyed having sex relations with whores, even though whores were prohibited by Moses' law, which law the holy saints cheerfully ignored. Nobody acted as though Moses' laws came from God at all. And in fact they did not. So the Jewish saints were less deceived by Moses than their religious followers are today.

Then the Philistine inhabitants of Gaza discovered that Samson was in their city, so they laid in wait to kill him at daylight. But the Bible tells us that Samson: "arose at midnight and took the doors of the gate of the city, and the two posts, and went away with them, bar and all, and put them upon his shoulders, and carried them up to the top of an hill that was before Hebron." (Judges 16:3) This was a first class insult to the men of Gaza.

HOW DELILAH DID IT TO HIM

After having sexual intercourse with the whore, it seems that Saint Samson again became more interested in women. They could be a lot of fun, he decided. So the saintly Bible writer tells us: "And it came to pass afterward, that he (Samson) loved a woman in the valley of Sorek, whose name was Delilah." (Judges 16:4) The Bible writer does not say that Delilah was Samson's wife, as many people assume. Yet he lived with her, unwed.

Delilah was a Philistine woman, so the lords of the Philistines came to her and said, "Entice him (Samson) and see wherein his great strength is, and by what means we may prevail against him, that we may bind him to afflict him: and each one of us will give you eleven hundred pieces of silver."

Well, with eleven hundred pieces of silver from each of the Philistine lords, Delilah would be a very wealthy woman. After thinking it over briefly, she decided to sell out Samson for the money. So she asked Samson what made him so strong, and how could he be bound so others could afflict him.

Samson replied, "If they bind me with seven green strings that have never been dried, then I shall be weak, and be as other men." Saint Samson looked at her closely to see if she believed him, and she seemed to. He laughed to himself at her gullibility.

The lords of the Philistines brought seven green strings to Delilah as she told them, and Samson let her bind him with them. He was highly amused by the whole procedure.

The saintly Bible writer tells us: "Now there were men lying in wait, abiding with her in the chamber. And she (Delilah) said unto him, 'The Philistines be upon thee, Samson.' And he brake the withs (strings) as a thread of tow is broken when it toucheth the fire. So his strength was not known." (Judges 16:9)

Delilah had been fooled, but she was not one to give up when so much money was at stake. So she came to Samson again and said "You mocked me and told me lies. Now tell me the truth as to how you can really be bound."

So Samson told her, "If thy bind me with new ropes that have never been used, then I shall be weak, and be as any other man."

Then Delilah tried again. She got new ropes and tied up Samson with them. Then she said, "The Philistines are coming, Samson." The saintly writer tells us that there were Philistines hiding in the room where she was with Samson. It must have been a large room with considerable furniture and drapes for them to hide behind.

But again Samson snapped the ropes as they though they were threads. Delilah was vastly disappointed. However, she had been promised plenty of money if she discovered Samson's secret source of strength, so she tried again.

The Bible tells us: "And Delilah said unto Samson, 'Hitherto thou hast mocked me, and told me lies: tell me wherewith thou mightest be bound. And he said unto her, 'If thou weavest the seven locks of my head with a web.'

"And she fastened it with the pin, and said unto him, 'The Philistines be upon thee, Samson.' And he awakened out of his sleep and went away with the pin of the beam, and with the web." (Judges 16:13,14)

Again Delilah was greatly disappointed. And she said to him, "How can you say that you love me, when your heart is not with me? You have mocked me these three times, and have not told me wherein your great strength lies."

And Delilah pressed him daily to reveal the secret of his strength. Finally, the Bible writer tells us that Samson's "soul was vexed unto death" by her nagging, so "that he told her all his heart, and said unto her, 'There hath not come a razor upon my head; for I have been a Nazarite unto God from my mother's womb: if I be shaven, then my strength will go from me, and I shall become weak and be like any other man.'"

"And when Delilah saw that he had told her all his heart, she sent and called for the lords of the Philistines, saying, 'Come up this once, for he hath shewed me all his heart.' Then the lords of the Philistines came up unto her, and brought money in their hand." (Judges 16:15-18)

Samson was as deceived as the other religious characters of his day. He firmly believed that his great strength was due to his not having his hair cut all these years. And this silly religious notion was his undoing, as we shall soon see.

Saint Samson's strength, of course, was due to his heredity. His father must have been a strong man, and his mother's father also a strong man, and his mother a strong woman. So naturally Saint Samson inherited this strength in a big and muscular body. Being a Nazarite holy man had nothing to do with it. But Samson was obsessed with this ridiculous Jewish religious idea, and thought that so long as he never had a haircut his strength would remain with him, and this was an egregious mistake.

Believe me, if growing a man's hair long would make him strong, every man in the world would be a Nazarite and have his hair growing down to his ankles. But the Philistines were taking no chances. They decided first to cut off all of Samson's hair from his head. And then they told Delilah what to do so Samson once his hair was cut off.

So Delilah petted Saint Samson and got him to doze off to sleep with his head in her lap. No sooner was he sound asleep then she had a Philistine barber cut all the hair off Samson's head. Then the saintly Bible writer tells us: "She began to afflict him (Samson) and his strength went from him." (Judges 16:19)

This statement in the Bible is completely contrary to fact. You and I know that when a man is afflicted or annoyed he becomes angry, and his adrenal glands pour adrenaline into his blood stream making him much stronger than he was before, and ready to fight. Affliction most certainly never drains a man of his strength. Instead it always increases a man's strength. So when the Bible claims that Delilah's affliction of Samson caused his strength to go from him, this statement is wrong and contrary to all knowledge.

However, the error is not due to what the saintly Bible scribe wrote in Hebrew, but is due to the mistake of the Bible translators. The word here translated "afflict" is from the Hebrew word "aw-naw", and may also be translated "force" (that is, to force one to have sexual intercourse), or similarly, "ravish." So now we are getting to the real understanding of the matter. The Bible translation should read: "She began to force him to have sexual intercourse, and his strength went from him." (Judges 16:19) This makes sense.

Of course, she undoubtedly did not use actual physical force against Samson, because she could not do that. But she just proceeded to have sexual intercourse with him without asking him if he was willing. And Saint Samson, being like most men, was very willing.

The human body is a big electrical battery that replenishes its strength every time we eat. A man's body generates more electricity than a woman's body, so a man is able to do strenuous physical work if necessity requires it. A woman's body contains a lower charge of electrical energy. Consequently, when a man and woman have sexual intercourse and the man has an orgasm, he not only ejaculates what the Bible calls "seed" (semen) into the woman, but a substantial amount of the man's electrical energy also, thus relaxing him. But too much sexual intercourse is very weakening to a man.

Every married man usually learns in the first two weeks of his married life, how much sexual intercourse he can engage in on any night without becoming pale, weak, and exhausted, and not worth ten cents at work the next day. So no matter how willing and cooperative and beautifully enticing his bride is, a married man soon discovers that he must use self-control in his sexual activity if he's going to avoid physical and mental exhaustion.

Each man's capacity for sexual intercourse varies from the next man. A few men have very great ability in bed. A famous lady said that one man she married boasted that he could have sexual intercourse with a woman seven times a night. She said that being married to this man was wearisome. Obviously if a man has sexual intercourse with his wife seven times in a night, neither one of them is going to get any sleep. It's like eating apple pie and ice cream. No matter how delicious it is, there is only so much a person can reasonably take.

Just how much sexual intercourse Saint Samson could engage in during one night we do not know. What we do know is that Delilah took off all her clothing, revealing all of her womanly beauty and seductiveness, and then proceeded to have sexual intercourse with Samson repeatedly, again and again and again, and this is how, as the Bible writer states, Samson's "strength went from him." (Judges 16:19) Samson lost his puissance. He became pale, weak and exhausted, and finally collapsed to the point where Delilah could no longer make Samson go "in unto her" as the Bible very factually describes it. (Judges 16:1) Saint Samson was finished. Delilah had done him in.

When Delilah saw that, she cried out, "The Philistines are coming, Samson!" Samson struggled to resist, but a gang of Philistines seized him. Samson found himself weak and unable to knock them flying as he had done at other times. So the Philistines took him and put out Samson's eyes, blinding him permanently. Then they chained him with fetters of brass, and forced him to grind grain in their prison.

This was an awful fate for a man like Saint Samson, but it shows what mistaken religious notions can do for a person. If Samson had realized that his strength lay in his heredity, he would not have recklessly allowed Delilah to weaken him so much. But instead, Saint Samson imagined that his strength was inexhaustible, being of divine origin. Now he found out differently, and was a prisoner of the Philistines.

However, just because Samson had too much sexual intercourse with his lady partner Delilah, and became pale, weak, and exhausted, did not mean that he would remain that way. If that were true, almost every man in the whole world would be permanently pale, weak, and exhausted, because most men overdo on sex at least once in their lifetimes. We have to live it up and learn.

But after getting a few square meals under his belt, Saint Samson revived and his strength quickly returned, as it does for all of us. Of course, the stupid religionists attributed Samson's returning strength to the fact that his hair began to grow out again. It's difficult for people to judge cause and effect rationally when their heads are full of religious nonsense.

Nevertheless, the Jews weren't the only ones who were superstitious. The Philistines were also muddle-headed religious rubbish. The saintly Bible writer tells us: "Then the lords of the Philistines gathered them together to offer a great sacrifice unto Dagon their God, and to rejoice, for they said, 'Our God hath delivered Samson our enemy into our hand." (Judges 16:23) The stupid Dagon worshippers didn't realize that it was their scheming and Delilah's cooperation that led to Samson's downfall. Their God Dagon had nothing to do with it, being a non-entity.

The Philistines had a great celebration over the capture and imprisonment of Saint Samson. Thousands of them gathered together in their assembly hall and surrounding area. The Bible tells us: "And they called for Samson out of the prison house; and he made them sport: and they set him between the pillars." (Judges 16:25) "Now the house was full of men and women; and all the lords of the Philistines were there; and there were upon the roof about three thousand men and women, that beheld while Samson made sport." (Judges 16:27) Samson was apparently doing some weight lifting and demonstrating other feats of strength for them, for he was no longer weak, pale and exhausted as when he was captured.

"And Samson said unto the lad that held him by the hand, 'Suffer me that I may feel the pillars whereupon the house standeth, that I may lean upon them." "And Samson took hold of the two middle pillars upon which the house stood, and on which it was borne up, of the one with his right hand, and of the other with his left. And Samson said, 'Let me die with the Philistines.' And he bowed himself with all his might and the house fell upon the lords, and upon all the people that were therein. So the dead which he slew at his death were more than they which he slew in his life." (Judges 16;26,27,29,30) So the saintly Bible writer tells us.

Samson did get revenge on the Philistines. However, there is considerable exaggeration here which we should examine, since the Bible claims to be the inspired word of God, and infallibly accurate. Here was this assembly hall of Philistines, built so large that they had three thousand people on the roof. This roof was held up by only two pillars. Let me ask you this: Have you ever been in an auditorium that could hold three thousand people? Then you know how enormous such a building is. Now here the Philistines are supposed to have had three thousand people on the roof of this building, and this roof was held up by only two pillars, so close together that Saint Samson could "take hold" of them with his hands.

In the first place, if these two pillars were to hold up as many as three thousand people, they would have had to be immense stone pillars at least three feet in diameter. No man could "take hold" of them with his hands, they could have to be so thick. Secondly, no flat roof that would hold three thousand people could be held up by merely two pillars. This is an architectural impossibility, and most certainly was in impossibility for the people of those days, considering the materials they had to work with. This part of Samson's story is an enormous exaggeration. Possibly the first writer of Saint Samson's story had thirty people on the roof. Then the scribe who copied the story onto the next scroll made it three hundred people on the roof, and so on, until the final copy had three thousand people on the roof, which baffled all rational people who read it. But we know the propensity of the Jewish scribes for exaggeration to make a good story better, and this is no exception. So much for the godly inspiration of the Bible and its saintly writers.

Saint Samson ruled Israel as judge for twenty years, which made him about forty years of age when he died. Like other athletes, his strength was well past its peak then, and his sexual ability likewise. No wonder Delilah did him in.

CHAPTER XXI. A GODLY MURDERER AND WIFE STEALER

Saul was king of Israel some years later and had a daughter named Michal. David was a commander in King Saul's army and a great hero in Israel because he had killed the Philistine giant Goliath, so Michal fell in love with David. (1 Samuel 18;20)

However, King Saul was no particular friend of David. It seems that Saint David had become so much of a folk hero among the Jews that King Saul had been thrown back in the shadows. Naturally the king became envious of David and hostile toward him, because Saul had been accustomed to receiving the adulation of the crowds, and now nobody paid attention to him anymore. Everybody was praising and glorifying David. Especially the women of the land who were dancing and singing: "King Saul has slain his thousands, but David has killed his ten thousands." This made Saul angry. "And Saul was very wroth and the saying displeased him; and he said, 'They have ascribed unto David ten thousands and to me they have ascribed but thousands. And what can he have more but the kingdom?' And Saul eyed David (suspiciously) from that day forward." (1 Samuel 18:6-8)

Nevertheless, with his daughter in love with David, King Saul thought he saw a way of getting rid of his rival. So Saul offered Saint David his daughter in marriage on conditions that would put David's life in danger. The Bible tells us: "And Saul said (to his servants), 'Thus shall ye say to David, "The king desireth not any dowry but a hundred foreskins (of the penises) of the Philistines, to be avenged of the king's enemies."' But Saul thought to make David fall by the hand of the Philistines." (1 Samuel 18:25)

Can you imagine this sort of barbaric and erotic thing happening in any civilized nation? That a ruler should offer his daughter in marriage to a man who would bring him one hundred of the severed private parts of his enemies? It's unheard of today. Yet here is the Bible, whom many regard as the "good Book," teaching people such barbaric practices as this. No wonder the majority have turned away from it.

When the Biblical hero Saint David heard King Saul's offer it pleased him well. "I'll cut off every one of the Philistines that pissess against the wall," he laughingly told the men under his command. This was one of David's favorite expressions. (See 1 Samuel 25:22 in the King James Version of the Bible.)

The Bible tale continues: "Wherefore David arose and went, he and his men, and slew of the Philistines two hundred men. And David brought their foreskins, and they gave them in full tale to the king, that he might be a king's son-in-law. And Saul gave him Michal his daughter to wife." (1 Samuel 18:27)

Here again King Saul thought to destroy David. "And Saul said, 'I will give him her, that she may be a snare to him, and that the hand of the Philistines may be against him,'" (1 Samuel 18:21) King Saul thought that his daughter Michal would give David so much in the way of sexual intercourse that David would be weakened physically and easily killed by the Philistines. But things didn't happen that way. Saint David proved he could take care of Michal and the Philistines both at the same time. He was, as they say, a super stud.

David had been hired by Saul to play music before him, as Saint David was quite a musician with the harp. However, now Saint Saul was enraged because none of his plans to destroy David had worked. Then one day while David was playing music for Saul, the king hurled his javelin at David, hoping to kill him. However, Saint David dodged and the javelin buried itself in the wall. Then David fled to his own house. (1 Samuel 19:10)

Thereupon King Saul sent officers to David's house to seize him, so King Saul could put him to death. However, Michal, David's wife, let David down out of the house on a rope from a window during the night, and so David made his escape. (1 Samuel 19:11,12)

Now Saint David fled to his sponsor, the prophet Samuel in Ramah, and told him about Saint Saul's attempts on his life. King Saul heard that David was at Naioth in Ramah, and so sent officers to seize David there. It so happened that Samuel was highly skilled in the occult arts, and was a psychic, a mind reader, and a hypnotist, and the people therefore regarded him as a prophet. Therefore when the king's officers arrived to seize David, the psychic Samuel hypnotized the entire company of them and forced them to dance and act foolishly, and then sent them back to King Saul. (1 Samuel 19:20,21)

This happened three times. Then King Saul decided to go himself to Ramah and kill David. But when Saul appeared, then Samuel also hypnotized King Saul and forced him to strip off all of his clothes and lie naked on the ground a whole day and night. So David escaped from Saul. (1 Samuel 19:24)

However, Saul's envy and anger against David could not be assuaged. Therefore Saint David gathered several hundred men to him in the wilderness and they lived as outlaws, dodging efforts of King Saul to capture them. Eventually David and his men fled the country and lived among the Philistines until King Saul and his sons were killed in warfare.

SAINT DAVID'S WAY TO GET ANOTHER WIFE

During his flight from King Saul, David had to leave his wife Michal behind. However, in spite of his precarious existence, he managed to acquire two more wives, Abigail and Ahinoam (2 Samuel 2:2) and this tided him over in the absence of Michal. After all, a man has to have one or more women no matter how difficult life is. Without them, life wasn't worth fighting for.

The story of how Saint David acquired Abigail as a wife is very interesting, not only for what the Bible tells us, but for what the Bible does not tell us, but only implies. After Samuel the prophet died, David went with his band of six hundred men, to the vicinity of Mt. Carmel. There he dwelt with his men and their wives, but Saint David had no wife with him. In fact, King Saul had given David's wife Michal to be the wife of another man, and this distressed David even more, as Saul hoped it would.

There was a wealthy rancher living in Saint David's vicinity who was reputed to have three thousand sheep and a thousand goats. So in the course of time David sent over to this rancher named Nabal and asked if he could contribute some animals as food for his men. David was a national hero, even though King Saul wanted to kill him out of envy, and most Israelites still thought very highly of David. So it was not uncommon for them to contribute toward the support of David and his men.

However, Nabal was not the type of man to idolize heroes or anything but his wealth, which he wouldn't give up to anybody except perhaps the tax collector. So when some of Saint David's emissaries came to him seeking contribution, Nabal refused to give them anything and sent them back to David with a brusque and surly answer. This was a foolish thing to do toward a hot-headed man like Saint David, who had killed thousands of men under less provocation than this

When David heard what him emissaries told him of Nabal's refusal, his anger soared. The Bible tells us, "And David said unto his men, 'Gird ye on every man his sword.' And they girded on every man his sword; and David also girded on his sword. And there went after David about four hundred men; and two hundred abode by their stuff. But one of the young men told Abigail, Nabal's wife, saying, 'Behold, David sent messengers out of the wilderness to salute our master: and he railed on them . . . .Now therefore know and consider what thou wilt do; for evil is determined against our master, and against all his household.'" (1 Samuel 25:13)

Abigail was frightened. David was a military hero of the nation of Israel and she admired him, but she also knew he was a man of great anger and combat. She know she had to act fast if she were to divert Saint David's anger and save her own life as well as the lives of the others in her household. The Bible tells us: "Then Abigail made haste and took two hundred loaves and two bottles of wine, and five sheep ready dressed, and five measures of parched corn, and an hundred clusters of raisins, and two hundred cakes of figs, and laid them on asses. And she said unto her servants, 'Go on before me; behold, I come after you.' But she told not her husband Nabal. And it was so, as she rode on the ass, that she came down by the covert of the hill, and, and, behold, David and his men came down against her; and she met them." (1 Samuel 25:18-20)

"Now David had said, 'Surely in vain have I kept all that this fellow hath in the wilderness, so that nothing was missed of all that pertained unto him: and he hath requited me evil for good. So and more also do God unto the enemies of David if I leave of all that pertain to him by the morning light any that pisseth against the wall." (1 Samuel 25:21,22 K.J.V.)

In other words, Saint David ran a "protection racket" with his outlaw gang, such as the other outlaw gangs operate in some large cities today. For their so-called protection of businesses they demand a fee from businessmen. If the fee is not forthcoming they attempt to destroy the business and sometimes the businessman. Here Saint David failed to receive his pay-off so he set out to destroy Nabal, the offending businessman.

Now if Saint David had been an honest man, he would not have attacked Nabal for failing to give him a contribution. After all, Nabal was under no legal obligation to give David anything. But Saint David was an outlaw and a vicious one at that. Abigail realized this and hurried to pay off David. She would do absolutely anything David demanded in order to save her own life.

Immediately when Abigail met Saint David and his men she got off her donkey and bowed herself to the ground before him, and made her apology to him. Then she gave them her gift of foodstuffs. She also told David that her husband was "a man of Belial (the devil)" and a fool. She wanted to put as much distance between her husband and herself as possible in order to save her own life.

Saint David had an eye for women, and he knew a beautiful woman when he saw one. The Bible says of Abigail: "She was a woman of good understanding, and of a beautiful countenance." (1 Samuel 25:3) Saint David instantly appraised her attractive appearance and the way in which she sought to please him. He was also a man who was currently without a wife, and that made her even more desirable to David. The Bible does not tell us all that went on between David and Abigail at that first meeting. However, considering subsequent events, there must have been a very good understanding between David and Abigail. Did he take her back with him to his tent? What did they do together when there? Did they coadunate? Did David do with her as he did later with another man's wife, have sexual intercourse with her? They must have had a very close and intimate agreement together because of what happened next.

Saint Abigail returned home afterward to her husband Nabal. Nabal was feasting and drunken, but the following morning when he sobered up, Abigail told him how she had persuaded David not to kill her husband. Nabal froze in fright. He had not previously realized how foolish he had been in refusing David's emissaries. Now he suddenly became aware that Saint David was a man of violence who would stop at nothing in destroying anyone who opposed him. He was not a man who was governed by the laws that bound other men. Saint David always did as he pleased. But Nabal was glad that his wife Abigail had deflected David's wrath.

Then Moses' Bible tells us: "And it came to pass about ten days after, that the Lord Jehovah smote Nabal, that he died." (1 Samuel 25:38) Does the Lord smite anybody dead? If God smote Nabal dead because he had a disagreement with David, why didn't God smite King Saul dead because he tried to kill David out of envy? Israel of that day was full of all sorts of criminals and God didn't smite them dead. The world today is also full of criminals, and God doesn't smite them dead, as we all know from observation. Why, then, would God single out Nabal to smite him dead?

This statement in the Bible doesn't hold up in the light of the facts.

Therefore what undoubtedly happened was, that Saint David gave Abigail some poison to put in her husband Nabal's food. Saint Abigail waited ten days before slipping Nabal the death cup so her crime would be less apparent. Then it was that she killed Nabal, whom David hated, and covered her tracks by telling her servants that God had struck her husband dead because of the way he had treated Saint David. The Slaves hated her husband too because he was a difficult man to work for, so they were not about to disagree with Abigail. So Saint Abigail and Saint David got away with their crime because there were not coroners in Israel to investigate suspicious deaths.

Immediately after Nabal her husband was dead, Abigail became David's wife. This was all too well arranged to be a coincidence.

DAVID'S FIRST THREE WIVES

Of course, polygamy was the rule among the Israelites, and this allowed Saint David to legally have three wives: Michal, Abigail, and Ahinoam. However, with one man having several women as wives, one wonders about some other men who wouldn't be able to find any women for wives. How did they get along? Because from a factual standpoint, there are about as many girls born as boys, so if one man had several wives he would almost surely deprive some other man of having even one wife. That's the way it is in a polygamous society, which the laws of the "holy" Bible established. This is just one more point that shows how senseless many laws of the Bible really are. And being senseless they are certainly not from God.

After King Saul and his sons were killed in warfare by the Philistines, David returned to Israel and to the territory of his own tribe of Judah, where he was proclaimed king. At the same time, one of King Saul's sons, namely Ishbosheth, was also proclaimed king in another part of Israel. This resulted in civil war for many years. Eventually Ishbosheth was betrayed, and Saint David became king over all the twelve tribes of Israel. In addition he managed to get his first wife Michal back, which made them both very happy. She earlier helped David escape death at the hands of Saint Saul's officers, and David loved Michal for her loyalty.

You would think that King David would now have been satisfied with his three wives, and not seek more. But that was not the way with David. The more the better, was his motto, and he gathered wives and concubines wholesale. He forsook his military campaigns and went on a campaign to acquire more and more women.

SAINT DAVID STEALS AGAIN

David's palace was one of the highest buildings in Jerusalem, and one day he was up on the roof of his palace by his penthouse. The Bible tells us: "And it came to pass in the eveningtide, that David arose from off his bed and walked upon the roof of the king's house. And from the roof he saw a woman washing herself; and the woman was very beautiful to look upon. And David sent and enquired after the woman. And one said, 'Is not this Bathsheba, the daughter of Eliam, the wife of Uriah the Hittite?'" (2 Samuel 11:2,3)

Well, David didn't care whose wive Bathsheba was, he wanted to have her, and not just to talk with or look at either. The Bible tells us of Saint David: "And David sent messengers, and took her. And she came in unto him, and he lay with her." (He had sexual intercourse with her, in plain language.) (2 Samuel 11:4) Saint David wasn't satisfied with all the wives and concubines he already had. Saint David had to steal another man's wife and commit adultery with her.

Bathsheba's husband Uriah was a captain in the army, and was then at the battle front. Consequently this left the coast clear for David to have repeated sexual intercourse with Uriah's wife without any likelihood of David's scandalous behavior being discovered. Or so David thought.

But then the roof began to cave in on Saint David's scheme. Bathsheba sent word to King David that he had got her pregnant. Oh, Lord! What could David do now? He worried and fumed, and consulted with his chief counsellor. Then he decided upon a plan. He sent for Captain Uriah to come home from the battle front. This way, he figured Uriah would immediately return to his wife Bathsheba, have sexual intercourse with her, and then the child that she bore would presumably be the child of Uriah. Saint David's perfidy would thus be covered up.

The Bible tale continues: "And David sent to Joab (his army commander), saying, 'Send me Uriah the Hittite.' And Joab sent Uriah to David. And when Uriah was come unto him, David demanded of him how Joab did, and how the people did, and how the war prospered." (2 Samuel 11:6,7) This made Uriah's recall from the battle front seem legitimate. So after receiving Uriah's report, King David told Uriah to go to his home and rest before returning to battle.

But here Saint David's scheme hit another snag. Uriah was a super patriot and filled with lofty ideas. He replied to the king, "My lord Joab and the servants of my lord are encamped in the open fields (in the army). Shall I then go into mine house to eat and drink, and to lie with my wife? As thou livest, and as my soul liveth, I will not do this thing." (2 Samuel 11:11)

Oh, Gad! thought David. This guy wasn't human! Then King David had another idea. "And David said to Uriah, 'Tarry here today also, and tomorrow I will let thee depart.' So Uriah abode him, he did eat and drink before him. And he (David) made him drunk. And at even he (Uriah) went out to lie on his bed with the servants of his lord, but went not down to his house." (2 Samuel 11:12,13) Even when Uriah was drunk he would not go down to his own house to spend the night with his wife.

Saint David was desperate. There was no way he could get Uriah to go to his house and have sex relations with his wife. And if he didn't have sexual intercourse with his wife, Saint David's adultery with Bathsheba would be discovered.

Well, there was one final scheme Saint David could use. If Uriah was killed in battle, Bathsheba his wife would be a widow. Then she could marry King David and their child would be legitimate. Since David was king, he could easily arrange this event. So the Bible tells us: And it came to pass in the morning, that David wrote a letter to Joab (his military commander) and sent in by the hand of Uriah. And he wrote in the letter, saying: 'See ye Uriah that he may be smitten and die.

So Uriah the patriot faithfully carried this letter to his commander Joab. Joab immediately obeyed the king's orders. Uriah was placed in the front line of battle. Later Joab sent a message to King David.

The Bible continues "And the shooters shot from off the wall upon thy servants, and some of the king's servants be dead. And thy servant Uriah the Hittite is dead also. (2 Samuel 11;24)

The Bible continues: "And when the wife of Uriah heard that Uriah her husband was dead, she mourned for her husband. And when the morning was past, David sent and fetched her to his house and she became his wife, and bare him a son." (2 Samuel 11:26,27) Thus for a second time Saint David arranged to have a husband killed in order to steal his wife. But this latter crime was not so easily covered up.

While we are royally condemning Saint David for his murderous conduct, let's not forget Bathsheba. This dame was not exactly a naive schoolgirl. Let's remember that if David could see Bathsheba from up at his penthouse, Bathsheba could also see the handsome and wealthy king David. Let's also remember that Bathsheba's husband had been away on military duty for quite awhile, and she had been denied her normal share of sexual intercourse. By now she desperately wanted a man, and what better man was there to have sexual intercourse with than King David? Let us also remember that there are few women who would strip off all their clothing and bathe nude, especially washing her private parts (2 Samuel 11:2-4) outdoors in the yard as Saint Bathsheba did. Obviously she was after King David and knew exactly how to get him, so she was no sweet little innocent victim in this sexcapade. She too bore guilt for her husband's murder, and for committing adultery with King David.

Most books on hagiography zealously report the story of David killing the giant Goliath. But how many book do you see detailing King David's adultery with Bathsheba and murder of her husband? Such books are almost non-existent. But here you finally have an honest book on hagiography. I pull no punches. You get the facts as straight as history gives them, with absolutely nothing covered up.

CHAPTER XXII. HOW THIS HOLY MAN AVOIDED
EXECUTION FOR MURDER

Some of us may wonder why the Bible sets forth in detail all these criminal and scandalous activities of Saint David. But was there any alternative? It was like the case of Abraham, who married his own sister. It was a ghastly scandal that everyone knew about, and it could not be covered up.

King David's adulterous conduct with Uriah's wife Bathsheba was known to all the members of David's court, and to all of his servants. You may be sure it was the choice morsel of gossip of that day. And from the palace, news of this scandal spread all through the nation of Israel.

Then the religious priesthood became involved. They were the conservators and purveyors of Moses' commandments. How could they stand quietly by and see the laws of Saint Moses so brazenly violated without protest? Here two of the Ten Commandments were openly broken by King David and Bathsheba: The commandment, "Thou shalt not commit adultery," and also "Thou shalt not commit murder." (Exodus 20:13, 14) And the punishment for violation of each of these commandments was death.

But here the priesthood was in a dilemma. Punishment for violation of these commandments was indeed death, but who could put King David to death? It was impossible. Saint David was king. Anyone attempting to put Saint David to death would be instantly slain himself. What could the priesthood do to enforce the law?

If God would only enforce these laws, all would be well. Law and order could be maintained. But with God himself ignoring the enforcement of Moses' laws, who could enforce the law against King David? It made thinking people wonder sometimes. Were these really God's laws after all?

In fact, was there even really a God? You couldn't tell by what went on with King David.

Of course, whenever there was a drought and a famine the priesthood always told the people this was their punishment for being unfaithful to God and their religion. Saint Moses had even said that many centuries before. (Leviticus 26:14, 19, 20) And they could do that again in David's case. However, there were always some wise guys who would point out that a drought and famine punishes the righteous along with the wicked, so this religious pretense didn't go over so well. The people didn't believe it.

So what could the priesthood do? All they could do was protest Saint David's sins and hope he would get into trouble later. Then they would be able to say that his troubles were due to his violation of Moses' laws.

The priesthood chose the prophet Nathan to take their protest to King David. This was a tricky proposition, because if David became angry at Nathan, the prophet could lose his head. So Nathan did not speak of Saint David's crimes directly, but approached David with a parable. The Bible tells us: "And he (Nathan) came unto him (David) and said unto him: 'There were two men in one city; the one rich and the other poor. The rich man had exceeding many flocks and herds. But the poor man had nothing, save one little ewe lamb, which he had bought and nourished up. And it grew up together with him and with his children. It did eat of his own meat and drank of his own cup, and lay in his bosom, and was unto him as a daughter."

"And there came a traveller unto the rich man, and he spared to take of his own flock and of his own herd, to dress for the wayfaring man that was come unto him, but took the poor man's lamb and dressed it for the man that was come to him."

"And David's anger was greatly kindled against the man. And he said to Nathan, 'As the lord Jehovah liveth, the man that hath done this thing shall surely die! And he shall restore the lamb fourfold, because he did this thing, and because he had no pity.'"

"And Nathan said to David, 'Thou are the man! . . . . Thou hast killed Uriah the Hittite with the sword, and hast taken his wife to be thy wife, and has slain him with the sword of the children of Ammon . . . . Thus saith the Lord Jehovah, 'Behold, I will raise up evil against thee out of thine own house, and I will take thy wives before thine eyes and give them unto thy neighbor, and he shall lie (sexually) with thy wives in the sight of this sun.'" (2 Samuel 12:1-7, 9, 11)

Here we see an alleged prophecy of evils that would befall Saint David in punishment for his sins. However, we must remember that the books of Samuel were not written until five hundred years after the time of David, so later events in David's life could have been "predicted" by putting a contrived "prophecy" in the mouth of Nathan. There is no proof that such a prophecy was actually uttered by Nathan to David.

Even so, the "Prophesied" punishment against David was not the punishment prescribed in the laws of Moses for the sins David and Bathsheba committed. Therefore the raping of David's wives later could not have been punishment for these sins. Death was the punishment Moses' laws prescribed for these sins; not the rape of David's wives. Such rape punished David's wives rather than Saint David.

Another point of interest is that the ancient Septuagint translation of the Bible, which pre-dates the Christian era, did not ascribe to Samuel the authorship of the books known as the books of Samuel. In the Septuagint version the books of Samuel are called the First and Second Books of Kings. There is actually no proof who wrote them. In Verse one of Chapter 25 of First Samuel it says: "And Samuel died." Yet there are thirty-one Chapters to the book of First Samuel, so with Samuel dead in Chapter twenty-five, who wrote the last six Chapters of First Samuel? Then comes the book of Second Samuel, but Samuel was already dead before the events recorded in the Second book of Samuel took place, including David's adultery with Bathsheba. How could Samuel write the book when he was already dead? Did they get it off a ouiji board or something? "Have faith, brother," the clergy tells us. We'd rather use our common sense.

Actually the Bible contradicts itself here in the matter of punishment for David's sins. First it prophesies punishment upon David by the rape of David's wives, etc., which was in reality punishing David's wives for his sins. But later it states that David's sin has been set aside. In 2 Samuel Chapter 12 and Verse 13 we read: "And David said unto Nathan, 'I have sinned against the Lord Jehovah.' and Nathan said unto David, 'The Lord Jehovah also hath put away thy sin; thou shalt not die!'"

This is worse yet. First Saint Moses says the punishment for adultery and murder is death. Then when the chips are down, the Bible says that its God conveniently sets aside his law when it involves a big-time politician like King David. In other words, the death penalty only applies to the taxpayers; the big politicians go scot-free. Doesn't this give you a great feeling about the justice and righteousness of Saint Moses' Bible?

In spite of the Biblical record of King David's murder of two men in order to steal their wives, and the evidence that he was a common criminal racketeer, and a vicious aggressor who killed thousands of the native inhabitants of Canaan--in spite of all that, the saintly Bible writers had the audacity to write in their Bible that David was "the sweet psalmist of Israel." (2 Samuel 23:1) Can you imagine the moral depravity of the Jewish saints who would write this of such a corrupt man?

These depraved Israelite saints wrote in the Bible: "Now these be the last words of David . . . . the sweet psalmist of Israel, said, 'The Spirit of the Lord Jehovah spake by me, and his word was in my tongue.'" (2 Samuel 23:1,2) Here is King David, who has broken his Jehovah God's law repeatedly, with murders and adulteries and more, claiming that after all this God still was doing business with him, and inspiring him with God's spirit, to speak. If this doesn't cure you of any regard for the inspiration of the Bible scriptures, nothing will. It's enough to make a decent person puke up his supper.

CHAPTER XXIII.   THE SAINT WHO RAPED TEN WOMEN ON A ROOFTOP

The larger a man's family is, the more chance there is for trouble between members of his family. This was true of Saint David. He had many wives and dozens of children by them. As these children grew up, their troubles multiplied and King David's problems increased.

Sex was the first cause of difficulty. Misuse of sex had caused a lot of misery for Saint David, and now it began to afflict his offspring.

Amnon was the son who now gave David trouble. Some may say they never heard of Saint Amnon, but this chap does appear in the Bible. And saint he was, because he had been circumcised and this sanctified him or set him apart as God's servant, according to Biblical usage. This differs from the rule followed by some churches today which only canonizes certain persons as saints after their decease.

The problem was that David's son Amnon fell desperately in love with his sister Tamar. His love for her actually made him sick because it could not be fulfilled legitimately. He madly desired to have sexual intercourse with his sister, but realized that he could get into a tremendous amount of trouble if he did so, even though Abraham and Sarah had set the pattern for this type of irregular conduct and had received Jehovah God's approval, according to the Bible. (Genesis 20:12; 26:5)

The Bible says: "And Amnon had a friend whose name was Jonadab, the son of Shimeah, David's brother; and Jonadab was a very subtle man. And he (Jonadab) said unto him (Amnon), 'Why are thou, being the king's son, lean (haggard) from day to day? Wilt thou not tell me?' And Amnon said unto him, 'I love Tamar, my brother Absalom's sister.'" (2 Samuel 13:4,5)

Well, Jonadab told him that was a simple thing to solve. He told

Amnon to trick Tamar into coming to his apartment, and then grab her and have sexual intercourse with her. Amnon was the king's son so he could get away with it. His father King David would pardon Amnon somehow, so there was nothing to worry about. Why should Amnon be sick day after day? He should get on with it and enjoy his sister's love.

So Amnon took courage. The Bible tells us that when his sister Tamar came to his apartment, "he took hold of her, and said unto her, 'Come lie with me (sexually), my sister.' And she answered him, 'Nay, my brother, do not force me (sexually); for no such thing ought to be done in Israel. Do not thou this folly.'" (2 Samuel 13:11, 12)

But Saint Amnon wouldn't listen to his sister. He pulled her down on his bed and raped her. "Howbeit, he would not hearken unto her voice, but being stronger than she, forced her and lay with her (sexually)." (2 Samuel 13:14) Moses Bible continues: "Then Amnon hated her exceedingly, so that the hatred wherewith he hated her was greater than the love wherewith he had loved her. And Amnon said unto her, 'Arise, be gone.'" (2 Samuel 13:15) If his sister had willingly had sexual intercourse with him, he would have loved her. But because she had refused him, and he had to rape her to have sexual intercourse with her, he therefore hated her. She had despised him, and now he despised her.

But she refused to get up from the bed. "And she said unto him, 'There is no cause (for me to be sent away.) This evil in sending me away is greater than the other that thou didst unto me.'" (2 Samuel 13:16) Since Saint Amnon had used her as his wife, she insisted that he should keep her as his wife.

However, Saint Amnon now hated her and would not have her in his house. He ordered his servant to put Tamar out, and lock the door behind her. "And Tamar put ashes on her head, and rent her garment of divers colors that was on her, and laid her hand on her head, and went on crying." (2 Samuel 13:19) She stumbled down the street in tears. It was a custom among the Jews to put ashes on their heads and tear their clothing when they were in grief or distress, and she followed this odd Biblical tradition.

After leaving Saint Amnon's house Tamar met her brother Absalom. "And Absalom her brother said unto her, 'Hath Amnon thy brother been with thee (had sexual intercourse with thee?) But hold now thy peace, my sister. He is thy brother. Regard not this thing.'"

So Tamar remained desolate in her brother Absalom's house." (2 Samuel 13:20) Brothers having sex relations with their sisters was a common thing in Israel. Therefore Absalom told her not to take it seriously.

When King David heard how Amnon had raped Saint Tamar he became very angry, but did nothing about it. Saint Absalom waited two years for King David to punish Amnon, and then took things into his own hands. He killed Saint Amnon and fled to an adjoining country for several years until his father's anger and grief had diminished, after which King David pardoned Saint Absalom.

WHOLESALE RAPE ON A ROOFTOP

Saint Absalom was King David's elder son, and by the laws of heredity he should be the one to become David's successor as king after David died. This was the law and custom of Israel. However, King David was not one to pay much attention to the law, as his adultery with Bathsheba and murder of her husband revealed. Saint David was a very religious person, but obeying his God's laws was not David's idea of religion. To Saint David religion was all talk and hymn singing. Decent conduct and obedience did not enter into it.

King David was getting old and Absalom could see that David intended to put his son Solomon on the throne, and not Absalom who lawfully should inherit it. Solomon was Saint David's youngest son, and was born of David's adulterous paramour Bathsheba. This outraged Saint Absalom, who laid careful plans to seize David's throne anyway, regardless of his father's wishes.

First Absalom sought to make himself prominent before the people. The Bible says: "And it came to pass after this, that Absalom prepared him chariots and horses, and fifty men to run before him." (2 Samuel 15:1) This was quite a display. It was almost like a parade when Saint Absalom went through Jerusalem with his chariots and horses and attendants. Everyone took notice. No one but royalty could put on a show like that.

"And Absalom rose up early and stood beside the way of the gate. And it was so, that when any man that had a controversy came to the king for judgment, then Absalom called unto him and said, 'Of what city art thou?'"

"And Absalom said unto him, 'See, thy matters are good and right; but there is no man deputed of the king to hear thee. Of, that I were made judge in the land, that every man which hath any suit or cause might come unto me, and I would do him justice!'" (2 Samuel 15:4)

In this manner Saint Absalom won the favor and attention of people from all the tribes of Israel. The people of the various tribes were already disgusted with the lawless and scandalous conduct of King David, so it was not difficult for Absalom to win numerous followers to himself.

Finally, as time went by and King David became older, Absalom decided it was opportune for him to strike. He left Jerusalem on a pretext and went to Hebron. "But Absalom sent spies throughout all the tribes of Israel, saying, 'As soon as ye hear the sound of the trumpet, then ye shall say, 'Absalom reigneth (as king) in Hebron.'" "And the conspiracy was strong, for the people increased continually with Absalom," (2 Samuel 15:10,12) So Moses' Bible tells us.

Then King David heard of the revolt. "And David said unto all his servants that were with him at Jerusalem, 'Arise, and let us flee, for we shall not else escape from Absalom. Make speed to depart, lest he overtake us suddenly and bring evil upon us, and smite the city with the edge of the sword." (2 Samuel 15:14)

Hastily King David and hundreds of his followers gathered up some of their belongings and fled from the city. "And all the country wept with a loud voice, and all the people passed over. The king also himself passed over the brook Kidron, and all the people passed over, toward the way of the wilderness." (2 Samuel 15:23) But King David left behind him ten of his concubines to take care of the palace.

Then Saint Absalom and thousands of his followers came to Jerusalem and the young king took over the throne vacated by his father David. In the palace King Absalom found the ten concubines or mistresses which his father had left behind.

The Bible tells us: "Then said Absalom to Ahithophel, 'Give counsel among you what we shall do.'"

"And Ahithophel (Absalom's counsellor) said unto Absalom, 'Go in unto thy father's concubines (sexually), which he hath left to keep the house. And all Israel shall hear that thou art abhorred of thy father. Then shall the hands of all that are with thee be strong.'" (2 Samuel 16:20,21)

This was an outrageous and daring thing for the new King Absalom to do: to rape his father's mistresses. But it was the sort of lawless and barbaric conduct that marked the Theocratic Kingdom of their God Jehovah. We are fortunate today that most of mankind has turned away from Moses' Bible and is no longer following such vicious conduct.

So then King Absalom ordered a large pavilion or canopy tent raised on the flat roof of his palace, and underneath the canopy was placed a large bed on a raised platform, so all the multitudes in the streets below could see what was taking place in the bed. Leading up to the bed was a ramp over which Absalom and David's concubines could go. There were no sides to the tent above the bed so the view from the streets below was unobstructed.

The Bible says: "So they spread Absalom a tent upon the top of the house (palace). And Absalom went in unto his father's concubines (sexually) in the sight of all Israel." (2 Samuel 16;22)

Oh, it was a gala event as the thousands of people in the streets surrounding the palace "oohed" and "aaahd" as Saint David's beautiful naked mistresses were sent up the ramp to Saint Absalom's bed, one by one, to be raped and inseminated by the new king. Of course, Saint Absalom could only have sexual intercourse with one or two of the women each day, or he would have become exhausted physically before he could rape them all. So the celebration lasted for a number of days before the insemination was completed.

Meanwhile in the streets below merchants hawked refreshments and souvenirs of the memorable event to the thousands of citizens jamming the thoroughfares around King Absalom's palace. The people were laughing and shouting as the naked women went up the ramp to Saint Absalom's bed, and later came down inseminated. Bets were placed as to how many women would become pregnant as a result of this event. But the more serious-minded older people shook their heads sadly, wondering what the world was coming to that such debauchery should take place in Jerusalem.

Meanwhile, thousands of men had rallied themselves to support the former king, David. And the new King Absalom gathered his thousands of men and attacked David's forces. "So the people went out into the field against Israel, and the battle was in the woods of Ephraim, where the people of Israel were slain before the servants of David. And there was there a great slaughter that day of twenty thousand men." (2 Samuel 18:6,7)

The battle went against Saint Absalom's forces and Absalom fled through the oak forest on a mule. But King Absalom's long dark curly hair caught in the limbs of an oak tree and he was dragged from the back of his mule and left hanging helplessly in mid-air. There General Joab found him and shot him through with darts, and Absalom died, ending the revolt. (2 Samuel 18:9,14,15)

King David thereupon re-entered Jerusalem and once more ruled as king of all the tribes of Israelites.

Concerning such wild tales of rape and incest in the Bible, Col. Robert G. Ingersoll had this to say: "The believers in the Bible are loud in their denunciation of what they are pleased to call the immoral literature of the world; and yet few books have been published containing more moral filth than this inspired word of God." Col. Robert Ingersoll was a former Attorney General of the State of Illinois.

CHAPTER XXIV.   HOW SAINT SOLOMON GOT HIS THOUSAND WOMEN

"Now King David was old and stricken in years; and they covered him with clothes, but he got no heat." (1 kings 1:1) He was about sixty-nine years old at the time, which is actually not terribly old but Saint David was not in the best of shape physically.

So what was the cure? Get another woman, naturally. That was Saint David's cure for everything. "Wherefore his servants said unto him, 'Let there be sought for my lord the king a young virgin, and let her stand before the king; and let her cherish him, and let her lie in thy bosom, that my lord the king may get heat." (1 Kings 1:2) So Moses' Bible tells us.

They hunted throughout Israel for an attractive young lady to share the king's bed. (None of his many wives would do, of course.) Finally a beauty was found. "And the damsel was very fair, and cherished the king and ministered to him. But the king knew her not (sexually)." (1 Kings 1:4)

Poor King David! Here he had a beautiful young lady in bed with him and was physically too far gone to have sexual intercourse with her! He was indeed headed for the last round-up. Anytime Saint David was unable to have sex relations with an attractive young lady, we may be sure his time was short in the land of the living.

David's next eldest son Adonijah was aware of this, and so sought to become king in his stead. "Then Adonijah the son of Haggith (and David) exalted himself, saying, 'I will be king.' And he prepared him chariots and horsemen and fifty men to run before him." (1 Kings 1:5) He would put on a display worthy of a king, and sieze that high office as King David's son and successor.

Meanwhile King David felt so forlorn, so wretched, so miserable because he was physically unable to enjoy sex relations with his new female playmate that he didn't care what happened to his kingdom or anything else. He paid no attention to Adonijah's claim to his throne, even though earlier he had indicated that he wanted Solomon to reign after him. Adonijah had clear sailing. "And his father (David) had not displeased him at any time saying, 'Why hast thou done so?'" (1 Kings 1:6)

However, there were others who supported Solomon's claim to the throne, and Nathan was one of them. "Wherefore Nathan spake unto Bethsheba the mother of Solomon, saying, 'Hast thou not heard that Adonijah the son of Haggith doth reign, and David our lord knoweth it not? Now therefore come, let me, I pray thee, give thee counsel, that thou mayest save thine own life, and the life of thy son Solomon. Go and get thee in unto King David and say unto him, "Didst not thou, my lord o king, swear unto thine handmaid, saying, 'Assuredly Solomon thy son shall reign after me and he shall sit on my throne? Why then doth Adonijah reign?'" (1 Kings 1:11-13)

So here is David lying in bed with his new young female when his favorite wife Bathsheba walks in. And what does she say? Ah-ha! You philandering rat, I've caught you at last?" No, under the laws of polygamy that they had in "holy" Israel she couldn't say that. Yet if David had caught her in bed with another man she would have lost her head. Literally. Such were the "holy" Bible laws they followed until the Romans forced them to quit polygamy in apostilic times.

David's wife Bethsheba had to put up with seeing him in bed with this very beautiful young woman. After all, Bethsheba had been young and beautiful once too, and had been in bed with David to the chagrin of the wives he had at that time. So perhaps turn-about was fair play here also.

All Bathsheba could do was ignore the young woman under the covers with David, and present her plea that Solomon should be made king after David's demise. Nathan also supported Bathsheba's request before the king. Thereupon Saint David finally founed himself from misery sufficiently to order that Solomon be anointed king in his place. This was done by Nathan and Zadok the high priest with a multitude of people watching. Then a great celebration was made as Saint Solomon ascended to David's throne.

The uproar of this celebration reached the ears of Adonijah and his supporters, and Adonijah feared for his life. "And all the guests that were with Adonijah were afraid, and rose up and went every man his way. And Adonijah feared because of Solomon, and arose and went and caught hold on the horns of the altar." (1 Kings 1:49, 50)

At first King Solomon pardoned his brother Adonijah, but later had him slain as a menace to his throne. Then as David approached death he advised Solomon to kill Joab who had been David's faithful military commander, but who had unfortunately backed Adonkiah's claim to the throne. He also advised that his enemy Shimei should be put to death. This, young king Solomon did, and his throne was established in a welter of blood. (1 Kings 2) Such was to be expected as Solomon's saintly father had been a wholesale murderer before him.

SAINT SOLOMON THE MARRYING MAN

Having established his throne, Solomon then sought to make an alliance with Egypt by marrying Pharoah's daughter. Thus he need not fear an attack upon Israel by Egypt. David had conquered and slaughtered and plundered his neighbors round about, and now King Solomon had all this wealth to enjoy. And enjoy it he did. The Bible tells us: "And Judah and Israel were many as the sand which is by the sea in multitude (a Jewish exaggeration, of course) eating and drinking and making merry." (1 Kings 420) The whole nation was happy, the military conquests were over, and joined with Saint Solomon in enjoying the plunder, taken from their dead victims.

Solomon ordered cedar timbers from Lebanon, and King Hiram shipped them to him so Solomon could build a religious temple and a palace for himself. "But Solomon was building his own house thirteen years, and he finished all his house . . . . Then he made a porch for the throne where he might judge, even the porch of judgment. And it was covered with cedar from one side of the floor to the other. And his house where he dwelt had another court with the porch, which was of like work. Solomon made also an house for Pharoah's daughter whom he had taken to wife, like unto this porch. All these were of costly stone." (1 Kings 7:1,7-9)

There is no record that King Solomon built special houses for each of his hundreds of wives. But he did provide an elaborate house for the daughter of Pharoah of Egypt, because after all, Egypt was the most powerful nation in that part of the world. Solomon knew he had better treat the princess of Egypt well, or there would be trouble.

Eventually the Queen of Sheba heard of Solomon's prosperity, and she came to visit him. "And she came to Jerusalem with a very great train, with camels that bare spices, and very much gold and precious stones. And when she was come to Solomon she communed with him of all that was in her heart . . . . And she gave the king an hundred and twenty talents of gold, and of spices very great store, and precious stones. There came no more such abundance of spices as these which the Queen of Sheba gave to King Solomon . . . . And King Solomon gave unto the Queen of Sheba all her desire, whatsoever she asked." (1 Kings 10:2,10,13)

One of the Queen of Sheba's desires was apparently to get pregnant by King Solomon. At least, the kings of Ethiopia have claimed to be descendants of King Solomon, whether that was the queen's desire of not. If the Egyptian princess who was King Solomon's wife knew about this romance, we have no knowledge. However, with polygamy the rule both in Egypt and Israel, the boudoir activities of their kings were unaccountable.

This was only a start for Israel's greatest loverboy. The Bible states: "But King Solomon loved many strange women, together with the daughter of Pharoah, women of the Moabites, Ammonites, Edomites, Zidonians, and Hittites. . . . And he had seven hundred wives, princesses, and three hundred concubines." (1 Kings 11:1,3)

However, this profusion of wives and mistresses provided little connubial bliss for any of the women, for no one man could get around to having sex relations with them all. At least, not frequently enough to satisfy any of them. So while the saintly Solomon had a great time sexually, his women suffered. But this was par for such righteous and godly Jews, who cared little for the feelings of their wives.

The Bible says: "And Solomon loved the Lord Jehovah, walking in the statutes of David his fatehr." (1 Kings 3:3) Such "walking in the statutes of David his father" gave Solomon wide leeway for wrongdoing.

CHAPTER XXV. WAS KING SOLOMON THE WISEST MAN ON EARTH?

King Solomon's nest move to establish his throne securely was to boost his own image. He has his public relations men advertise him as the smartest man in the world. As the Bible states: "And Solomon's wisdon excelled the wisdom of all the children of the east country, and all the wisdom of Egypt. For he was wiser than all men . . . . And he spake three thousand proverbs; and his songs were a thousand and five. And he spake of trees, from cedar tree that is in Lebanon even unto the hyssop that springeth out of the wall. He spake also of beasts and of foul and of creeping things and of fishes." (1 Kings 4:30-33) He was so smart about plants and trees that he saw nothing wrong with the Bible's claim that God created fruit trees growing on the earth before God created the sun, even though trees can't grow without sunlight. (Genesis 1:11-19) Solomon would fail any grade school biology or argriculture class today.

He really liked to show off what he thought he knew, and made sure his sayings were all advertised. "And there came of all people to hear the wisdom of Solomon, from all the kings of the earth which had heard of his wisdom." (1 kings 4:34) He made sure that everyone heard of his so-called wisdom and had a staff of public relations men writing and hawking his proverbs everywhere. Solomon's object, of course, was to make his subjects believe he was so smart that he was indispensable, so they would want to keep him in his job of being king.

He also threatened his subjects in his proverbs. He wrote: "The wrath of a king is as messangers of death, but a wise man will pacify it." (Provrbs 16:14) He also wrote in the Bible: "The king's wrath is as the roaring of a lion, but his favor is as dew upon the grass." (Proverbs 19:12) And "The fear of a king is as the roaring of a lion. Who so provoketh him to anger sinneth agianst his own soul." (Proverbs 20:2) In other words, "Toe the mark, you birds, or I'll have your heads.!" He repeated his threate frequently in his proverbs to keep the Israelites thoroughly intimidated.

At the same time he sought to ease the fear of his nobles and palace officers, who remembered how David his father had stolen the wife of Uriah the Hittite, his faithful army officer, and then had Uriah murdered. King Solomon made it clear that he was absolutely against anything like adultery. He would never do such a vicious thing as his father had done. He wrote many chapters of proverbs on this subject in an effort to assure his officers that he, Solomon, was opposed to such immorality. In Chapter 5 of Proverbs he wrote: "For the lips of a strange woman drop as an honeycomb, and her mouth is smoother than oil, but her end is bitter as wormwood, sharp as a two-edged sword." (Proverbs 5:3,4) Quite graphic!

Then he adds: "Let thy fountain be blessed and rejoice with the wife of thy youth. Let her be as the loving hind and pleasant roe. Let her breasts satisfy thee at all times, and be thou ravished always with her love. And why wilt thou, my son, be ravished with a strange woman, and embrace the bosom of a stranger?" (Proverbs 5:18-20) Good thoughts indeed, especially coming from a king whose father had strayed far from such a course!

In Chapter 6 of Proverbs, Saint Solomon continues at versus 24-29: "Keep thee from the evil woman, from thy flattery of the tongue of a strange woman. Lust not after her beauty in thine heart; neither let her take thee with her eyelids. For by means of a whorish woman a man is brought a piece of bread, and the adulteress will hunt for the precious life . . . . So is he that goeth into his neighbor's wife. Whosoever toucheth her shall not be innocent." You note that Saint Solomon blamed the woman for seducing the man to excuse his father; but it takes two to do it, as the saying goes. The blame can hardly be placed on just the woman, no matter how beautiful she is.

In addiiton to Chapter 5 of Proverbs, Solomon also wrote Chapters 7, 9, and 6:26-29 on the same subject against adultery and fornication in general. King Solomon had to bear down heavily on this angle in order to keep his officers pacified so they wouldn't overthrow him in a revolt. Solomon was, after all, the son of Bathsheba, the woman with whom King David had committed adultery, and for whom he had murdered one of his army officers, her husband. Consequenty every one of Solomon's officers was watching him very closely.

Saint Solomon wrote numerous proverbs embracing many subjects in order to promote his alleged wisdom, but in doing so he sometimes forgot what he had previously written and contradicted himself. People talk about the contradictions in the Bible, and here are some of them: Solomon writes: "The fear of the Lord Jehovah tendeth to life, and he that hath it shall abide satisfied; he shall not be visited with evil." (Proverbs 19:23) "No ill befalls the righteous, but the wicked are filled with trouble." (Proverbs 12:21) Very nice if that were true! But according to other writings of Solomon, it isn't true. And the facts of life agree.

Look at Saint Solomon's writing in Ecclesiastes Chapter 8 and verse 14: "There is a vanity which is done upon the earth, that there be just men unto whom it happeneth according to the work of the wicked. Again there be wicked men to whom it happeneth according to the work of the righteous." And again in Verse 15 of Chapter 7: "There is a just man that perisheth in his righteousness, and there is a wicked man that prolongeth his life in his wickedness." So righteousness doesn't pay off with an absense of suffering or long life either. Therefore Solomon's previous proverbs are lies. And the Bible as well as Solomon both contradict themselves!

Such was Saint Solomon's alleged wiseom. He wasn't so smart after all.

Proof of his folly are his vast public works programs. King Solomon taxed his people heavily to pay for all the public buildings, palaces, and the temple that he built. "And they brought every man his present, vessels of silver and vessels of gold, and garments and armor and spices, horses and mules, a (tax) rate year by year." (1 Kings 10:25) "And the king made silver to be in Jersalem as stones." (1 Kings 10:27) In other words, Solomon's public works expenditures in Jerusalem were so great that silver became as plentiful there as stones (and the Jerusalem area, in fact all Isreal, is nothing but a rock pile.) This made prosperity for the inhabitants of Jerusalem, but the other Israelites were impoverished by all this taxation and resented it greatly.

In additon to this, Solomon drafted Israelite men to work on his palace building projects as the Bible tells us: "And King solomon raised a levy out of all Isael, and the levy was thirty thousand men. And he sent them to Lebanon, ten thousand a month by courses: a month they were in Lebanon, and two months at home. . . . And Solomon had three score and ten thousand that bare burdens, and fourscore thousand hewers in the mountain; beside the chief of Solomon's officers which were over the work, three thousand three hundred which rules over the people that wrought the work." (1 Kings 5:13016) A draft of men is never popular wether it is a military draft, or a labor draft. And a labor draft is the more obnoxious of the two, because the people do not have an enemy to fight, but a dictatorial politician to curse. This made Solomon all the more unpopular among the Israelites.

Moses' Bible says: "So King Solomon exceeded all the kings of the earth for riches and for wisdom." (1 Kings 10:23) This was nothing but propaganda put out by Solomon's henchmen, another Bibilcal lie on both counts. Solomon was obviously not richer than Incas in America, whose vast wealth in gold was unequalled anywhere in the ancient world.

FOLLY DESTROYS THE KINGDOM

Finally King Solomon's folly and lack of wisdom became apparent. After Solomon's death his son Rehoboam ascened to the throne. The Bible says: "And Jeroboam and all the congregation of Israel came and spake unto (King) Rehoboam saying, 'Thy father made our yoke grievous. Now therefore make thou the grievious ervice of thy father and his heavy yoke which he put upon us lighter, and we will serve thee.'"

"And he (King Rohoboam) said unto them, 'Depart yet for three days, then come again to me.' And the people departed." (1 Kings 12:3-5)

Then the young King Rohoboam consulted with his counsellors who had formerly served his father. These advisors had been opposed to King Solomon's heavy taxation program, but could not prevail against Solomon's determination to carry out his scheme of lavish public construction. These counsellors advised the young king that enough palaces had been built. Now was the time to ease the peoples' burdens of taxation and labor drafts, and thus win the support of the people.

But this did not suit the grandios ideas of Rehoboam, who was truly a duplicate of his father. So the young king followed the advice of his younger counsellors, who urged him to continue in his father's footsteps.

Moses' Bible tells us: "So Jeroboam and all the people came to (King) Rohoboam the third day as the king had appointed . . . . And the king answered the people roughly, and forsook the old men's counsel that they gave him. And spake to them after the counsel of the young men saying, 'My father made your yoke heavy and I will add to your yoke. My father also chastised you with whips, but I will chastise you with scorpions." (1 Kings 12:12-14)

You can imagine how those words were received by the people of the outlying tribes of Israel. They had suffered long under King Solomon's rule, and now his son promised them worse oppression. Solomon's public construction program had brought great wealth to Jerusalem and his own tribe of Judah, but the heavy taxation had impoverished the outlying ten tribes of Israel. They wanted no more of it.

So when the delegates saw that the young king would only increase their burdens they cried, "To your tents, O Israel!" And they departed. So Israel rebelled against King Rohoboam and cut themselves off from the tribe of Judah where Rohoboam reigned.

King Rohoboam could not bring himself to believe that the ten tribes of Israel had actually revolted and rejected his rule. He thought it was just talk. So in due course King Rohoboam sent his tax collector named Adoram down amoung the tribes of Israel to collect the tribute. To make sure that the taxes were collected, King Rohoboam followed at a distance behind his tax collector, to give added authority to the procedure.

But the Israelites had enough of King Rohoboam's rule and Solomon-like oppresion. They immediately killed Adoram, the tax collector. Seeing this from a distance, King Rohoboam leaped into his chariot and fled for his life. (1 Kings 1218)

Then the ten tribes of Israel who had defected chose the leader of their delegation, Jereboam, to be their king. These then came to be known as the Isrealites, while the tribe of Judah under King Rehoboam became known as the Jews. The tribe of Benjamin which lay next to Judah also served King Rehoboam. So the unified kingdom of the twelve tribes lasted only a bare 120 years under three kings.

As a sidelight on this situation, over the centuries the prophets of Moses' Bible religion often denounced Babylonia as a wicked nation that God would destroy. However, Babylon had existed many thousands of years already, and here the so-called righteous kingdom of Jehovah and the Israelites only managed to survive a little more than one century. If on that basis we judge a nation's righteousness, certainly the Babylonians were far more upright than the Israelite Moses worshipers. Certainly if the Jews were truly the "chosen people of God" as the Bible likes to boast, they should have been able to hold their government together for longer than 120 years.

Following the political break-up there was also a split in the religious ranks. The religion of Moses centered in Jerusalem and its temple where Rohoboam ruled. Of course, King Jereboam would not want his subjects travelling to Jerusalem to worship under the political rule of his rival, King Rehoboam. Consequently King Jereboam set up his own religion, the worship of the golden calf of Bethel and another in Dan. As the Bible tells us: "Whereupon the king took counsel and made two calves of gold, and said unto them, 'It is too much for you to go up to Jerusalem. Behold thy gods, O Israel, which brought thee up out of the land of Egypt.'" (1 Kings 12:28; Exodus 32)

From then on there was not only political rivalry, but religious rivalry between the two factions of priests. Religious curses and denunciations were uttered by priests, and on their rival political rulers. And priests were involved in many plots to overthrow kings who ruled the two kingdoms. Such was life under the divided kingdom of godly saints.

CHAPTER XXVI.   THE PROPHET AND THE PRETTY
YOUNG WIDOW

One of the prophets of the Moses religous cult was a chap named
Elijah. Now Saint Elijah was known as a weather prophet, and he went to
King Ahab who ruled over the ten tribes of Israel, telling Ahab that there
was not going to be any rain for several years. Furthermore, this Elijah
took credit for the drought, saying that only he could make it rain. (1
Kings 17:1)

Naturally, King Ahab took umbrage at this statement and Elijah's
boast that he controlled the drought. So Elijah had to flee from the king's
presence to save his neck. Another thing made King Ahab hostile to Elijah.
King Ahab was not a follower of the Moses religion that Elijah represented,
and Ahab knew that Elijah was his enemy.

The prophet Elijah therefore fled deep into the desert wilderness,
and claimed that crows fed him there. Who knows if they did or didn't?
Later Elijah decided he must flee the country, and he went to the
neighbring kingdom of Sidon. Droughts were frequent in Palestine and
sometimes lasted for years, so Elijah's stay in Sidon also was to last for
several years.

In his wanderings on foot Elijah came to a small town and met a
widow lady near the gate of the city where she was gathering firewood.
Striking up a conversation with her, since she was young and undoubtedly
a nice looking woman who would inspire coversation from a single man,
Elijah found out that she had a room he could rent. (1 Kings 17:10)

Saint Elijah apparently located an entrance to a grain depository
and olive oil storage house from which he obtained sustenance for himself
and the young widow and her small son. There was a serious drought by
that time so that the crops failed and food was difficult to get, but this

undercover supply of nourishment kept the three of them alive and happy for several years of the drought.

Of course, Elijah's saintly happiness was increased by the fact that this young widow lady was looking for a husband, as most widow ladies are. And what's more, she knew from experience what men liked and how to give it to them. So the Prophet Elijah was delighted with all the benefits a pretty widow lady could bestow on a handsome single man whom she hoped to ensnare in marriage. During several long years of living unchaperoned with this young widow, we may be sure that the saintly Elijah enjoyed all the physical delights of connubial existence.

Of course, it is true that the young widow did not get pregnant, but they could have engaged in oral sexual intercourse or anal sexual intercourse, or they may have used the linen condoms manufactured by the Egyptians in those days. Sidon had a busy trade with Egypt that brought all sorts of benefits to the people of that area. So pregnancy was not at all unavoidable by her.

This idyllic condition continued for three years until Elijah saw from the sky that the drought would soon end in a rainstorm. He then departed from the widow and resumed his prophetic mission by notifying King Ahab that now it was going to rain again. Very clever, these weather prophets!

Of course the Bible puts it in religious phrase, saying that "the word of the Lord Jehovah came to Elijah in the third year saying, 'Go, show thyself unto (King) Ahab, and I will send rain upon the earth.'" (1 Kings 18:1) When a religious person sees a cloud in the sky he will of course say, "God revealed to me that it would rain." This is how the religious mind functions. The rest of us would merely say, "it looks as though it's going to rain."

After this great prophetic triumph, Saint Elijah managed to murder four hundred and fifty priests of the Baal religion that King Ahab followed. This was in keeping with the teachings of Moses who said, "He that sacrificeth unto any God, save unto the Lord Jehovah only, he shall be utterly destroyed." (Exodus 22:20) Saint Moses' Bible is indeed the source of the most vicious and bloody sort of bigotry. Elijah's stroke of murderous religious intolerance made it necessary for Elijah again to flee for his life from the officers of King Ahab. (1 Kings 18:40; 19:1-3) Murdering 450 people was no small crime the government could overlook.

After some years of dodging the officers of the government, the murderer Elijah decided he had to flee the country of Israel again. So he left his coat with his apprentice prophet Elisha, and told Elisha that when the government officers would come looking for him, to tell them that a whirlwind had carried him Elijah away. This Elijah hoped to stop the officers from trying to track him down. Then Elijah left Israel and went to a foreign country to live. There he may have found another young widow lady in the country to which he fled, who would make him forget the troubles of his saintly past life.

Moses' Bible of course insists that Saint Elijah was indeed picked up by a whirlwind and carried out of his disciple Elisha's presence. (2 Kings 2:11) Yet if the wind was strong enough to pick up Elijah, why did it not also pick up Elisha too who was with him at the time? This is another distortion of the physical facts which makes the Bible story dubious. This yarn was undoubtedly fabricated to conceal Elijah's flight from the king's arresting officers.

MORE SAINTLY RELIGIOUS MURDERS

When Elisha took over as prophet of the Moses religious cult after Elijah had fled, Elisha was more tricky than his master. Elisha wanted to destroy all the worshippers of other religions which did not recognize the Jews as being the "chosen people of God," but he himself was afraid to do the killing. He had seen how Elijah his master had to flee the country to escape being executed as a murderer because he had slain 450 priests of Baal. Elisha did not want a similar murder charge laid against him and risk being put to death, so he put into motion a more subtle plan.

Elisha knew that Jehu was an ambitious captain in the army, who would like to become king. Furthermore, Jehu was not a worshipper of Baal. Why not get a soldier such as Jehu to kill the priests of Baal? Thus if anything went wrong, Jehu would be punished and not himself.

The first move Elisha made was to anoint Jehu to become king. Elisha was afraid to do this himself, so he sent a simple son of one of the other prophets to do the job. The Bible says: "And Elisha the prophet called out one of the children of the prophets and said unto him, 'Gird up thy loins and take this box thither, look out Jehu the son of Jehoshapat the son of Nimshi, and go in and make him arise up from among his brethren, and carry him to an inner chamber. Then take the box of oil and pour it on his head, and say, "Thus saith the Lord Jehovah, 'I have appointed thee king over Israel.' Then open the door and flee, and tarry not.'" (2 Kings 9:1-3)

So the young man took the oil and harried to do as he was told by the great prophet Elisha. The Bible tells us: "And he poured the oil on his head and said unto him, 'Thus saith the Lord Jehovah God of Israel, "I have anointed thee king over the people of the Lord, even over Israel. And thou shalt smite the house of Ahab thy master, that I may avenge the blood of my servants the prophets, and the blood of all the servants of the Lord at the hand of Jezebel. For the whole house of Ahab shall perish, and I will cut off from Ahab him that pisseth against the wall, and him that is shut up and is left in Israel."'" So spoke Jehovah God according to the Bible at 2 Kings Chapter 9 and Verses 6-8, as translated directly from the Hebrew in the King James Version.

After the young man anointed Jehu and fled, the fellow army officers with Jehu found out that Jehu had been anointed king. This suited them well, and they blew the trumpets to announce this great event. Then the conspiracy waxed hot. Jehu shot an arrow and killed Joram, king of Israel, who had supported the religion of Baal. And Jehu's fellow soldiers slew King Ahaziah of Judah. Jehu also had the queen mother of Israel, Jezebel, slain, and all seventy of King Ahab's sons killed too. So the throne of Israel was his.

Regarding this slaying of the seventy sons of the late King Ahab the Bible tells us: "Then he (Jehu) wrote a letter the second time to them, saying: 'If ye be mine, and if ye will hearken unto my voice, take ye the heads of the men your master's sons, and come to me Jezreel by tomorrow this time.' Now the king's sons being seventy persons were with the great men of the city which brought them up. And it came to pass, when the letter came to them, that they took the king's sons and slew seventy persons and put their heads in baskets, and sent them to Jezreel. And there came a messenger and told him (Jehu) saying, 'They have brought the heads of the king's sons.' And he said, 'Lay ye them in two heaps at the entering in of the gate until the morning.'" (2 Kings 10;6-8)

Thomas Paine, in his book, "The Age of Reason," wrote concerning this event: "The cruelties that the Jews had accustomed themselves to practice on the Canaanites, whose country they had savagely invaded under the pretended gift from God, they afterward practiced as furiously on each other. Scarcely half their kings died a natural death, and in some instances whole families were destroyed to secure possession to the successor; who, after a few years, and sometimes only a few months or less, shared the same fate. In the tenth Chapter of the second book of Kings, an account is given of two baskets full of children's heads, seventy in number, being exposed at the entrance of the city; they were the children of Ahab, and were murdered by the order of Jehu, whom Elisha, the pretended man of God, had anointed to be king over Israel, on purpose to commit this bloody deed, and assassinate his predecessor. And in thr account of the reign of Menahem, one of the kings of Israel who had murdered Shallum, who had reigned but one month, it is said, 2 Kings, Chapter XV., Verse 16, that Menahem smote the city of Tispah, because they opened not the city to him, and all the women therein that were with child he ripped up."

"Could we permit ourselves to suppose that the Almighty would distinguish any nation of people by the name of <u>His chosen people</u> we must suppose that people to have been an example to all the rest of the world of the purest piety and humanity, and not such a nation of ruffians and cut-throats as the ancient Jews were; a people who, corrupted by the copying after such monsters and impostors as Moses and Aaron, Joshua, Samuel and David, had distinguished themselves above all others on the face of the known earth for barbarity and wickedness. If we will not stubbornly shut our eyes and steel our hearts, it is impossible not to see, in spite of all that long-established superstition imposes upon the mind, that the flattering appellation of <u>His chosen people</u> is no other than a lie which the priests and leaders of the Jews had invented to cover the baseness of their own characters, and which Christian priests, sometimes as corrupt and often as cruel, have professed to believe." Thus wrote Thomas Paine, who signed the Declaration of Independence, and was the contemporary and associate of George Washington, first president of the United States.

CHAPTER XXVII. ISRAELITE SAINTS WHO ATE THEIR CHILDREN

However, Thomas Paine barely scratched the surface when he referred to the ancient Jews as "a nation of ruffians and cut-throats." One ghastly practice followed by the Israelites was that they ate their own children. Moses' Bible tells us: "And the king said unto her, 'What aileth thee?' And she answered, 'This woman said unto me, "Give thy son, that we may eat him today, and we will eat my son tomorrow." So we boiled my son and did eat him. And I said unto her on the next day, "Give thy son that we may eat him." And she hath hid her son.'" (2 Kings 6:28,29)

For people under any circumstances to kill and eat their own children is ghastly cannibalism, murder and depravity of the foulest sort. And these are the Jews whom the Bible calls God's "chosen people." (Deuteronomy 7:6) No civilized people could believe that the Bible is God's word when it says that.

Now we return to the religious murders committed by Jehu, the agent of Elisha, the great prophet of Jehovah, Moses' God. The next move of Jehu was to destroy the priests of the Baal religion who had supported King Joram. Moses' Bible states: "And Jehu gathered all the people together and said unto them: 'Ahab served Baal a little, but Jehu shall serve him much. Now therefore call unto me all the prophets of Baal, and his servants, and all his priests. Let none be wanting, for I have a great sacrifice to do to Baal. Whosoever shall be wanting, he shall not live. But Jehu did it in subtlety, to the intent that he might destroy the worshippers of Baal." (2 Kings 10:18,19)

So all the priests and worshippers of Baal came to the temple of Baal, and it was packed with people. Then they brought forth the religious garments and had all the people clad in these vestments of Baal. The Bible tells us: "And it came to pass as soon as he had made an end of offering the burnt offering, that Jehu said to the guard and to the captains, 'Go in and slay them; let none come forth.' And they smote them with the edge of the sword." (2 Kings 10:25) Human blood ran deep on the floor of the temple as the people were hacked to pieces by the swords of the soldiers, and the blood ran out at the doors of the temple. It was like the carnage in a slaughter house. It was a massacre.

This reminds one of the massacre of St. Bartholomew's night in Paris, France, on the twenty-second day of August, 1572. Charles IX., the King of France, belonged to the Roman Catholic religious sect there. He ordered his army to slaughter all members of another Christian religious sect in Paris, the Huguenots, which they did. His soldiers broke open the doors of houses and hacked to death men, women and children. The king had learned this sort of bigoted murderous conduct from Moses' Bible. This slaughter lasted several days, and the streets of Paris and the Seine river ran red with human blood. Then from Paris the religious massacre spread through all the corners of France.

The chief difference between the king's Christian sect and the Christians he slaughtered was that in the king's sect when the Eucharist or Lord's supper was observed, the priest drank all the wine and the congregation ate the crackers. In the Christian sect that he slaughtered, the congregation drank the wine and ate the crackers both. This may seem insignificant to you, but to zealous religionists these are the things that inflame the mind to rage and to commit murder, just as Moses raged and committed wholesale religious murders many centuries before. Judeo-Christian religion never changes.

An account of the St. Bartholomew's night religious massacre appears in detail in the "Book of Martyrs" by John Fox, which also describes millions of similar murders perpetrated during the centuries of Biblical religious rule in Europe. The Christian religionists had learned well the lessons of religious intolerance and murder taught in Moses' Bible, and by their priests. Fortunately religious rule has been put down, and no civilized nation today would permit such religious murders.

DIVORCE BY GOVERNMENT COMMAND

As the years went by the mighty king of Babylon came with his army and took the Jews captive to Babylon. Since their kingdom was divided they could no longer put up a resistance to an invader. Then after many decades the captives were allowed to return to Palestine. A Jewish government was set up under Ezra and Nehemiah in Jerusalem, but still under Babylonian rule.

These local Jewish governors had a lot of latitude as to what laws they could enforce. So one day Ezra and Nehemiah proclaimed a law that all Jews must divorce their wives if their wives were not of Jewish blood.

Now this caused great consternation among the Jews who had returned to Jerusalem from their captivity in Babylon. Many had married Babylonian women and were happy with their wives and children. Now that happiness was to be destroyed.

Many are the claims of religionists that the Bible teaches interracial harmony and tolerance, but this is not true. Here Moses' Bible itself gives a Biblical law forbidding intermarriage with other races. "And Shechiniah, the son of Jehiel, one of the sons of Elam, answered and said unto Ezra, 'We have trespassed against our God, and have taken strange wives of the people of the land. Yet now there is hope in Israel concerning this thing. Now therefore let us make a covenant with our God to put away all the wives, and such as are born of them, according to the counsel of my lord, and of those that tremble at the commandment of our God. And let it be done according to law.'" (Ezra 10:2,3)

This law was passed, and followed by most Jews who returned from Babylon to Jerusalem. "Then all the congregation answered and said with a loud voice, 'As thou hast said, so must we do.'" (Ezra 10:12) Of course, some Jews undoubtedly packed up and returned to Babylon rather than submit to such an outrageous law.

This law ordering the divorce of all non-Jewish wives was made in conformity with Moses' law given in Deuteronomy 7:3 prohibiting miscegenation, that is, marriage of Jews with non-Jews. Although Moses gave this law to others, he did not keep it himself. He had married a black African woman, an Ethiopian woman (Numbers 12:1; Jer. 13:23) The saintly Moses was a typical religious hypocrite who did not obey the laws he claimed were from God undoubtedly because he knew his laws were not from God at all. Moses was a facinorous individual who liked to make trouble for other people.

Moses' Bible tells us: "And Miriam and Aaron spake against Moses because of the Ethiopian woman whom he had married; for he had married an Ethiopian woman. And they said, 'Hath the Lord indeed spoken only by Moses? Hath he not spoken also by us?' And the Lord heard it . . . . And the anger of the Lord was kindled against them; and he departed. And the cloud departed from off the tabernacle; and, behold, Miriam became leprous, white as snow: and Aaron looked upon Miriam, and behold, she was leprous. And Aaron said unto Moses, 'Alas, my lord, I beseech thee, lay not the sin upon us, wherein we have done foolishly, and wherein we have sinned. Let her not be as one dead." . . . . And Moses cried unto the Lord, saying, 'Heal her now, O God, I beseech thee.' . . . . And Miriam was shut out from the camp seven days: And the people journeyed not till Miriam was brought in again." (Numbers 12:1, 2, 9-13, 15)

Here Moses played one of his hypnotic tricks, for Moses was a hypnotist, and had learned the art from the Egyptians who used Hypnotism to maintain control of the uneducated people. (Acts 7:22) Miriam and Aaron knew nothing of hypnotism, and did not know that Moses had hypnotized them and made them imagine that Miriam had been struck with leprosy because she opposed Moses' unlawful conduct; and also caused them to imagine that God had spoken to them. Moses was like some politicians in our day who do not obey the laws that they themselves enact. He did as he pleased, regardless of any law.

Moses had married an Ethiopian black woman because he felt more kinship to blacks than to Jews and Jewish women. Moses felt closer to the blacks both instinctively and intellectually. And as the old saying goes: "Birds of a feather flock together."

SAINTLY ERRORS IN THE BIBLE

Not only is the Bible a source of insane laws that cause misery for humanity, but the text of the Bible itself is full of contradictions. For example, here is an account of the history of the Jews given in Moses' Bible, and the saintly Bible writers can't get it straight:

In 2 Chronicles Chapter 28 and Verse 5 in the Bible it says: "Wherefore the Lord Jehovah his God delivered him (King Ahaz) into the hand of the king of Syria and they smote him (King Ahaz) and carried away a great multitude of captives . . . . And he (King Ahaz) was delivered into the hand of the king of Israel who smote him with a great slaughter. For Pekah the son of Remeliah slew in Jeday an hundred and twenty thousand in one day."

However, when you read the history of the same event in the Bible at 2 Kings Chapter 16 and Verse 5 it says: "Then Resin king of Syria and

Pekah son of Remeliah king of Israel came to Jerusalem to war; and they besieged (King Ahaz) but could not overcome him."

So the first story contradicts the second. In the first Bible account King Ahaz was defeated and his people slaughtered, and in the second Bible account they besieged King Ahaz but could not over come him. Which is right? The Bible writers claim to be inspired by God and their every word true, but one of these stories is obviously a lie. They can't both be right. Yet some people continually proclaim that they "believe the Bible." All right, which yarn do they believe here?

Now let's look further into the saintly errors of the Bible. Here is another example of contradictory Bible statements. In 2 Kings Chapter 16 and Verses 7 to 9 it says: "So (King) Ahaz sent messengers to Tiglathpilezer king of Assyria saying . . . . come up and save me out of the hand of the king of Syria and out of the hand of the king of Israel, which rise up against me . . . . And the king of Assyria hearkened unto him; for the king of Assyria went up against Damascus (Syria) and took it, and carried the people of it captive to Kir, and slew Rezin (the king of Israel)."

But in 2 Chronicles Chapter 28 and Verse 20 the Bible says: "And Tilgathpilneser king of Assyria came unto him (King Ahaz) and distressed him, but strengthened him not." (Tiglathpilezer and Tilgathpilnezer are the same king according to leading Biblical authorities. It's just that the two inspired saints who wrote these contradictory accounts couldn't agree on the spelling of the Assyrian king's name either.)

So in the first story the Bible says King Ahaz was delivered from his enemies, and in the second story the Bible says he was not. Which are we supposed to believe?

In the midst of all this confusion of lies the saintly Bible writers have the nerve to say, as does the apostle Saint Paul at 2 Timothy Chapter 3 and Verse 16, K.J.V.: "All scripture is given by inspiration of God." Since these are examples of how the Bible God inspires his scriptures, it gives thoughtful persons little confidence in anything written in the Bible. Instead, they are compelled to conclude that God indeed had nothing to do with the writing of the Bible, and that Moses' Bible is merely a man-made piece of nationalistic propaganda put out by the Israelites and Jews.

ORIGIN OF THE BIBLE

Where did the Bible come from? Some superstitious people imagine that the King James Version Bible in English was handed to Moses by God on Mount Sinai, but this is hardly the case. It is said that Moses himself wrote parts of the first five books of the Bible, and various later Israelite saints wrote the remaining books. After Jesus and the apostles died there were many books in use among Christians. Some had been written by the apostles and others of their day, and some by later Christians. Finally the Bishop of Alexandria, Egypt, in 367 A.D. declared the twenty-seven books now found in the New Testament to be canonical. Thirty years later the Council of Carthage agreed with him. But the eastern wing of the Christian church could not decide what they believed for some centuries thereafter. So there was confusion among Christians as to which New Testament books should be in the Bible and which not.

Sixty-six books today constitute the Protestant Bible, both Old Testament and New Testament. The Roman Catholic church has a Bible that contains an additional eleven books that the Protestants do not recognize. Why is that? This difference dates back to about 1545 A.D. at the Council of Trent where the Catholic church accepted these eleven apocryphal books of the Old Testament as Canonical.

In Jesus' Time the Septuagint Version of the Old Testament contained even more books yet. It contained fourteen more books than the Protestant Old Testament. In addition to these, the Bible speaks of the book of Nathan, the book of Gad the Seer, the book of Jasher, the book of Shemaiah, and the book of Jehu. None of these are in the Bible. So who knows what books really belong in the Bible and which do not? Even Bible followers can't agree. (1 Chronicles 29:29; 2 Chronicles 9:29; 12:15; 20:34; and Joshua 10:13) Besides that, God doesn't seem to care if any of the books are in the Bible or not. Why? Because it's not his book.

CHAPTER XXVIII.   SOME SAINTLY PORNOGRAPHIC PROPHECIES

There were many Jewish saints who specialized in producing prophecies for the Bible. They were quite prolific, for Moses' Bible contains more ambiguous prophecies than any other religious book. The King James Version of the Bible is composed of sixty-six books, written by dozens of different saints, and of these, seventeen contain nothing but prophecies, and of the remaining books, more than half of them also contain prophecies.

The way some Bible prophets obtained their prophetic visions was through fasting, as Saint Daniel writes: "And I set my face unto the Lord Jehovah God, to seek by prayer and supplications, with fasting . . . " (Daniel 9:3) Fasting causes delirium, and while delirious these fasting Hebrew prophets saw their visions which were supposedly from their tribal God.

Bible prophecies at times have some spicy zing to them. Take the prophecy at Revelation Chapter 17 and Versus 1 to 3 which says: "And there came one of the seven angels which had the seven vials, and talked with me, saying unto me, 'Come hither, I will shew unto thee the judgment of the great whore that sitteth upon many waters; with whom the kings of the earth have committed fornication, and the inhabitants of the earth have been in the spirit into the wilderness: and I saw a woman sit upon a scarlet colored beast, full of names of blasphemy, having seven heads and ten horns."

This is real pornography according to the dictionary, which defines pornography as material dealing with prostitutes.

And here is another saintly pornographic prophecy, this one written by the prophet Ezekil: "Thou didst turn in thine own beauty, and playedst the harlot because of thy renown, and pouredst out thy fornications on every one that passed by; his it was. And of thy garments thou didst take, and deckedst thy high places with diverse colors, and playedst the harlot thereupon . . . . And in all thine abominations and thy whoredoms thou has not remembered the days of thy youth, when thou wast naked and bare, and wast polluted in thy blood . . . . Thou hast build thy high places at every head of the way, and hast made thy beauty to be abhorred, and hast opened thy feet to every one that passed by, and multiplied thy whoredoms." (Ezekiel Chapter 16 and Verses 15, 16, 22, 25) Then again the "holy" Bible says: "For a whore is a deep ditch; and a strange woman is a narrow pit." (Proverbs 23:27) Very graphic! Pornographic.

Thus the Bible gives us various pornographic prophecies for our so-called edification, and because this material is in the "holy" Bible, religious people accept it without a murmur or complaint. But just think what a denunciation Nostradamus would get from these same church people if he had written a pornographic prophecy! Yet when it appears in the Bible it is all very holy and it's okay, we are told.

PROPHETIC DRAGONS YET

Many saintly Bible prophecies include descriptions of weird dragons and beasts, which are supposed to represent something. Here is a sample from the Bible book of Revelation, Chapter 13, and Verses 1 to 3: "And I stood upon the sand of the sea, and saw a beast rise up out of the sea, having seven heads and ten horns, and upon his heads the name of blasphemy. And the beast which I saw was like unto a leopard, and his feet were as the feet of a bear, and his mouth as the mouth of a lion: and the dragon gave him his power, and his seat, and great authority. And I saw one of his heads as it were wounded to death; and his deadly wound was healed: and all the world wondered after the beast." Having this kind of nightmarish material to work with, you can see how easy it is for religionists to come up with all sorts of interpretations for their followers to swallow. And swallow they do.

Bible prophecy is a subject very popular among religious organizations nowadays. Such prophecies tend to frighten people into joining the church by threatening them with destruction at the Battle of Armageddon, which some claim is supposed to be a sort of world war and end of the world. In past generations everlasting torment in hellfire, used to scare people into joining the church. Now few people believe in hellfire torment, but are definitely afraid of the Battle of Armageddon described by the Bible saints, and for that reason join the church.

One sect made the mistake of putting their predictions about the end of the world in print for all to see, so their errors came back to haunt them. In their earlier books they claimed that Armageddon and the end of the world would come in 1914 with World War I, but it didn't. Then at the start of World War II they said that Armageddon and the end of the world was surely at hand and therefore their church members should not marry, but should concentrate on distributing their religious pamphlets instead. Of course, Armageddon did not arrive then either, but it did help to get their religious propaganda out. And after World War II the leader of this sect himself finally married, so he apparently decided Armageddon was still a long way off, and they had guessed wrong again.

Many other Christian sects have made errors in their predictions also. It is quite to be expected, considering the ambiguous nature of Bible prophecies. In fact, error in interpreting Bible prophecy dates back about 2,000 years to the apostle Saint James, who confidently wrote (allegedly under inspiration of the Holy Ghost), "The coming of the Lord draweth nigh." (See James Chapter 5 and Verse 8 in the Bible.) How nigh is "nigh?" Saint James so far has missed predicting the second coming of Jesus by about 2,000 years. Other Christians have been predicting Jesus' second coming and the end of the world ever since, and with equal accuracy.

One of the prophecies most popular with religionists appears in the Bible book of Daniel, Chapter 11, and particularly Verses 11 to 15, and has to do with the king of the north and the king of the south. Saint Daniel writes: "And the king of the south shall be moved with choler and shall come forth and fight with him, even with the king of the north; and he shall set forth a great multitudes; but the multitude shall be given into his hand. And when he hath take away the multitude, his heart shall be lifted up; and he shall cast down many ten thousands: but he shall not be strengthened by it. For the king of the north shall return, and shall set forth a multitude greater than the former, and shall certainly come after certain years with a great army and with much riches. And in those times shall many stand up against the king of the south; also the robbers of thy people shall exalt themselves to establish the vision; but they shall fall. So the king of the north shall come, and cast up a mount, and take the most fenced cities: and the arms of the south shall not withstand, neither his chosen people, neither shall there be any strength to stand." There is more to this prophecy, but this is enough to show you how it goes.

Some fifty years ago one Christian sect claimed that this was fulfilled by Napoleon, who was the king of the south, they said, and by Britain which was the king of the north. But during World War II they changed their tune and said Germany was the king of the north, and the United States was the king of the south. It didn't bother this Christian sect that Canada and not Germany is north of the United States. They apparently had failed in their geography lessons when in school. In the Bible, though, the king of the south is defeated by the king of the north. They did not dare to put that statement in print in their literature, because they had named the United States as the king of the south. Their interpretation was entirely wrong though. The United States won the war.

But today this sect has changed its tune again. Now they say the king of the north is Soviet Russia, and the king of the south is the United States. The fact that Russia is not at all north of the United States does not faze them in the least.

And so it goes with the peddlers of Bible prophecies of the saints. They will say anything to terrify people into joining their church organizations. You would think that after a religious outfit had bungled its interpretations of Bible prophecies so many times, their followers would quit them in disgust. But not so. Only a few smart ones do.

So much for all the Bible prophecies of the saints, who are like the proverbial Jews' - harp upon which any melody can be played. Actually most saintly prophecies were a propaganda device used by the nation of Israel to give hope to their people while they were conquered and held captive by the many stronger nations that surrounded them. The prophecies foretold a future time when Israel would be victorious. They were like the cry of a defeated football team: "You beat us today, but wait until next time!"

The prophets of Israel had no interest in foretelling events pertaining to other nations such as the United States, Russia, or various world wars. Their effort was to encourage the Jews to hold fast until some future time when things would be better for them. Even Jesus was a Jew who had no interest in nations outside of Israel. So he prophesied to his apostles: "I appoint unto you a kingdom, as my Father hath appointed unto me: That ye may eat and drink at my table in my kingdom, and sit on thrones judging the twelve tribes of Israel." (Luke 22:29, 30) Jesus himself confidently believed that his kingdom would be set up in full power during the lives of his apostles. The Bible says: "And he (Jesus) said unto them, 'Verily I say unto you, that there be some of them that stand here which shall not taste of death till they have seen the kingdom of God come with power.'" (Mark 9;1) The apostles desperately hoped for fulfillment of these prophecies until they died, but Judea continued to be a captive nation under the power of the Roman Empire. God's kingdom did not come, and has not come to this day, nearly two thousand years later.

In spite of this, many Christian churches continue to insist that Christ's kingdom is always about to be established, and that the Battle of Armageddon is at hand. However, some sects say that Armageddon is at the beginning of the one thousand year reign of Christ's kingdom, and other sects insist that the Battle of Armageddon will not come until the end of Christ's one thousand year reign. These various sects are only one thousand years apart in their interpretation of the Bible prophecies of the saints.

There are about 265 different Christian sects in existence, and each one has different interpretations for the saintly Bible prophecies, and other Bible matters. Each sect claim to be right, and that all the others are wrong. Also many sects claim that all other Christian churches but theirs are "of the devil." So with Christian religious leaders in this state of hostility and confusion, what chance has anyone else of understanding this hodge-podge called Bible prophecy, or anything else in the Bible? Yet we are supposed to roast in hellfire for not believing what they preach. Do you sense a trifle insanity in all this?

And how do we know that the Bible is true? Why, saint Moses said so. He wrote part of it. The apostles of Jesus said so. They wrote part of it. The fact remains that if you believe that the Bible is true, you do so because your parents told you it is true. Or your priest or preacher or rabbi said the Bible is true. But where is the proof that what the ignorant barbarian saints wrote in the Bible is true, or that it is the inspired word of God? Rather, the evidence shows that the Bible is not inspired of God, because it is full of errors of the most elemental facts of existence.

For these reasons, and also because of the history of murderous bloody conduct by Bible followers, the Judeo-Christian religion is rejected by most people today. And numerous churchgoers today are known as "Golden Rule Christians;" that is, they try to follow the Golden Rule, and believe little else if found in the Bible.

When I was young I went into a bookstore looking for some reference books on the Bible. The middle-aged Jewish couple who owned the store told me not to take religion too seriously. I wasn't ready to accept their advice then, but after I studied the Bible thoroughly I understood why they had said what they did. They undoubtedly had studied it also, and found the Bible to be far less than what the saints claimed it was: too full of errors to be inspired by God.

According to statistics more than half of the people in the United States and Europe do not belong to any Christian church or Jewish synagogue and do not believe that the Bible is the inspired word of God.

CHAPTER XXIX.   SUSANNA AND THE LECHEROUS ELDERS

Previously we learned that not all the Bible books are found in today's Bible. In the days of Jesus and the apostles, the Septuagint Version of the Bible contained fourteen books that are not found in most Bibles today. However, we are going to examine one of the tales of scandalous saints that appears in these Bible books because they are really a part of ancient Bible writings. This tale in fact appears in Roman Catholic Bibles today.

Our story takes place in the time when the prophet Saint Daniel was in Babylon. How is it that a Jewish prophet was in Babylon? This was because, after the ten tribes of Israel split off from the tribes of Judah and Benjamin, then Nebuchadnezzar, the emperor of Babylon, came with his army and took the Jews of Judea captive. Jehoiakim was king of the Jews in those days, and they then became a subject province of Babylonia. But King Jehoiakim rebelled against Nebuchadnezzar. Then Jehoiakim died and his son Jehoiachin became king in his place.

Again Emperor Nebuchadnezzar of Babylonia came with his army against Jerusalem and finally the Jewish King Jehoiachin surrendered to the Babylonians. Empower Nebuchadnezzar then took King Jehoiachin and his wives and officials and all the chief men of the land, a total of ten thousand captives, to Babylon. He also took away their treasures of gold and silver to Babylon with him.

Then Emperor Nebuchadnezzar appointed Zedekiah to be king over Judea. However, King Zedekiah rebelled against Nebuchadnezzar also. Why Zedekiah imagined that his rebellion could succeed against Babylonia where his predecessors had failed is not clear. All we know is that the Jews were a warlike and rebellious class of people who acted emotionally instead of using their heads. Again Emperor Nebuchadnezzar came to Jerusalem to put down the rebellion, and he was very annoyed by the Jews this time. When Nebuchadnezzar captured the king of the Jews, he had King Zedekiah's eyes put out, and carried him in chains to Babylon. Then the temple of the Jews was burned to the ground and the city of Jerusalem destroyed and its walls torn down, and a multitude of captives were taken to Babylon. So this is why the prophet Daniel was in Babylon, along with many thousands of other Jews. (2 Kings 25:7-11)

THE NAUGHTY ELDERS APPEAR

So our tale of Susanna and the elders took place in Babylon where she was with her husband as a captive of the Babylonians. This story was formerly appended to the book of Daniel, which you find in the Bible, but is now separated therefrom. Many Bible scholars feel that this tale is not properly a part of Daniel's book of prophecies.

The Bible story begins: "There dwelt a man in Babylon, and his name was Joakim; and he took a wife, whose name was Susanna, the daughter of Helkias, a very fair woman, and one that feared the Lord. Her parents also were righteous, and taught their daughter according to the laws of Moses. Now Joakim was a great rich man, and had a fair garden joining unto his house: and to his resorted the Jews; because he was more honorable than all others." (Susanna 1-4)

The Jewish congregation to which they belonged appointed two elders to judge their people in matters of law. These law cases were judged in Joakim's palatial house every day, and the two elders kept much of their legal records also at Joakim's mansion. The ancient text tells us: "These (elders) kept much at Joakim's house; and all that had any suits in law came unto them." (Susanna 6)

But now trouble of a sexy nature began to rear its head. These two elders were good at judging the law, but not so good at keeping it, we are told. The story of Susanna continues: "Now when the people departed away at noon, Susanna went into her husband's garden to walk. And the two elders beheld her going in every day, and walking; and they were inflamed with love for her." (Susanna 7 and 8)

According to the story, Susanna was "a very fair woman", to put it mildly. She was a real looker, an outstanding beauty, the kind of woman that a man of Joakim's wealth would be able to marry. And these elders were not so elderly that they would ignore her beauty. They were elders in name only. And being in the house with her daily they were exposed to her beauty all the time and couldn't get her out of their minds. She was the kind of a woman who could seduce men without half trying.

The tale continues: "And the two elders beheld her going in (the garden) every day, and walking; and they were inflamed with love for her . . . . And albeit they both were wounded with her love, yet durst not shew another his grief. For they were ashamed to declare their lust, that they desire to have to do with her (sexually)." (Susanna 8, 10, 11)

Things were getting serious when the elders desired to have sex relations with her. It was no longer a matter of simply admiring her outstanding beauty, but it had got right down to the point where they desperately wanted her. And here she was a married woman, and they knew they would be breaking Moses' law against adultery if they had sex relations with her. But they had got to the stage where they were willing to break the laws of their Bible God, or anything else, in order to join themselves to Susanna physically.

The story continues: "Yet they wanted jealously from day to day to see her." (Susanna 12) In Babylon all the buildings were made of sun dried brick, like the old Spanish adobe brick buildings in California. The Babylonians had plenty of asphalt pitch oozing from the ground in that country (now know as the oil rich land of Iraq) so they cemented their bricks together with pitch. Even the walls around the garden where Susanna walked were made of these sun dried brick, for they had no other building material for such purpose. So when the lecherous elders were watching Susanna on her daily walks in her garden, they were climbing up and peering over these garden walls of sun dried brick.

The Bible story tells us that as the elders were both watching her: "The one said to the other, 'Let us now go home: for it is dinner time.' So when they were gone out, they parted the one from the other, and turning back again they came to the same place." (Susanna 13,14) Imagine their embarrassment when they both returned to the wall to continue watching and met each other! The tale continues: "And after that they had asked one another the cause (why they came back), they acknowledged their lust: and then appointed they a time both together, when they might find her alone." (Susanna 14, 15) Now it was really getting serious. Why do you suppose they wanted her alone? So they could have sex relations with her, of course.

Finally their great opportunity came. The Bible tale says: "And it fell out, as they watched (for) a fit day, she went in as aforetime (into the garden) with two maids only, and she was desirous to wash herself in the garden: for it was hot." (Susanna 15) The climate around Babylon was hot, but the mighty Euphrates river ran through the middle of the great city of Babylon, so there was plenty of water for all purposes. Joakim being a wealthy man, of course had a swimming pool on his estate, and his wife Susanna decided to do a bit of skinny dipping to cool herself. The garden was surrounded by high walls so nobody could see her, ordinarily. "And there was nobody there save the two elders, that had hid themselves, and watched her." (Susanna 16)

The Bible story tells us: "Then she said to her maids, 'Bring me oil and washing balls, and shut the garden doors, that I may wash me.' And they did as she bade them, and shut the garden doors, and went out themselves at the side doors to fetch the things that she had commanded them: and they saw not the elders, because they were hid." (Susanna 17,18) So Susanna took off her clothing piece by piece until she was completely naked.

Oh, wowie! The two elders were in ecstasy as they watched her take off all her clothing and appear nude before them. They could restrain themselves no longer.

"Let's go get her!" exclaimed Abe. And they dove over the brick wall and dropped into the garden behind some bushes.

The Bible story continues: "Now when the maids were gone forth, the two elders rose up, and ran unto her, saying, 'Behold, the garden doors are shut, that no man can see us, and we are in love with thee: therefore consent unto us, and lie with us (sexually).'" (Susanna 19:20)

Susanna was frightened to see the two elders running toward her, and grabbed her pantyhose or something and held them in front of her to conceal her major assets. "Are you crazy?" she demanded. "You want I should wreck mine marriage to one of the richest men in Babylon just to give you guys some jollies? If you knew how hard I hadda work to catch Joakim, you wouldn't talk like that. Every woman in town was trying to get him."

"No, listen Susy," Said Saint Abe. "It ain't gonna wreck your marriage, because nobody'll know about it. The garden gates are shut, and Jake here will be a lookout while you and I crawl back in the bushes and make it together. Then after we've made it, I'll be the lookout to let you know if anybody's coming, while you and Jake make it together. That way nobody will ever find out."

"No way," replied Susanna. "If I did it once with you creeps you'd be in here every day after me, and sooner or later we'd be caught wrestling together. I wasn't born yesterday, guys. Try some other dame. Go get yourselves a whore or something."

Saint Jake scowled. "If thou wilt not, we will bear witness against thee, that a young man was with thee: and therefore thou didst send away thy maids from thee." (Susanna 21) "You better give us what we want, or your marriage will be wrecked for sure. You know that under Moses' law you will be put to death for adultery."

Saint Susanna paled. "You can't do that. You got no proof."

"Oh, yes we can," replied Saint Abe. "Remember: we're elders. We don't need proof. Everybody believes what we say."

The Bible tells us: "Then Susanna sighed, and said, 'I am straightened on every side: for if I do this thing, it is death unto me: and if I do it not, I cannot escape your hands. It is better for me to fall into your hands, and not do it, than to sin in the sight of the Lord.'"

"With that Susanna cried with a loud voice: and the two elders cried out against her." (Susanna 22-24)

The elders grabbed Saint Susanna, naked as she was, and dragged her toward the gate while she screamed for help. "Then ran the one (elder), and opened the garden doors. So when the servants of the house heard the cry in the garden, they rushed in at the side door, to see what had befallen her. But when the elders had told their tale, the servants were greatly ashamed: for there was never such a report made of Susanna." (Susanna 25-27)

"They're lying!" cried Susanna. "They propositioned me, and when I refused to have sex with them, they told these lies to get revenge on me."

"Tomorrow we'll bring our charges against her before the whole congregation," said Abe. Then the two saintly elders left the place and went home.

Well, Saint Susanna's whole household was in an uproar. When her husband Joakim came home, Susanna told him about what happened. He could not believe the charges that the elders had brought against her. And when her father and mother and the rest of the family heard about it, they also stood by Susanna, since they all knew that Susanna had never been accused of any wrongdoing.

Then the Bible tells us: "And it came to pass on the morrow, when the people assembled to her husband Joakim, the two elders came full of their wicked intent against Susanna to put her to death; and said before the people, 'Send for Susanna, the daughter of Helkias, Joakim's wife.'"

"So they sent; and she came with her father and mother, her children, and all her kindred. Now Susanna was a very delicate women and beauteous to behold. And these wicked men commanded her to be unveiled, (for she was veiled) that they might be filled with her beauty. Therefore her friends and all that saw her wept." (Susanna 28-33)

"Then the two elders stood up in the midst of the people, and laid their hands upon her head . . . . And the elders said, 'As we walked in the garden alone, this woman came in with two maids, and shut the garden doors, and sent the maids away. Then a young man, who there was hid, came unto her, and lay with her (sexually). And we, being in a corner of the garden, saw this wickedness, and ran unto them. And when we saw them together, the man we could not hold: for he was stronger than we, and opened the doors, and leaped out (of the garden). But having taken this woman, we asked who the young man was, but she would not tell us: these things do we testify." (Susanna 34-40)

The Bible story continues: "Then the assembly believed them, as those that were elders of the people and judges: so they condemned her to death."

"Then Susanna cried out with a loud voice, and said, ...'They have borne false witness against me, and behold, I must die; whereas I never did such things as these men have maliciously invented against me.'" (Susanna 41-43) This was really nothing but a kangaroo court, a lynch mob trial, in which the testimony of the accusers was believed without cross-examination or proof. Very often Plaintiffs and prosecution witnesses lie in court, even today. Though today, many times such fraudulent convictions can be overturned on appeal to higher courts. But there were no such appellate courts among the Jew. If a person was convicted, that was final. So Saint Susanna faced death by execution.

But suddenly a young man in the audience cried out against this travesty of Justice. The Bible tells us he was "a young youth, whose name was Daniel: and he cried with a loud voice, "I am clear from the blood of this woman!'"

Now this saint Daniel was of great reputation among the Jews in Babylon, because he was a member of the court of Emperor Nebuchadnezzar. The Bible says: "Then all the people turned toward him, and said, 'What mean these words that thou hast spoken?'"

"So he (Daniel) standing in the midst of them said, 'Are ye such fools, ye sons of Israel, that without (cross) examination or knowledge (proof) of the truth ye have condemned a daughter of Israel? Return again to the place of judgment: for these have borne false witness against her.'"

"Wherefore all the people turned again in haste, and said unto him, 'Come, sit down among us, and show it to us (that is, show us our errors).'" (Susanna 47-50)

Saint Daniel had been in the court of Emperor Nebuchadnezzar of Babylonia and had learned how proper court trials must be conducted. Plaintiffs and all witnesses must be cross-examined, whether they are witnesses for the prosecution, the accusers, or witnesses for the defense. Otherwise the truth of their statements could not be determined. And now this Daniel took it upon himself to act as attorney for the defense.

The Bible story tells us: "Then said Daniel unto them, 'Put them (the accusing elders) asunder one far from another, and I will examine them.'" So they took one of the elders out of the room while the other was to be cross-examined. The tale continues: "So when they were put asunder one from another, he (Daniel) called one of them, and said unto him, ... 'Now then, if thou sawest her, tell me, under what tree sawest thou them companying together (having sexual intercourse together)?'"

And the first accusing elder said, "Under a mastic tree." (Susanna 51, 52, 54, 55)

So then Saint Daniel dismissed the first accusing elder. The Bible story continues: "So he (Daniel) put him aside, and commanded to bring the other (accusing elder), and said unto him, ... 'Now therefore tell me, under what tree didst thou take them companying together?'"

And the second accusing elder said, "Under a holm tree."

"Then said Daniel unto him, 'Right well hast thou also lied against thine own head.'" (Susanna 56, 58, 59)

Then the story says: "With that all the assembly cried out with a loud voice . . . . And they arose against the two elders, for Daniel had convicted them of false witness out of their own mouth: and according to the law of Moses they did unto them in such sort as they maliciously intended to do to their neighbor: and they put them to death. And the innocent blood was saved the same day."

"Therefore Helkias and his wife praised God for their daughter Susanna, with Joakim her husband, and all the kindred, because there was no dishonesty found in her."

"And from that day forth was Daniel had in great reputation in the sight of the people." (Susanna 60-64)

WHY SO MUCH SEX IN THE BIBLE?

Folks often wonder why the Bible contains so many stories about illicit sex. Well, for one thing, the Bible is a history of many saints who were involved in scandalous sexual intercourse. And then again, the Bible writers knew what kind of stories most people like to read. So they figured that if you want to get people to read the Bible, you've got to give them what they want to read about.

Proof of that is in the way the bishops decided which stories should go into the Bible, and which shouldn't. Of all the fourteen books that were rejected by the Protestant clergy and relegated to apocryphal status, only one was sexy, and that's the one you just read about "Susanna and The Lecherous Elders." The reason "Susanna" was rejected by Protestant is that it cast aspersions on the church officials, the elders. And the bishops thought that it would cause whole congregations to look with suspicion at elders and the clergy. So they rejected it.

The thirteen other apocryphal books are quite drab and boring and not sexy at all. But the Protestant bishops included the sexiest books in the text of their Bible. However, the Roman Catholic Bible includes eleven of these apocryphal books, most of them boring but one not, in addition to the books in the Protestant Bible.

AND NUDE SAINTLY STATUES YET!

Another thing: back in the Dark Ages when few people knew how to read, the clergy attracted people into church with statues of nude male saints. Many statues of male Christian saints in France were nude, revealing oversize penises. These were greatly admired and venerated by the Christian populace. Included among these many nude statues were those of St. Giles of Brittany and St. Greluchon at Borges. The clergy here were using the same scheme the saintly Bible writers had, by employing sex to attract people to the Christian Church. In the early centuries of the Dark Ages most Europeans were pagans, and it was a real problem for the Christian clergy to lure people into their churches.

The Christian church members often used these nude statues in ways that people today might not suspect. In other words, the statues of nude saints were not merely bowed to or looked at. They were actually employed in ways that some women today use vibrators, and with the same results!

Humanity hasn't changed much over the centuries, has it? Except that in the Dark Ages this sort of erotic message was associated with the Christian religion, and today it is associated with electricity! However, it is reported that even today such nude statues of the saints are still being used as they were in centuries past, in some places. Woohoo! Who ever thought that Christianity could be thus!

CHAPTER XXX.   WHO DISRUPTED THIS LADY'S VIRGINITY?

Who done it? This is the old cry in all the detective stories, and here in the Bible we have a similar puzzle. Who ended Saint Mary's virginity? Did her Jewish fiancee Joseph do it? Or did a guy named the Holy Ghost do it? So here are the facts, as the Bible gives them.

You have heard the religious claim repeatedly made that Jesus was born miraculously due to insemination of Saint Mary by the Holy Ghost, but the Bible doesn't always say that. In fact, the Bible piles confusion on confusion as it gives two tales of how Mary got pregnant. Three tales, in fact.

At the start of the New Testament in the Bible, in the Book of Matthew, Chapter 1, and Verses 1 to 16 we have a list of Jesus' Jewish ancestors from the time of Abraham down to the birth of Jesus, and the key is verse 16 which says: "And Jacob begat Joseph the husband of Mary of whom was born Jesus, who is called Christ." So there is no confusion thus far. Jesus' ancestors included Abraham and David and finally Joseph the husband of Mary, the Jewish mother of Jesus. That's what the Bible says. It's plain, and it's simple. As verse one states, "The book of the generation of Jesus Christ, the son of David, the son of Abraham," and eventually the son of Joseph. This genealogy is the record of Jesus' ancestors and it includes Saint Joseph, for it is also Joseph's genealogy.

But now comes the confusion. Right after giving this simple account of the Jewish ancestral line of Jesus, we have another story. At Verse 18 in Chapter 1 of Saint Matthew's gospel above quoted we have this statement: "Now the birth of Jesus Christ was on this wise: When as his mother Mary was espoused to Joseph, before they came together (that is, had sexual intercourse) she was found with child (pregnant) of the Holy

Ghost."

Holy altar smoke! If a thing like that happened today would you believe it? Suppose a girl you knew said she got pregnant by having sexual intercourse with an angel or with the Holy Ghost. Would you believe it? Well, hardly. You'd probably laugh till you fell on the floor! That is, if you weren't one of the girl's parents. Of course, people were superstitious in those days and were more inclined to believe such nonsense. But this is the yarns the Jewish Saint Mary came up with when her folks found out she was pregnant and not married.

Fortunately she was engaged to Joseph and he agreed to marry her even if she was pregnant. Yes, it was scandalous, but lots of pregnant girls were married by men who are willing to raise some other guy's baby in order to marry a very pretty and popular girl. This happens every once-in-awhile, and it may have happened in Mary's case.

On the other hand, some say Mary and Joseph could have been doing some very close and intimate heavy petting and didn't realize that a girl can get pregnant sometimes even if they barely touch each other. You note, I say "bare-ly touch," and you know where.

Anyway, here Saint Mary was fecund before she and Joseph were married. This was a very nasty scandal, as some people thought, including Joseph, who almost broke off his engagement to Mary. So first the Bible admits Joseph was the father of Jesus and the Bible gives Joseph's Jewish genealogy. Then the Bible gives Mary's wild tale of getting pregnant through sexual intercourse with the Holy Ghost.

(I wonder if they asked her if the Holy Ghost was a real stud, and if she had an orgasm when it happened. It's certain that her female relatives must have asked her how it felt to have sexual intercourse with a ghost. Whatever answer Mary gave them doesn't appear in the Bible, but it would have been interesting to know. And I would not be a faithful hagiographer if I did not raise these questions.)

However, if the Holy Ghost was actually the father of Jesus Christ, then this whole list of ancestors of Jesus including Joseph could not be Jesus' genealogy at all, because it is also Joseph's genealogy. The only way a genealogy could trace Jesus' ancestry back to Abraham would be through Mary's list of Jewish ancestors, but that is not given here. Also the Holy Ghost does not have Abraham as one of his ancestors, and no such claim is made in the Bible.

So these two stories of Jesus' ancestors are completely at odds with each other. One Bible story contradicts the other Bible story completely. And you can take your choice as to which you believe. Or you don't have to believe either story, because the fact that the Bible contradicts itself shows that it is not a reliable source of information.

TALE NUMBER THREE

Now we get to the third tale of Jesus' birth, as if two were not more than enough. And this contradicts the other two. This yarn appears in the gospel of Luke, Chapter 3, and beginning at Verse 23. Here the Bible says: "And Jesus himself began to be about thirty years of age, being (as was supposed) the son of Joseph, which was the son of Heli, which was the son of Matthat, which was the son of Levi, which was the son of Melchi, which was the son of Janna," etc., all the way back to Adam.

But woah! Something is wrong here. Luke writes that Jesus' father Joseph was the son of Heli, in the above quotation, but back in Matthew Chapter 1 and Verse 16, Matthew says that Jesus' father Joseph was the son of Jacob. And the whole list of Jesus' ancestors in the Book of Luke is different from that in Matthew, with a few exceptions. Obviously either Matthew's genealogy is false, or Luke's genealogy is false. They both cannot be true. Joseph could not have two fathers.

Of course, some of the clergy insist that the reason for this difference is that one list of ancestors pertains to Joseph and one list belongs to Mary, but this can't be true. Neither list mentions Mary. Both lists trace themselves down to Joseph, the father of Jesus. Thus the alibi of the clergy cannot be correct.

So here we have two different lists of Jewish ancestors for Jesus, and a third tale that throws both lists overboard and claims that the Holy Ghost fathered Jesus. So you have three genealogies for Jesus, and you can choose whichever one you want: Eenie, meenie, minee, moe. It would seem that with a person as prominent as Jesus, the Bible could at least get his ancestral lineage straight. If the Bible can't do that, how can we believe anything else it says about Jesus?

There is an explanation for the claim that the Holy Ghost fathered Jesus. If you read the four Gospels, you will note that they often give Jesus' claim: "I am the son of God," as he says at John 10:33-36. There was much controversy with the Jewish priesthood over this issue, and Jesus was ultimately put to death because of this claim. Even after Jesus' execution this controversy raged between the Jewish clergy and the disciples of Christ.

It is not surprising then that some ambitious saint may have inserted this tale of the Holy Ghost fathering Jesus into the books of Luke and Matthew. This would settle once and for all the issue of Jesus being the son of God, even though the original writings of Matthew and Luke apparently did not contain this Holy Ghost story. The original manuscripts were undoubtedly written with only the Jewish ancestry of Jesus traced through Joseph as his father. Then along came this invented tale about the Holy Ghost fathering Jesus, and this was added to the manuscripts at a later date.

Obviously if Jesus had indeed been fathered by the Holy Ghost then there would have been no point in giving a list of his alleged Jewish ancestry through Joseph, because Joseph would have had no blood relationship to Jesus at all. The Holy Ghost story is manifestly a forgery.

Concerning this Thomas Jefferson, third president of the United States, wrote: "The day will come when the mystical generation of Jesus . . . . in the womb of a virgin will be classed with the fable of the generation of Minerva in the brain of Jupiter."

The idea of the gods fathering humans was not a new one. The kings of many nations were alleged to be descendants of the gods, and Greek mythology is full of such tales. The idea of Jesus being fathered by God could have been borrowed from Greek mythology to give stature to Jesus.

FURTHER EXAMPLES OF ALTERATIONS

If you want to see an example of forgery into the Bible text, just turn to 1 John 5:7 in your King James Version of the Bible, which most of you have. Here this verse reads: "For there are three that bear record in heaven, the Father, the Son, and the Holy Ghost: and these three are one."

Now turn to the same version in the American Standard Version which is different because it was translated from older Greek manuscripts of the Bible that were made before this forgery was added.

Therefore you see proof right here that forgeries and changes have been made in the Bible text over the centuries. In just that matter the spurious story of Jesus' being fathered by the Holy Spirit may have been inserted into the original Bible manuscripts.

A modern example of changing the Bible text is found at 1 Kings 14:10. Here the King James Version of the Bible quotes God as saying that he "will cut off from Jeroboam him that pisseth against the wall." This is exactly what God is supposed to have said, as quoted directly from the Hebrew Bible manuscript, where the Hebrew word for "pisseth" is "shaw-than".

However, the translators of the Standard Version thought that quotation too blunt and factual for modern readers, even if God did say it, and God shouldn't be so vulgar anyway, so they changed this text to say that God "will cut off from Jeroboam every man-child." But this is not what God actually said, according to the Hebrew text. As a matter of fact, females can also urinate against a wall if they want to; it is not at all physically impossible nor difficult for them to do so. And the insertion of the pronoun "him" into the King James Version text is not at all certain; the pronoun could be "her". So how can anyone rely on what he reads in any Bible translation?

IS CHRISTMAS JESUS' BIRTHDAY?

Christmas is not a celebration established by the Bible, but a church holiday dating from about 350 years after Christ's death. December 25 is not the birthdate of Jesus. Many Bible scholars today believe Jesus was born some time in October. The December 25 date was chosen by the Roman Catholic church apparently because it was one of the chief non-Christian celebrations of the year.

On December 25 the Scandinavians celebrated the return of the sun, since the days began lengthening after the winter solstice. Also the Romans celebrated the harvest feast of Saturnalia on this day, which the Christian saints sought to usurp and use as the date to celebrate Jesus' birthday, which date is not given in the Bible.

All over Europe the white race celebrated the return of the sun as the days began lengthening after winter solstice on December 21. After all, Europe is almost all north of the fortieth parallel (or about New York City) and mostly opposite Canada and Alaska, therefore the return of the sun meant a great benefit to the white people. So they had their celebrations with Yule logs burning in the fireplace, and fir trees decorated with ornaments, and a jolly old fat man in a red suit who brought gifts in his sleigh pulled by reindeer.

You can read the Bible all you want and you will never find any mention of Yule logs and fir trees decorated with ornaments, and a jolly old fat man in a red suit. These things belonged to the European people who celebrated the return of the sun. After all, who ever heard of a Jewish Santa Clause with a hooked nose and a black beard cut off square across the bottom according to the Moses' law? The Jews never had any fir trees or holly in Palestine and never heard of any jolly gift giving Santa Clause, or sleighs pulled by reindeer. The ancient Jews wouldn't know a reindeer from a rhinoceros, and never heard of a sleigh. All these things belong to the white race and have nothing to do with the celebration of Christ's birthday. But the Roman Catholic church usurped the European celebration of the festival of the returning sun and used it as a celebration of Christ's birthday, even though they didn't know when Christ was born. So today we find the celebration of the return of the sun mixed with the Jewish Jesus religion, to the detriment of both.

During the first century following the deaths of Jesus and his apostles, the Christian disciples believed that Jesus was born in the early part of March. The sun is in the Stellar constellation of Pisces at that time, and the Latin word "pisces" means "fishes". Therefore carved on many of the tombs of these early Christians was a picture of a fish, which was the secret symbol of Jesus used by Christians at that time. In those days the Roman rulers severely persecuted Christians, throwing them to the lions or putting them to death in other ways. Consequently Christians had to be careful in identifying themselves to each other. Thus when two people met, and one wanted to know if the other was a Christian, he would casually draw a picture of a fish. If the other recognized it, the two people then knew they were both Christians. From this widespread custom of the first Christian disciples it is apparent that Jesus was generally believed to have been born in early March, and this seems to be the most reliable information we have regarding the birthdate of Jesus, since it was undoubtedly given to the disciples by the apostles.

CHAPTER XXXI. THIS SAINT SAID THEY WOULD ROAST IN HELL

When Jesus grew up into manhood he found the Jewish nation in a ferment. They had been conquered years before by the Romans and made subject to the rule of Rome, to which they had to pay taxes. The Jews were seething with ideas of revolt against Rome, and looked for a leader or deliverer to rise up and restore their independent kingdom as the prophets promised.

The Jewish religious sect of the Pharisees led the nation in this expectation. The Pharisees had the idea that the Jews under the Messiah or Christ would set up a government that would rule over the entire world, with Jerusalem as the capital city. This notion inflamed the Jews to a religious fanaticism that made them almost impossible to govern. They were constantly plotting revolt against Rome, heedless of their national weakness and inability to succeed against the vastly superior Roman army.

In the midst of this fanatical uproar Jesus publicly began to preach, claiming himself to be the son of God and Messiah whom God had anointed to be the Jewish king. Furthermore he promised to set up God's Kingdom, with his apostles to be his chief officers governing the Jewish kingdom. (Luke 22:29, 30)

If someone had set off a bomb in Jerusalem it would have had far less effect than Jesus presenting himself as the king of the Jews. Here is what the Pharisees had been promising for generations, and now the people had their king in their midst. All the prophets had also long before promised that a mighty prince would arrive, who would deliver the nation of Judea from their captivity. Now at last their prince or king had arrived, and the shackles of the hated Romans would be thrown off!

No wonder the multitudes flocked after Jesus to hear him preach.

At least the Jewish multitudes hoped that Jesus fulfilled the words of the prophets. Jesus of course knew these prophecies too and slanted his preachings and Messianic claims to fit the prophetic words. The only question remained: Were Jesus' claims valid? And would he indeed set up the Jewish kingdom as promised? But thousands of the Jewish people were not inclined to doubt Jesus' claims. The nation had become so inflamed with the idea of revolt against their captors they were ready to follow anyone who rose up to lead them with a promise of victory. They had followed the Maccabees in revolt several generations before this, and now they were ready to rise and do battle again.

The Maccabees had been patriots who had risen up against Judea's Syrian conquerors, and more particularly the Syrian king, Antiochus Epiphanes. This Syrian ruler attempted to do away with the Jewish religion and substitute the Greek worship of Jupiter. A Jewish priest named Mattathias and his five sons led the Jews in a revolt against Syria and were successful, due to the intervention of Rome on their side. Rome of course was not interested in the Jews' religion, but wanted Syria out of Judea, as Rome had its own designs on that area. As a result, the Syrian king had to withdraw his troops from Judea. This allowed the Jews to resume their national form of religion, the Moses religion, with all its barbaric niceties, in the year 165 B.C.

Now, nearly two hundred years later, the Jews remembered their triumphant revolt against Syria, and hoped for another triumph in a new revolt, this time against Rome. However, they forgot one element in their previous success. Rome had intervened, and the threat of the power of Rome had forced the Syrian king to withdraw from Judea. But today, what nation was strong enough to intervene and force the mighty Roman armies to withdraw? There was no nation as strong as Rome in those days. If even Syria and Egypt trembled before the might of Rome, how could the tiny nation of Jews possibly succeed in war against Rome. But the religious fanaticism of the Jews would admit no obstacle too great for them to surmount. If the Jews would rise up in the name of their God Jehovah, they were bound to conquer! Or so they thought.

When Jesus appeared on the Jewish national scene, claiming to be the son of God, and the Jewish Messiah or Christ, a vast multitude of people immediately flocked to his standard. He was to them the great Prince who should deliver them from the rule of Rome and restore to them their lost national sovereignty.

But Jesus brought with him a new and different kind of religion than Moses had taught. Moses had taught the Israelites to fight and kill, and slaughter non-Jewish people, men, women, and children, as we have documented earlier in this book. But Jesus had a completely different teaching. Jesus said, 'Ye have heard that it hath been said, 'An eye for an eye, and a tooth for a tooth.' But I say unto you, that ye resist not evil, but whosoever shall smite thee on thy right cheek, turn to him the other also." (Matthew 5:38,39) "Ye have heard that it hath been said, 'Thou shalt love thy neighbor and hate thine enemy.' But I say unto you, love your enemies, bless them that curse you, and pray for them which despitefully use you and persecute you." (Matthew 5:43,44)

This was completely at variance with Moses' teachings and immediately aroused opposition among those who sought to revolt against Rome. How could the Jews fight Rome if they were going to follow Jesus' teachings? So there was a sharp split among the Jews. Some realized that for a small nation like Judea to attempt to fight against the mighty Roman Empire would be suicidal, and they followed Jesus. But the majority followed the war party, the Pharisees.

Jesus had other teachings that were completely different from what the Jews had been taught in the Moses religion. Saint Moses had promised blessings of prosperity in this life if his followers obeyed him. (Leviticus 26:3-12) Unfortunately, these blessings did not materialize as Moses promised, and the people saw that evildoers such as King David prospered and were wealthy, while those who obeyed Moses' laws often perished. (Ecclesiastes 8:14) Jesus realized this, and made no promises for this life. But in the life to come Jesus promised them blessings in heaven. (Luke 16:20-23)

This was the sort of promise nobody could argue with, because who could go to heaven and come back and say what went on there? Who could even prove there was or was not a heaven?

On the other hand, Jesus promised those who disobeyed or disbelieved him a future life after death in hellfire torment. (Matthew 25:41,46) This was a promise of punishment nobody could dispute, for who could go to hellfire and then come back and say what went on there, or who was in there? Nobody could disprove his claim that there was such a place as hellfire after death; but of course, on the other hand, nobody could prove that hellfire existed.

This threat of hellfire torment was developed at least one thousand years before Christ in Persia. The clergy showed their followers volcanic eruptions and told them they would roast underground in hell if they disobeyed the priesthood. Thus was born the idea that hellfire is down below. In the same way the clergy had also claimed that thunder in the clouds was the voice of God, and thus heaven was conceived as being up in the sky. (Job 37:5) This was the religious dogma taught by Jesus also. (Matthew 7:11)

A PROPHECY OF TERROR

Jesus himself sought to terrify people into following him by causing them to fear a final judgment in which he, Jesus, would be judge, and those who did not follow him would be punished in fire. The Bible tells us that Jesus said of the end of the world: "When the son of man (Jesus) shall come in his glory, and all the holy angels with him, then shall he sit upon the throne of his glory; and before him shall be gathered all nations; and he shall separate them one from another, as a shepherd divideth his sheep from the goats; And he shall set the sheep on his right hand, but the goats on the left. Then shall the King (Jesus) say unto them on his right hand, 'Come, ye blessed of my Father, inherit the kingdom prepared for you from the foundation of the world.' . . . . Then he shall say also unto them on the left hand, 'Depart from me, ye cursed, into everlasting fire, prepared for the devil and his angels.'" (Matthew 25:31-34, 41)

This teaching was not original with Jesus. He copied it from the priesthood of Persia and the other various Indo-European peoples. These Aryan priests taught that there would be a final Judgment and destruction of the world by fire for something like a thousand years before Jesus decided to incorporate it into the Jewish religion. But Jesus considered it useful, as the Persian priests considered it useful, in frightening the people into obedience to religion and the priesthood. After all, if you can frighten people into believing in a final judgment after death, where they will be punished if they have been found disobedient to what their priests have told them, you then have control over a mass of superstitious people who will do anything the priests require of them. And if the priests ask for a money payment in order to deliver such superstitious people from this imaginary and fictitious future punishment, the people will gladly hand over their money to the priests. Jesus knew a good thing when he saw it, and so included this Persian eschatological doctrine in his religion. Money, money, money! It makes the world go around, even when people are swindled out of it.

JESUS CAN WAIT

However, if heaven is so good, how is it that Christians are building so many hospitals and filling up all the hospitals? They're sure trying to avoid seeing Saint Peter and Jesus as long as possible. Even when Saint Peter was alive, the Bible tells us the same thing was going on. It says: "Now there was at Joppa a certain disciple named Tabitha which by interpretation is called Dorcas: This woman was full of good works and almsdeeds which she did. And it came to pass in those days, that she was sick, and died; whom when they had washed, they laid her in an upper chamber. And forasmuch as Lydda was nigh to Joppa, and the disciples had heard that Peter was there, they sent unto him two men, desiring him that he would not delay to come to them. Then Peter arose and went with them. When he was come, they brought him into the upper chamber: and all the widows stood by him weeping, and shewing the coats and garments which Dorcas made, while she was with them. But Peter put them all forth, and kneeled down, and prayed: And turning him to the body said, "Tibatha, arise.' And she opened her eyes: and when she saw Peter (in her bedroom) she sat up. And he gave her his hand, and lifted her up, and when he had called the saints and widows, presented her alive." (In the Bible see Acts 9:36-41)

We don't know for sure what Saint Peter did to her after he ordered all the others out of her bedroom and closed the door, but it probably went something like this:

This nice lady let out a scream. "There's a strange man in my bedroom! Sir, how dare you touch me there?"

"The others told me you were dead, and touching you there was the only sure way I knew would wake you up. It worked too. I should introduce myself. My name's Peter."

"Well, that figures. Holy altar smoke, I wasn't dead! I just had one drink of wine too many, and I guess I must have passed out."

(But don't laugh at the ancients for not knowing when a person is dead. Even nowadays somebody they have pronounced dead will revive in the hospital or even in the morgue. After all, they don't pronounce you "brain dead" unless they need your body parts so they can perform an expensive surgical operation on somebody else.)

So Christians were trying to avoid going to heaven in those early days too. Apparently they weren't too sure heaven was as good a place as it was cracked up to be.

The only heaven men are sure of is being with their wives. But in the heaven that Jesus told about, wives were forbidden. Jesus said of those in heaven: "They neither marry, nor are given in marriage, but are as the angels of God in heaven." (See Matthew 22:30 in the Bible.) Before men and women were admitted to Jesus' heaven they all had to be castrated or ovariotomized. That's what Jesus' teachings showed. (Learning of this, most people say, "To hell with that kind of a heaven!")

JESUS CONTRADICTS HIMSELF

Many Jews saw vast contradictions in Jesus' teachings, just as thoughtful people do today. Jesus talked frequently about "loving one another." The apostle John writes in the New Testament: "God is Love." (1 John 4:8) On the other hand, Jesus also taught absolutely the opposite of love. In Matthew 25:31 and 41 Jesus says: "When the Son of man (Jesus) shall come in his glory and all the holy angels with him, then shall he sit upon the throne of glory. Then shall he say also unto them on the left hand, 'Depart from me, ye cursed, into everlasting fire, prepared for the devil and his angels.'" The New Testament further states at Revelation 14:10, 11 about those whom Jesus disapproves: "He shall be tormented with fire and brimstone in the presence of the holy angels and in the presence of the Lamb (Jesus). And the smoke of their torment ascendeth up for ever and ever; and they had no rest day or night."

Consider now how vicious this doctrine is. If a person in the United States were to torture a dog for five minutes in fire, he would be thrown in jail. Yet here Jesus says that he will torture people in fire and brimstone forever. If Jesus attempted to do such a thing in the United States he would be thrown in prison immediately, and rightly so. Such a teaching and such an attitude is cruel and savage in the extreme. What value would there be in tormenting people in fire forever? If they had sinned, torment forever could not be for the purpose of correcting them, because they would never escape from the fire. Of what value was such torment then? Only a barbaric Israelite could see any value in it.

Charles Darwin, the great biologist who set forth the teaching of evolution in his book, "The Origin of The Species," wrote: "I can hardly see how anyone ought to wish Christianity to be true, for if so the plain language of the text seems to show that the men who do not believe, and this would include my father, brother, and almost all my best friends will be everlastingly punished. And this is a damnable doctrine."

The teachings of Jesus about heaven and everlasting hellfire torment were all new and different from anything the Jews had been taught in the Moses religion. Saint Moses and the prophets had never even mentioned anything like heaven and hellfire torment. It is true that the word "hell" appears in the English translation of the Bible Old Testament.

However, this word translated "hell" comes from the Hebrew word "Sheh-ole", which literally means "grave" or "pit", a place where the dead are buried. There is no other word translated "hell" in the Old Testament except this one Hebrew word above given. And there is no place in the Bible Old Testament that mentions hellfire torment after death. Heaven and hellfire torment after death were entirely new ideas to the Jews. Where did Jesus get these new and different teachings?

CHAPTER XXXII.   THE HOLY MAN WHO WAS A HYPNOTIST

There is a very great similarity between Jesus' teachings and Buddhism. The teachings of non-violence, pacifism, and ostensible love for all are paramount in both Buddhism and Biblical Christianity. The teachings of heaven and hellfire torment are part of both religions. Of course, Buddhism is not satisfied with one hell, but provides numerous hells, and both Christianity and Buddhism provide many heavens. Paul, the apostle of Jesus, writes of "the third heaven" (2 Corinthians 12:2) And we have no idea how many other heavens he and other early Christians may have believed in.

The Apostle Saint Peter later enlarged upon the doctrine of hell, writing in the Bible: "God spared not the angels that sinned, but cast them down to hell" (2 Peter 2:4) While in most places in the New Testament the word "hell" is translated from the word "Gehenna", here the word "hell" is translated from the Greek word "tartarus." This is the only time this word "tartarus" is used for the word "hell" in the entire Bible. Saint Peter here shamelessly stole the tale written by the ancient Greek author, Homer, in which the Greek god Zeus hurled his enemies into a pit far below Hades, and the pit Homer named "targarus." Thus it is seen that Christianity is an opportunistic conglutination of Greek myths combined with Buddhism and some traditional Jewish teachings.

Buddhism and Biblical Christianity both prohibit murder, stealing, adultery, drunkenness, and personal ornamentation with jewelry. Both hold up poverty and evangelism as virtues. Jesus told his disciples: "Sell what you have and give alms . . . . for where your treasure is, there will your heart be also." (Luke 12:33, 34) The early Christians did exactly that. The Bible tells us: "And all that believed were together, and had all things in common; and sold their possessions and goods, and parted them to all men as every man had need." (Acts 2:44, 45) The fact that this might eventually reduce the entire congregation to poverty was disregarded or not forseen by early Christians. In any case, poverty was a virtue to Christians and Buddhists alike.

Jesus had no use for the rich, and made his views very clear in the following words: "There was a certain rich man, which was clothed in purple and fine linen, and fared sumptuously every day. And there was a certain beggar named Lazarus, which was laid at his gate, full of sores. And desiring to be fed with the crumbs which fell from the rich man's table; more over the dogs came and licked his sores.

"And it came to pass that the beggar died, and was carried by the angels into Abraham's bosom. The rich man also died, and was buried; and in hell he lift up his eyes, being in torments, and seeth Abraham afar off, and Lazarus in his bosom. And he (the rich man) cried and said, 'Father Abraham, have mercy on me and send Lazarus, that he may dip the tip of his finger in water and cool my tongue; for I am tormented in this flame'"

"But Abraham said, 'Son, remember that thou in thy lifetime receivedst thy good things, and likewise Lazarus evil things; but now he is comforted, and thou art tormented.'" (In the Bible see Luke, Chapter 16 and Versus 19 to 25)

Note carefully that Jesus did not say that the rich man was immoral or dishonest or failed to attend the synagogue or church. All Jesus said of the rich man was, "Thou in thy lifetime receivedst thy good things, and likewise Lazarus (the beggar) evil things. But now he is comforted and thou art tormented." In other words, Jesus showed that in his view it is wicked to be rich, and that the rich automatically go into hellfire torment when they die.

But before ordinary folk become too smug in smirking at the plight of the millionaires heading for hellfire, just listen to this next command that Jesus gave, as quoted from Luke Chapter 3 and Versus 10 and 11: "And the people asked him, saying, 'What shall we do then?' He (Jesus) answereth and saith unto the, 'He that hath two coats, let him impart to him that hath none.'"

So now Christians who keep more than one coat aren't Christians at all. They're in the same boat with the millionaires, heading for hellfire, according to Jesus' words. And remember that Jesus also said: "Not everyone that saith unto me, 'Lord, Lord,' shall enter into the kingdom of heaven; but he that doeth the will of my Father, which is in heaven."

(Matthew 7:21) So if they have anything more than the coat on their backs, they are not Christians, and will surely roast in hellfire forever, according to Jesus' teachings. They can't own an extra coat, an extra shirt, a television set, an automobile, or anything.

With this kind of teaching it is a wonder that any people attend church. The reason they do, obviously, is because they do not know what Christianity teaches. In the opinion of Jesus poverty was a virtue, and the rich and anybody owning more than the coat on his back were condemned unless they sold all they had and made themselves extremely poor.

There were other similarities between Buddhism and Biblical Christianity. Gautama Buddha, in India, the founder of Buddhism, instituted the practice of confession. Similarly the Christian teaching in the Bible at James 5:16 says: "Confess your faults one to another, and pray for one another." Again Buddhism gives the Golden Rule as its teaching, saying, "Hurt not others in ways that you yourself would find hurtful." Jesus put this in positive phrase, saying: Therefore all things whatsoever ye would that men should do to you, do ye even so to them." (Matthew 7:12)

Christians may of course say that Buddha was just copying Jesus' teachings, but not so. Buddha lived 600 years before Jesus began to teach. So Jesus obviously had come into contact with some zealous Buddhist evangelists, of which there were many. He learned from them well, and adapted their teachings to the society of the Jews. Just as Moses had copies most of his religion from the Babylonians, Jesus copied most of his religion from the Buddhists of India.

Apparently Jesus forgot the Bible statement that God is supposed to have made, which says: "Therefore, behold, I am against the prophets, saith the Lord, that steal my words every one from his neighbor." (Jeremiah 23:30) Stolen words or not, Buddhism was more civilized than the bloody religion Moses had taught.

Both Buddha and Jesus used faith healing along with their preaching. Buddha used Hypnosis to make the faith healing more effective. Jesus also used hypnosis. Note the Bible account at Luke 9:28-32: "And it came to pass about an eight days after these sayings, he (Jesus) took Peter and John and James and went up into a mountain to pray. And as he prayed the fashion of his countenance was altered, and his raiment was white and glistening. And behold there talked with him two men, which were Moses and Elias, who appeared in glory and spake of his decease which he should accomplish at Jerusalem. But Peter and they that were with him were heavy with sleep; and when they were awake, they saw his glory and the two men that stood with him."

Here is a prime example of the way Jesus used hypnotism to produce hallucinations in the minds of the three disciples, so they saw visions. Note particularly the statement that the disciples "were heavy with sleep." Why should they be asleep in midday? Because Jesus hypnotized them. Hypnosis puts people in a sleepy state of mind during which they may have hallucinations, dreams of things that do not really exist.

Dr. H. Bernheim was one of the world's leading authorities on hypnosis, and in his book, "Suggestive Therapeutics," he tells us: "Between a perfectly conscious condition and deep sleep all transitions exist. It is certain that in many subjects belonging to these different categories, intelligence and sensibility remain active during hypnosis. Others have only certain symptoms of sleep: the lack of initiative, inertia, sensation of drowsiness and the closed eyelids, or their minds reacting to the operator whom they answer and obey, seem uninfluenced by other people whom they do not appear to hear, and to whose questions they give no answers."

Sleep is not always necessary to produce hypnotism. Dr. Bernheim writes: "To define hypnotism as induced sleep, is to give a too narrow meaning to the word -- to overlook the many phenomena which suggestion can bring about independently of sleep. I define hypnotism as the induction of a peculiar psychical condition which increases the susceptibility to suggestion. Often, it is true, the sleep that may be induced facilitates suggestion, but is not the necessary preliminary. It is suggestion that rules hypnotism."

Since sleep is not necessary to invoke hypnotic phenomena such as healing of various ailments, we begin to see how Jesus used hypnotism to perform alleged "miracles' of healing, just as Buddha had done, even though Buddha had actually put ill people to sleep in order to effect a cure. Dr. Bernheim was a medical doctor, one who used hypnosis extensively in treating illnesses. He has this to say about miracles of healing: "What a powerful worker of miracles is the human imagination! Upon it is based the therapeutic virtue of talismans and amulets."

"'From the time' says Charpognon, 'that stones were worn attached to the breastplates of the Jewish priests and to the girdles of the priests of Cybele, from the time that beetle-shaped, hand-shaped, and circular stones were worn by the Orientals, Greeks, and Romans, down to the cameos of our modern ladies, all these objects have represented the magic talisman of ancient and mysterious power.'"

"'Paracelsus, the great partisan of occultism, recognized,' this author goes on to say, 'the cause of the effects produced by magnets and similar objects, for he wrote these wise words: "Whether the object of your faith be real or false, you will nevertheless obtain the same effects. Thus if I believe in St. Peter's statue as I would have believed in St. Peter himself, I will obtain the same effects that I would have obtained from St. Peter; -- but that is superstition. Faith, however, produces miracles, and whether it be a true or a false faith, it will always produce the same wonders.'"

"Let us compare the words uttered by Pierre Ponponazzi of Milan, an author of the sixteenth century, with these. They are given by Hack Tuke:

"'We can easily conceive the marvelous effects which confidence and imagination can produce, particularly when both qualities are reciprocal between the subjects and the person who influences them. The cures attributed to the influence of certain relics, are the effect of this imagination and confidence. Quacks and philosophers know that if the bones of any skeleton were put in place of the saints' bones, the sick would none the less experience beneficial effects, if they believed that they were near veritable relics.'

"The magnetic stone which the Egyptians used in the preparation of their prophylactic amulets, has cured gouty pains, headaches, toothaches, and hysteria from time immemorial."

"Before touching upon the heart of our subject, which is therapeutic suggestion, let us give a few observations upon cures obtained through the influence of the imagination, according to these authors; facts, which although well known everywhere, it is well to have before our eyes, because they show that what we are doing has always been done. Therapeutic suggestion is not new; what is new, is the mode of applying it methodically, and its final adoption in general medicine.

"Sobernheim, city of Charpignon, tells the story of a man with a paralysis of the tongue which had yielded to no form of treatment, who put himself under a certain doctor's care. The doctor wished to try an instrument of his own invention, with which he promised himself to get excellent results. Before performing the operation, he introduced a pocket thermometer into the patient's mouth. The patient imagined it to be the instrument which was to save him; in a few minutes he cried out joyfully that he could once more move his tongue freely.

"Among our cases, facts of the same sort will be found. A young girl came into my service, having suffered from complete nervous aphonia for nearly four weeks. (She couldn't speak.) After making sure of the diagnosis, I told my students that nervous aphonia sometimes yielded instantly to electricity, which might act simply by its suggestive influence. I sent for the induction apparatus. Before using it I wanted to try simple suggestion by affirmation. I applied my hand over the larynx and moved it a little, and said, 'Now you can speak aloud.' In an instant I made her say a, then b, then Marie. She continued to speak distinctly; the aphonia had disappeared.

"'The "Bibliotheque chosie de medicine,"' says Hack Tuke, 'gives a typical example of the influence experienced by the imagination over intestinal action, during sleep. The daughter of the consul at Hanover, aged eighteen, intended to use rhubarb, for which she had a particular dislike, on the following day; she dreamed that she had taken the abhorred dose. Influenced by the imaginary rhubarb, she waked up, and had five or six easy evacuations.'

"The same result is seen in a case reported by Demangeon. (De l'Imagination, 1879). 'A monk intended to purge himself on a certain morning. On the night previous he dreamed that he had taken the medicine, and consequently waked up to yield to nature's demands. He had eight movements.'

"But among all the moral causes which, appealing to the imagination, set the cerebral mechanism of possible cures to work, none is so efficacious as religious faith. Numbers of authentic cures have certainly been due to it.

"The princess of Schwartzenburg had suffered for eight years from paraplegia, for which the most celebrated doctors in Germany and France had been consulted. In 1821, the Prince of Honenlohe, who had been a priest since 1815, brought a peasant to the princess who had convinced the young prince of the power of prayer in curing disease. The mechanical apparatus which had been used by Dr. Heine for several months to overcome the contracture of the limbs was removed. The prince asked the paralytic princess to join her faith to both his and the peasant's. -- "Do you believe you are already helped?" -- "Oh, yes! (she said) I believe so most sincerely." -- "Well! Rise and walk."

"At these words the princess rose and walked around the room several times, and tried going up and down stairs. The next day she went to church, and from this time on she had the use of her limbs. (Charpignon.)

"The reader of course understands that this was one of those very common nervous paralyses which often exist only in idea, (ideal paralysis), and which are at times susceptible to cure through violent emotion.

"The same thing may occur in hysterical contractures. Charcot says, 'Deep moral emotion, a concurrence of events which strikes the imagination vividly, the return of monthly periods which have not occurred for a long time, etc. -- are frequently the cause of these prompt cures.'"

"In this hospital I have seen three cases of this kind, of which I will give a brief resume:"

"1st. The first case was a contracture of a lower limb, dating back four years at least. On account of the patient's bad behavior I was obliged to give her a vigorous talking to, and to assure her that I would send her away if she did not do better. The next day her contracture disappeared entirely."

"2nd. The second case was also one of contracture limited to one limb. The hysterical causes, properly so-called, had been absent for a long time. The woman was accused of robbery, and the contracture, which had lasted more than two years, suddenly vanished on account of the moral shock which this accusation produced."

"3rd. In the third case, contracture had taken a hemiplegic form; the right side was affected, and the upper limb especially. The cure came suddenly, eighteen months after the appearance of the contracture, being brought about by a very animated controversy."

"In this connection, Charcot cites an article by Littre, published in the "Revue de philosophie positive,' and entitled, 'Un fragment de medicine retrospective (Miracles de Saint Louis,)' in which is found the history of several cases of paralysis cured after pilgrimages to Saint-Denis, to the tomb where the remains of the King, Louis IX, had just been placed."

"I come now to the study of therapeutic suggestion. If in the waking condition violent moral emotions, lively religious faith, everything which strikes the imagination, can drive away functional troubles and work cures, it must nevertheless be said that active therapeutics done not often reap advantage from this means. In the waking condition, many imaginations are refractory to the suggestive shock of the moral emotions. Credulity is moderated by the superior faculties of the understanding. Hypnotism, like natural sleep, exalts the imagination, and makes the brain more susceptible to suggestion." So writes Dr. Bernheim.

In Jesus' case he found it unnecessary to put people to sleep with hypnotism in order to effect so-called "miraculous" cures to their illnesses. Jesus was regarded as the Jewish Messiah, the great king whom the nation had looked forward to for centuries. He therefore had tremendous prestige. He was believed to be the son of God, even God himself. Consequently, when he told a Jew that he was healed, the Jew believed he was healed. And he was therefore healed. But it was no miracle. It was simply a type of mental suggestion, hypnosis without sleep.

Dr. Bernheim explains: "The brain, influenced by suggestion, tends to realize the phenomena commanded with an energy varying according to the individuality; in some it is already docile in the waking condition; it becomes so in almost all cases when in the hypnotic condition, or a condition analogous to it, has put to sleep or dulled faculties of reason, judgment, and control which moderate and restrain the cerebral automatism. Then the brain, more powerfully impressed by the formulated order, accepts the idea and transforms it into action."

The religious faith of Jesus' followers dulled their critical faculties so they believed they were healed, and they were healed. It was as simple as that. Similar healings are performed by hypnotists now every day. So much for Jesus' miraculous powers. He was a capable hypnotist and psychic, and the ignorant people of his day equated such skill with being God.

However, the so-called miracle working power that Jesus had was nothing more than hypnotism. It was not absolute power. So it was that when Jesus was among people who had no respect for him, his power as a hypnotist waned. The Bible tells us that Jesus' own neighbors and kinfolk in his home town of Nazareth had no respect for him. They said, "Is not this the carpenter, the son of Mary, the brother of James and Joses and Juda and Simon? And are not his sisters here with us? And they were offended at him."

"But Jesus said unto them, 'A prophet is not without honor except in his own country, and among his own kin, and in his own house.' And he could there do no mighty work (miracle.)" (Mark 6:3-5)

This is the same problem that all hypnotists face, so to offset it professional hypnotists hire press agents to build up their reputations as hypnotists, and this enables them to influence people successfully when they give their hypnotic stage performances. Similarly Jesus found his hypnotic power effective all over Judea, where he was regarded as the messiah from God, but in his home town "he could do no mighty work" because there he was thought of as nothing but a carpenter.

From these facts we can see that the much proclaimed miracles of healing ascribed to Jesus Christ were only the effects of hypnotism on his followers. Yes, hypnotism has healing effects in some types of illness as Dr. Bernheim has pointed out, but miracle it is not.

As Thomas A. Edison, the inventor of the incandescent electric light bulb, moving pictures, the phonograph, and hundreds of other inventions said: "So far as the religion of the day is concerned, it is all a fake." Edison was a life-long infidel.

CHAPTER XXXIII. "CUT OFF YOUR HANDS," THIS SAINT COMMANDS

When you look at the pictures of Jesus in your Bible or in most religious books, you will see a Jesus who has light brown hair, blue eyes, a European face with a white skin and a straight European nose. I have a Bible at hand here with just such a picture of Jesus in it. But this is a complete fraud and a deception. What the churches are trying to do is to sell you a foreign religion disguised to make it appear that it is the native religion of the white race, which it absolutely is not. The churches are lying and are practicing fraud when they do this. In any other business but the religion business they would be jailed for such misrepresentation of their merchandise.

The Bible tells us that Jesus was a full-blooded Jew. His ancestry was not crossed over with any other race. His father was of the Israelite tribe of Judah, and his mother likewise. Consequently he had very dark blackish curly hair on his head, and a curly black beard cut off straight across at the bottom in conformity with Moses' law. His skin was somewhat yellowish, and his nose was large, hooked and bulbous. His eyes were very dark and glittered as he spoke. He looked like a real full-blooded Jew, and was accepted as such by his own people. If Jesus had the appearance of a European as the Christian churches like to depict, he would have been completely ignored by the Jewish people. Instead, Jesus was well received by thousands of the Jews who became his followers, and accepted his teachings.

However, Jesus' teachings are loaded with inconsistencies that make a thinking person wince. Jesus repeatedly admonished his disciples to love one another, and even to love their enemies. (John 13:35; Matthew 5:44) Yet when a non-Jewish woman begged him to heal her daughter,

Jesus told her, "It is not fit to take the children (of Israel's) bread and to cast it to dogs." (Matthew 15:26) In other words he said, 'You non-Jews are dogs. Why should I do anything for you?" How would you like to have Jesus call you a dog? Calling people dogs who were not Jews is hardly an expression of love. Jesus was insolent, arrogant and conceited in calling this woman a dog. So in actual practice, Jesus the saint was not so saintly after all. The facts show that Jesus actually hated those who were not Jews.

Tacitus, the Roman historian who lived in the days of Jesus' apostles, wrote that the Jews of his day were ready to help each other, but were full of hatred toward all those who were not Jews. Saint Moses had taught the Jews to be conceited bigots who thought themselves better than all other races of people, and the fact that all the nations surrounding the Jews had conquered them and made subjects of them made the Jews hate other nations all the more. Thus the hateful attitude of Jesus toward those who were not Jews was similar to that of the rest of his nation.

Saint Paul writes, allegedly under inspiration of God, "Jesus Christ the same yesterday, and today, and for ever." (Hebrews 13:8) So if you were planning to go to heaven to be with the loving Jesus, and you are not a Jew, you had better think it over again.

However, the Jews should have been thankful that the great nations surrounding them had not practiced genocide on the Jews, as the Jews had practiced genocide on the people of the small kingdoms of Palestine, slaughtering all men, women, children, and infancy, and even the unborn infants in the bellies of the pregnant women whom they ripped up. If indeed the surrounding great nations had massacred the Jews as the Jews had massacred the people they had conquered, there would have been no Jesus and no other Jews left to hate their neighbors.

This hateful attitude taught by Saint Moses' religion is still evident in the way many Israeli Jews treat people of other races in this day. Some former members of the terrorist Stern gang of Jews are in high government places in Israeli politics today, and one recently boasted that he was part of a group of terrorists that murdered Swedish Count Bernadotte, who was in Jerusalem to bring about peace between Jews and Arabs. Earlier Count Bernadotte had saved many Jews from death in concentration camps. All this was ignored by the hateful religious Jews who murdered the Count, since the Count was Swedish and not Jewish. "Thou shall smite them and utterly destroy them." (Deuteronomy 7:2) So said Moses of other races of people.

ANOTHER INCONSISTENCY

Another inconsistency is found in John 1, Verses 1 to 3 where the Bible says of Jesus: "In the beginning was the Word (Jesus) and the Word was with God, and the Word was God. The same was in the beginning with God. All things were made by him; and without him was not anything made that was made."

This is a bold claim that Jesus was the actual Creator of the universe, the world, and everything on earth: people, animals, trees, plants, etc.

But here comes the difficulty, which the non-thinking disciples of Jesus did not perceive. If Jesus indeed created all things as the Bible claims, then Jesus is responsible for creating poisonous snakes, scorpions, and disease germs. Is this an expression of Jesus' love for humanity?

Some sectarians assert that Jesus did not create these vicious enemies of mankind, but that the devil did it. However, not so. The Bible definitely says the devil did not create anything. Note Saint John's statement in the Bible: "All things were made by him (Jesus); and without him was not anything made that was made." (John 1:3) The Bible says Jesus made everything. And that includes rattlesnakes, scorpions, and disease germs. As they say, "Jesus loves you, brother." You'd have to be insane to believe it, or very ignorant of what the Bible teaches.

Luther Burbank, the great plant scientist, wrote: "As a scientist, I cannot help feeling that all religions are on a tottering foundation. None is perfect or inspired. As for their prophets, there are as many today as ever before, only now science refuses to let them overstep the barrier of Common Sense . . . . The Hebrews have credit of inventing the conception of our monotheistic Jewish Christian God, who however is represented as having the most weaknesses and bad habits of primitive man. . . . . I am an infidel. I know what an infidel is, and that's what I am!"

Most scientists reject the Jewish Christian religion, and all other religions. Their interest is solely in facts.

A RELIGION OF PESSIMISTS

The Christian Bible as well as the Buddhists whom Jesus copied take a dim view, a very pessimistic view, of life on this earth. The saintly Apostle John writes in the Bible: "Love not the world, neither the things that are in the world. If any man love the world, the love of the Father is not in him. For all that is in the world, the desire of the flesh, the desire of the eyes, and the pride of life, is not of the Father, but it of the world." (1 John 2:15, 16)

Christians are supposed to suppress all desires of the flesh, such as enjoyment of sexual relations, enjoyment of food and drink, and levity and entertainment. (1 Corinthians 7:29; Titus 2:2) They are supposed to be ascetics. To Buddhists also life is considered miserable and undesirable, and a curse rather than a blessing. Even though nature has blessed mankind with pleasure in cohabitation to ensure the survival of the human race, and pleasure through eating for the same reason, and pleasure through mirth and entertainment, these are all rejected by Christianity and Buddhism. Their outlook on life on this earth is gloomy. Like the hypochondriac who glories in his fancied illnesses, these saints gloried in their dour outlook on life. "And he (Jesus) said to them all, 'If any man will come after me, let him deny himself, and take up his cross daily and follow me." (Luke 9:23) Sad, sad, sad.

Of course, most Christians ignored this viewpoint, although many hid their pleasure in sex and other things to put on a pretended ascetic front. They tirade against trends that reveal the beauty of the human body, calling it "obscene" (while at the same time insisting that their god made this "obscene" thing).

'EAT FOOD WITH DIRTY HANDS'

Jesus' teachings were hardly those that would attract people of much stature to his religion. Few people of importance and owners of property would want to sell all they had and give it to the poor or anyone else. Money and property were too hard to come by to toss them away as lightly as that. And few people would want to stand passively and turn the other cheek while some bully or robber knocked them down or killed them. The average person with normal common sense valued his own welfare and would fight to protect himself and his family. This pacifist doormat type of religion was not for them.

But for every kind of religion under the sun there will be a following, and there were multitudes who followed Jesus. Most of them were poor, who favored the idea of having someone else sell his property and give the money to them. Many of them were women who could not fight back successfully if anyone attacked them anyway, so Jesus' pacifist doctrine was no obstacle to them. And so the followers of Jesus increased in number.

The ignorant also followed Jesus, because many of Jesus' teachings would turn away all but the ignorant. For example, Jesus taught his disciples to eat food with dirty hands, and not to wash before eating. Saint Mark reports this in the Bible: "Then came together unto him (Jesus) the Pharisees, and certain of the scribes, which came from Jerusalem. And when they saw some of his (Jesus') disciples eat bread with defiled, that is to say, with unwashen hands, they found fault. For the Pharisees, and all the Jews, except they wash their hands oft, eat not, holding the tradition of the elders. And when they come from market, except they wash, they eat not. And many other things there be, which they have received to hold, as the washing of cups, and pots, brasen vessels, and of tables. Then the Pharisees and scribes asked him (Jesus), 'Why walk not thy disciples according to the tradition of the elders, but eat bread with unwashen hands?'" (Mark 7:1-5)

Everyone knows that handling food with dirty hands is a good way to catch a disease and become ill. But here was the great Messiah, alleged to be the son of God, and even God himself, teaching people dirty habits that would result in illness and sometimes death. How could Jesus be God and be so ignorant? But he was ignorant, and the smarter Jews criticized him for it.

Some attempt to alibi for Jesus by saying that Jesus was only objecting to the ceremonial washing of hands, but this is not true. The Bible clearly states that Jesus and his disciples did not wash their hands before they ate, either ceremonially or otherwise. The Bible says they ate their bread "with defiled, that is to say, unwashen hands." (Mark 7:2) Jesus and his disciples belonged to the great fraternity of the dirty and the unwashed.

Likewise Jesus taught his followers to drink from a community cup. (Matthew 26:27) This is also a first class way to catch a serious disease and even die from it, but Jesus who was said to be God, insisted that this is the way his followers should live. Is it any wonder that the majority of Jews rejected him? And is it any wonder that the majority of people today reject Jesus, the Bible and Christianity also?

'CUT OFF YOUR HAND,' SAYS JESUS

You would never expect a religious leader to tell his followers to cut off their hands and feet, and gouge out their eyes, but that is exactly what Jesus told Christians to do. Here are his exact words, quoted from the Bible: "And if thy hand offend thee, cut it off: it is better for thee to enter into life maimed than having two hands to go into hell, into the fire that never shall be quenched: where their worm dieth not, and the fire is not quenched. And if thy foot offend thee, cut it off: it is better for thee to enter halt into life, then having two feet to be cast into hell, into the fire that never shall be quenched: where their worm dieth not and the fire is not quenched. And if thine eye offend thee, pluck it out: it is better for thee to enter into the kingdom of God with one eye, than having two eyes to be cast into hell fire: where their worm dieth not, and the fire is not quenched." This is written in the Bible book of Mark, Chapter 9, and Verses 43 to 48; and also at Matthew 18:8,9.

This is such a ridiculous teaching that most people laugh at it as silly, but not everybody laughs. Many devout religionists believe these words of Jesus should be followed, and every once in a while we learn in the news that some Christian has actually cut off his hand and gouged out an eye because of this teaching of Jesus.

It is a reckless thing for Jesus to put forth such a teaching as this. He certainly knew that when he taught this some of his followers would cut off their hands and feet and gouge out their eyes. And it also shows Jesus' colossal ignorance. Almost everyone knows that hands and feet have no will of their own, and therefore cannot of their own volition offend anyone. It is the brain, the human mind, that orders hands and feet to do what they should or should not do. But Jesus was obviously ignorant of this basic fact, even though he was supposed to be God. Some God! He didn't even know how the brain and body works!

(Incidentally, the scripture text above quoted, saying, "where their worm dieth not," has been called by the irreverent, "the doctrine of the immortal worms." This text has been used to prove that worms never die, and are therefore immortal!)

WOMEN FOLLOWERS OF JESUS

In the days of Jesus women were greatly debased by the Jewish rabbis. For instance, when walking to a synagogue for religious services, women were required to use the back streets so the men could not see them. Yet where did they suppose all the men would be if all the women were on the back streets? The rabbis were not thinking very clearly. And once at the synagogue, women were required to sit apart from men in a separate section of the synagogue, and with their backs to the men, so the men could not see them. It seems that the Jewish men couldn't keep their minds on religion if they could so much as see a woman. In a nation that had no laws against rape, the men were thought to be little better than dogs in the street, and always ready to run after and copulate with any unattached female in sight. It was also required of rabbis that they never speak to a woman in public, not even if she was his own wife. So prudish were the rabbis -- like Moses, another queer character.

However, Jesus did not follow the rules of the Pharisees and spoke to women in public whenever he chose. Jesus and his disciples were followed by a large group of women as they went about the nation of Judea preaching. Some of these women were the wives of the disciples, and they cooked and washed clothes for their menfolks while the men attended to teaching and preaching. (Matthew 27:55; Luke 23:27, 49; Mark 1:30)

Women were more attracted to the teachings of Jesus than men, and it is the same today. Women today constitute the majority of Christian churchgoers. This is only natural. Jesus promised his followers that they would be with him in heaven. As Jesus told the thief dying on the cross beside him: "Verily, I say unto thee, 'Today shalt thou be with me in paradise.'" (Luke 23:43) The idea of being in heaven with Jesus appealed to women, but obviously had less appeal for men. On the other hand, if Jesus had promised the men some women companions in heaven, Jesus would have had more men followers in his religion. As it was, the men had little to look forward to except playing on harps, which is not exactly the most attractive way to spend eternity from a man's viewpoint. They'd just as soon go to hell as live like that!

Some have claimed that Jesus was a homosexual because of his friendship with John. However, homosexuality was vigorously condemned by Moses' law (Leviticus 20:13) and none of Jesus' opponents was able to convict him of violating any of the laws of Moses. Jesus even challenged his religious enemies, saying, "Which of you convicteth me of sin?" (John 8:46, A.S.V.) Jesus would not have escaped punishment if he had been a homosexual.

However, Moses' Bible law was very liberal in other directions. Bible law nowhere punishes a man for patronizing prostitutes, even though this spreads dangerous diseases among the population. Jesus could have all the sex relations he wanted with women prostitutes and still have been considered "holy, harmless, undefiled, separate from sinners" as the Jewish apostle Saint Paul says of Jesus in his epistle to the Hebrews, Chapter 7 and Verse 26. Of course, the Bible does not say that Jesus did patronize prostitutes, but neither does the Bible deny that Jesus had sexual intercourse with women prostitutes. The Bible does not always report the sexual activity of its saints. For example, the apostle Saint Peter (Cephas) was married, but his sexual activity with his wife is never mentioned in the

Bible. (1 Corinthians 9:5) So Jesus could have had sexual intercourse with women prostitutes without any mention of it appearing in the Bible either.

We must also take note here that although Jesus changed Moses' law permitting divorce, so that Jesus banned divorce, Jesus did not change Moses' law permitting men to copulate with women prostitutes without being charged with sin or punishment. In other words, Jesus approved Moses' law permitting men to copulate with prostitutes. This makes you wonder about Jesus' own sex life, doesn't it?

Such saintly Jewish-Christian practices and Biblical laws are a disease-spreading menace to society. However, not only the members of the churches and synagogues are led astray by these corrupting Biblical teachings, but even the clergy are led into immoral and foolish conduct. For example, according to recent news reports in the United States, the preacher heading a vast Christian preaching enterprise, although he was married, was alleged to be having repeated sexual encounters with his secretary. In one episode exposed by an indignant associate clergyman, the news report alleged that the offending preacher had sexual intercourse with his woman secretary, and then this preacher's assistant also had sexual intercourse with her. Then a third man entered the room intending to have sexual intercourse with her too, but by that time she was naked and prostrate on the floor and "unable to respond." To the credit of the church organization to which this clergyman belonged, he was discharged from being their preacher, because the morality of the church members exceeded the morality taught in the Bible.

Then in another case, seven "celibate" Christian priests were alleged in the news reports to have engaged in repeated sexual intercourse with one young woman. She removed all of her clothing until she was entirely nude, and then each of the seven priests "went in unto her" repeatedly, as the "holy" Bible describes it (Judges 16:1). When she finally became pregnant, she sued the seven priests and their diocese for one million dollars. There is no report that the priests were dismissed from the priesthood for such conduct. The Catholic church apparently adheres strictly to the Bible for its code of morality or lack of same. Jews and Christians are known to provide the major support for prostitutes in this country.

Such is the baneful influence of the Bible saints in leading their followers into unwise conduct that may result in their infection with disease, and sometimes death.

CHAPTER XXXIV.   A FAKE EARTHQUAKE AT THIS GODLY FUNERAL

Finally when several years went by and the nation of Israel as a whole did not flock to his side, Jesus became exasperated. He lashed out harshly at his religious opponents: "Woe to you, scribes and Pharisees, hypocrites!" Jesus cried, "For ye shut up the kingdom of heaven against men; for ye neither go in yourselves, neither suffer ye them that are entering to go in. Woe to you scribes and Pharisees, hypocrites! For ye devour widow's houses, and for a pretense make long prayer. Therefore ye shall receive the greater damnation. Woe, unto you, scribes and Pharisees, hypocrites! For ye compass sea and land to make one proselyte, and when he is made, ye make him twofold more the child of hell than yourselves!" (Matthew 23:13-15, et seq.)

This sort of tongue lashing further enraged Jesus' religious enemies, and they determined to kill him. "O Jerusalem, Jerusalem?" Jesus exclaimed. "Thou that killest the prophets and stonest them which are sent unto thee! How often would I have gathered thy children together, even as a hen gathereth her chickens under her wings, and ye would not! Behold, your house is left unto you desolate." (Matthew 23:37,37)

Jesus knew that he had not succeeded in turning the Jews away from their determination to revolt against Rome. They had rejected his pacifist teachings. He knew they could not stand before the mighty Roman legions and would be destroyed, just as the Babylonian emperor Nebuchadnezzar had destroyed Jerusalem centuries before. But the Jews were a warlike and rebellious class of people, and a leopard never changes its spots says the Bible. (Jeremiah 13:23) They were the same in Jesus' time as they had been centuries before. Neither would they learn from the lessons of history.

Recognizing that he had failed to turn the Israelites from their self-destruction in war, Jesus left the Temple. "And Jesus went out, and departed from the temple. And his disciples came to him for to show him the buildings of the temple. And Jesus said unto them, 'See ye not all these things? Verily, I say unto you, there shall not be left here one stone upon another that shall not be thrown down!'" (Matthew 24:1,2)

Throwing down the stones of the temple seemed like an impossibility to the average onlooker. They were huge building stones. The Jewish historian Flvius Josephus who lived at the time of Christ's apostles, wrote: "The Temple was built of white stones of great size -- the length of each about thirty-seven and a half feet, some even forty-five-feet, and thickness twelve feet, and the breadth eighteen." The Roman ruler Herod had build this might temple for the ungrateful Jews, and the Roman armies tore it down when they later crushed the Jewish revolt as Jesus predicted.

Jesus spoke further of the outcome of the rebellion against Rome, which he could see approaching. "And when ye shall see Jerusalem compassed with armies, then know that the desolation thereof is nigh . . . . And they shall fall by the edge of the sword, and shall be led away captive into all nations. And Jerusalem shall be trodden down of the Gentiles." (Luke 21;20, 24) "Verily I say unto you, This generation shall not pass away till all be fulfilled." (Luke 21:32) This prophecy of Jesus was no great psychic vision or revelation from God. It was just a plain common sense evaluation of the situation as Jesus could see it developing.

As Jesus had forseen the trend of events, the Jews rebelled against Rome some forty years later, and the Jewish nation was destroyed by the Roman army. But Jesus' warning helped his disciples escape destruction when that rebellion took place. Instead of joining in the futile war against Rome they fled the country and escaped with their lives.

The question now arises, if Jesus was Almighty God as they claim, why did he not give the Jews victory over the Roman army? The answer is simple, and the Bible gives it at Judges 1:19 which says: "And the Lord God was with Judah; and he drove out the inhabitants of the hill country; for he could not drive out the inhabitants of the valley, because they had chariots of iron." Obviously the Romans also had chariots of iron and this made the Almighty God of the Jews powerless and unable to give them victory over the Romans. So when you get through laughing at that incongruous situation, we'll go on with the rest of this tale . . . .

The night following Jesus' tirade against his religious enemies, Jesus was seized by the Jewish Temple officers as he and his disciples camped in an olive orchard outside Jerusalem. The next day Jesus was hauled before Pilate the Roman ruler. The Bible says: "Pilate saith unto them, (the Jewish mob) 'What shall I do then with Jesus which is called Christ?' They all say, 'Let him be crucified.'"

"And the governor said, 'Why? What evil hath he done?' But they cried out the more saying, 'Let him be crucified.' When Pilate saw that he could prevail nothing, but that rather a tumult was made, he took water and washed his hands before the multitude saying, 'I am innocent of the blood of this just person. See you to it.'"

"Then answered all the people and said, 'His blood be on us and on our children.' . . . . And when he (Pilate) has scourged Jesus, he delivered him to be crucified.'" (Matthew 27:22-26)

So Jesus died nailed to a cross of wood by his hands and feet, murdered by religionists who followed the bloody bigotry taught by Saint Moses in his Bible.

If Jesus were in the United States today he could not easily be put to death by the Government. However, he would undoubtedly spend many years in both Federal and State prisons for healing people without a license, because of the thousands he would heal. Many medical associations are very wealthy here, and medical lobbyists spend millions of dollars each year influencing both politicians and the judges of the courts to protect medical doctors from any and all competition with their business. But the constitution might block the medicos from having Jesus put to death, since it guarantees freedom of and from religion, and is therefore far superior to the laws of Saint Moses in his Bible.

As an interesting sidelight on the value of the medical treatment supplied by some physicians and surgeons today, in Los Angeles County recently doctors went on strike for a period of two weeks, and during this strike the deaths in Los Angeles County decreased by fifty percent! And it would have been a worse showing if there had not been some good doctors out there.

At least, there is no record that Jesus' work of healing ever killed anybody.

However, there are ways in which Jesus could have been executed in the United States in spite of Constitutional guarantees of freedom of religion. Jesus' claims of being a religious leader could have been denied, and he could have been branded a political agitator who talked of setting up his own kingdom. Because he denounced the rich he could have been charged with being a foreign spy and executed. So the medical mafia could have had Jesus put to death even today.

Not all religious claims are accepted by the courts. We have to remember that religious conscientious objectors to war were jailed in the United States during World War I, even though the Quakers had taken this position over one hundred years before the United States came into existence. And during World War II, conscientious objectors were put into concentration camps in the United States, which was just the same as the Nazis in Germany did. So Jesus' claims of religious freedom under the United States Constitution could have been tossed aside by the authorities just as easily, and Jesus could have been put to death here today as surely as he was in Judea about 2,000 years ago.

THE UNNOTICED EARTHQUAKE

There are many obvious falsehoods inserted into the tale of Jesus' life, and here at the account of Jesus' death we find another one. The Bible tells us at Saint Matthew Chapter 27 and Versus 50 to 53: "Jesus, when he had cried again with a loud voice, yielded up the ghost. And behold, the veil of the Temple was rent in twain from the top to the bottom. And the earth did quake, and the rocks rent. And the graves were opened, and many bodies of the saints which slept arose, and came out of the graves after his resurrection, and went into the holy city (Jerusalem) and appeared unto many."

There are four accounts of Jesus' life and death in the Bible in books by Matthew, Mark, Luke, and John. You would think that with a stupendous event such as a mighty earthquake at Jesus' death, and dead saints rising out of their graves and walking about the city, that all four accounts of Jesus' life and death would record this remarkable miracle. But do they? No. Matthew's book is the only one that mentions this event. The others are silent about it.

All four of these writers of Jesus' life and death were supposed to have been present when Jesus died, and yet only Saint Matthew's book mentions the earthquake and the raising of the dead saints. If you had seen such an event, would you have failed to write about it later when compiling a record of Jesus' life? Hardly. Earthquakes and the raising of the dead don't occur so often as to make them commonplace. Of course you would have told about it.

So when Mark, Luke and John fail to mention this mighty event at all, it throws immense doubt in its occurrence. If such a tremendous thing had actually happened all four of these gospel writers would have reported it. The fact that only one account, that in the book of Matthew, tells about it, is positive evidence that this earthquake and raising of the dead never occurred. This is the conclusion of Thomas Paine in his notable critique of the Bible, his book, "The Age of Reason," and that conclusion has been shared by countless other students of the Bible text, including this one. The account of the earthquake and raising of the dead was obviously a wild fictional tale inserted into the text of Saint Matthew's gospel by some well-intentioned religious forger who thought to make a good story better.

It is difficult to believe that much of the account of Jesus' life is true and accurate when obvious falsehoods like this occur in the Bible text. This and the contradictory jumble that purports to give the genealogy of Jesus are clearly not true. Much of the rest of the texts of these four gospel accounts of Jesus' life and death contradict each other completely. What can we safely believe to be true? This throws much of the story of Jesus into great doubt.

CHAPTER XXXV. SAINTS WHO MURDER FOR MONEY

After the untimely death of Jesus his disciples were thrown into confusion. Their hope that Jesus would somehow deliver the Jewish nation from Roman rule and set up his own independent kingdom of God was dashed. "But we trusted that it had been he (Jesus) which should have redeemed Israel," moaned the disciples. (Luke 24:21) What was left?

Simon Peter the apostle saw no hope. "I'm going fishing," he told the others, so they also went with him (John 21:3) They had to make a living somehow, and fishing had been their trade before they began to follow Jesus. Of course, fishing was not as good a way to make money as being a rabbi. Christian Rabbis only had to talk to make a living, but in this fishing business a man had to be out often at night in the wind and cold, pulling in icy fish nets and handling slimy cold wet fish. They didn't like it at all. They had become spoiled by the easy life of Christian preachers, where people would come up and hand them money contributions and there were no aching muscles or frozen hands. Besides that, the fish weren't running well, and you can't make money unless you can pull in plenty of fish.

They were disgusted. This fishing business was no good when compared to the life of a rabbi. But wait a minute! There were thousands of people out there who were devoted followers of Jesus. They would still like to follow a religion such as Jesus had taught. They had no use for the Pharisees. They would welcome rabbis who would continue to teach the new religion Jesus had brought them.

But Jesus their leader was dead. What could the apostles say about that? Well, they would tell the disciples that Jesus had gone to heaven and was running things from up there. In due time Jesus would return to the earth and set us his kingdom. (Luke 22:29, 30) Meanwhile the disciples on earth had to continue in the teachings that Jesus had given them.

Great! So Saint Peter and the others tossed aside their fishnets, changed their clothes, and went back into the preaching business.

Surely as they had surmised, thousands of Jesus' followers flocked to support the apostles in a continuation of the work that Jesus had begun. They gathered a large Jewish Christian congregation together in Jerusalem which listened to the preaching of the apostles such as Saint Peter, Saint James and Saint John. And the contributions continued to pour in, which fortunately enabled the apostles to forget about their miserable fishing business.

A NEW ECONOMIC THEORY

Then the saintly apostles had a bright idea. Jesus had told them, "Sell what you have, and give alms." (Luke 12:33) What could be better than if all the disciples sold their possessions, lands, houses, whatever, and gave the money to the church? Meaning, to the apostles. Then the apostles could divide up the money among all the church members and they'd all have plenty to eat without working. All they'd have to do was sit in church and listen to the apostles preach. After all, hadn't Jesus said, "Consider the lilies . . . . they tell not," the congregation would do likewise.

But wouldn't they eventually run out of money? Never. As they used up the money, the new members coming into the congregation would sell all they had too and give to the church. So they could all continue to eat indefinitely. Besides, Jesus had said he would return to earth soon and set up his kingdom. Their money would surely hold out until that happened.

So this Christian program was put into effect among the members of the early church. The Bible tells us: "And all that believed were together, and had all things in common. And sold their possession and goods and parted them to all men, as every man had need." (Acts 2:44,45) "Neither was there among them any that lacked, for as many as were possessors of lands or houses sold them and brought the prices of the things that were sold and laid them down at the apostles' feet. And distribution was made unto every man according as he had need." (Acts 4:34,35)

That this plan had a great similarity to a plan put out by a later financier named Ponzi was not then known.

On the other hand, many regard this as an early attempt at communism, as advocated by the ancient Greek philosopher Plato. The Jewish Christian apostles were apparently not only followers of Jesus, but disciples of Plato as well.

Plato, however, not only favored having goods in common, but having wives in common too. Plato obviously was not satisfied with his own wife, but was one of these characters who likes to try out other men's wives too. He was also an armchair philosopher who had not the slightest understanding of normal human motivations.

Plato was not truly interested in benefitting the poor. Economic communism has always been promoted as a means of improving the lot of the poor by doing away with the accumulation of wealth by individuals. However, if that is what Plato intended, the simple and direct way of achieving this goal was to limit the amount of wealth any individual could possess. But this would not give Plato an excuse under state law to force other men's wives to go to bed with him. So you see Plato's real motive in pushing for communism was not to promote economic equality, but to force other men's wives to have sexual intercourse with him, under his law requiring wives also to be held in common.

However, wives are not always as docile as this armchair philosopher Plato might have thought. If he had tried to force some high spirited filly into bed with him under color of law, he would undoubtedly have got a carving knife stuck through his brisket, resulting in <u>terminus vitae</u> for himself and his depraved notions.

Plato's idea of holding wives in common has been tried many times in private communes in the United States, and it has always failed. Eventually the men and women begin to pair off. One man and one woman prefer each other to everybody else in the commune, and no longer want to have sexual intercourse with the others. So they pair off and leave the commune to set up their own home and begin to raise a family. This happens with one couple after another until nobody is left in the commune. According to statistical records, most communes where promiscuous sexual intercourse was practiced have failed and disappeared within two years or less. A few have continued for a year or two longer. The reason is, of course, that the majority of the human race are monogamous by instinct, with the exception of the Semites, i.e., the Jews and Arabs, who are traditionally polygamous, and some black Africans who follow one of the Semite religions. That is, the men are polygamous; but we don't know what the women think about it as they don't seem to have much to say.

Actually, Plato did not succeed in persuading any Greek government to adopt his ideas. They probably reasoned that Plato's armchair philosophy was fine as long as it was confined to his armchair. The Greeks didn't want to share their wives or their bank accounts with

Plato or anybody else. Only the Christian Jews in Jerusalem were willing to follow Plato, since most of Jesus' followers were poor and had nothing, so sharing money with anyone else would be a gain for them. And the difference between the polygamy of the Jews and holding wives in common was minuscule. They already herded their women like cattle.

The big question here is: Did the early Christians follow Plato by having their wives in common? Most of the clergy will undoubtedly deny that, but let's look at the matter fully. Yes, Jesus had prohibited adultery, but Jesus had also prohibited divorce, saying: "It hath been said, whosoever shall put away his wife, let him give her a writing of divorcement. But I say unto you, that whoever shall put away his wife, saving for the cause of fornication, causeth her to commit adultery, and whosoever shall marry her that is divorced committeth adultery." (Matthew 5:31, 32) In spite of Jesus' prohibition of divorce, Christians of all sects have divorces as frequently as the rest of the population. So how do they get around the commandment of Jesus? It is simple. Jesus said, "Whosoever shall put away his wife, saving for the cause of fornication causeth her to commit adultery." So Christians frequently use the allegation of fornication as a pretext to get a divorce. Also one large sect permits divorce by euphemistically calling it an "annulment." One couple even got an "annulment" after having four children! The going price for an "annulment" in this Christian sect is about $400.00 paid in hand to the priest, according to some of those obtaining this form of divorce, in defiance of the teaching of Jesus.

The same kind of sophistry could have been used by early Christians wanting to have their wives in common. Adultery was regarded as one marriage partner sneaking around behind the back of the other marriage partner, and secretly having sexual intercourse with someone else. However, with wife-trading -- that is, holding wives in common -- both marriage partners knew what was going on and consented to it, so in this view it wasn't really adultery. Besides, hadn't Saint Paul commanded that wives should be obedient to their own husbands? (Titus 2:5) So if their husbands ordered wives to have sexual intercourse with their neighbors, the wives were only obeying the Christian commandment when doing so.

Therefore with this sort of specious reasoning it is very likely that some Christians held their wives in common, as the Bible says: "All that believed were together -- (note that) -- and had ALL things in common." (Acts 2:44) They not only held ALL things in common, but "were together." This is a very revealing Bible statement in light of Plato's teachings.

Here again we see that Christianity is a weird mixture of Greek Philosophy, Buddhism, and some traditional teachings of Moses.

FRAUD IN THE CHRISTIAN CHURCH

Wherever there is money involved, there is sure to be fraud and cheating. The Bible relates: "And in those days, when the number of the disciples was multiplied, there arose a murmuring of the Grecians against the Hebrews, because their widows were neglected in the daily ministration." (Acts 6:1) Some were getting more of the pie than others when the congregational money was being handed out. Their preaching of the high moral principles of Jesus was not allowed to get in the way of playing favorites. So the saintly apostles had to contend with that.

Then again, some were joining the church just to get in on the money that was being handed out daily to the members. These would pretend to sell all they had, but would give only part of the money to the apostles and hide the rest. So the apostles put in a spy arrangement to determine if the new members were handing in all their money or holding some back. The apostle Saint Matthew had once been a tax collector, and he knew ways of checking up on people to see that they turned in all the money that was owed. But even this scheme failed to stop the swindlers.

The Bible tells: "But a certain man named Ananias, with Sapphira his wife, sold a possession, and kept back part of the price. His wife also being privy to it. And brought a certain part and laid it at the apostles feet."

"But Peter said, "Ananias, why hath Satan filled thine heart to lie to the Holy Ghost, and to keep back part of the price of the land? While it remained was it not thine own? And after it was sold was it not in thine own power? Why hast thou conceived this thing in thine heart? Thou hast not lied unto men, but unto God.'"

"And Ananias, hearing these words fell down and gave up the ghost. And great fear came on all them that heard of these things." (Acts 5:1-5)

According to the Bible, the apostles then hurriedly called in young men of the congregation to bury the dead Ananias. Three hours later the wife of Ananias, Sapphira by name, came to the apostles wanting to be admitted as a member of the church. She did not know what had happened to her husband. The Bible says:

"And Peter answered unto her, 'Tell me whether ye sold the land for so much?' and she said, 'Yea, for so much.'"

"Then Peter said unto her, 'How is it that ye have agreed together to tempt the Spirit of the Lord? Behold, the feet of them which have buried thy husband are at the door, and shall carry thee out.'"

"Then fell she down straightway at his feet, and yielded up the ghost: and the young men came in, and found her dead, and carrying her forth, buried her by her husband. And great fear came upon all the church, and upon as many as heard these things." (Acts 5:6-11)

In those days the authorities never looked into deaths of people very much. There were no coroners or autopsies. So when Ananias and his wife Sapphira died, there was no inquest to determine if the deaths were naturel, or whether they were murdered. And they had been hastily buried to prevent anyone seeing their wounds.

Note carefully that the Bible account does not say what caused the deaths of these two people. It merely says they fell down dead, and religious people without reason assume that God struck them dead. But there is no Bible statement that God struck them dead. Many other people throughout the Bible record were very great sinners and God had not struck them dead. King David murdered two men in order to steal their wives, and God did not strike David dead. Why then should God strike Ananias and Sapphira dead?

This reminds us of Col. Robert Ingersoll, the famous atheist son of a Congregational minister. Ingersoll had also been the Attorney General of the State of Illinois. Robert Ingersoll used to lecture against Christianity, and while on the platform would often challenge God to strike him dead. God of course did not do so, although if God had done so he could have easily proved his existence. The fact that God did not do so was evidence that the Bible God did not exist; or if he did exist, was unwilling to prove it and also unwilling to strike anybody dead.

So there is no reason for us to assume that God struck Ananias and Sapphira dead. It is far more probably that one of the apostles struck Ananias and Sapphira dead.

Religious people may recoil in horror at this idea, but look at the facts. When the officers came to arrest Jesus to haul him off to be executed, the Apostle Peter drew a sword and struck at one of the arresting officers and cut off his ear. Apparently the man's helmet was the only thing that saved his skull from being split in two. So if the apostle Saint Peter was quick with his sword, you may be sure the other saintly apostles were also. Whether they used a sword on Ananias and Sapphira, or a dagger, or a bludgeon, the result was the same. The apostles killed these two people, because history shows that God would not do it. (Mark 14:47,

John 18:26)

Religious murders by saintly Bible followers occurred quite commonly both in Bible times and since then. Saint Moses was an infamous religious murderer who caused the deaths of three thousand people because of religious differences. (Exodus 32:26-28) Saint Elijah the prophet murdered four hundred and fifty priests of a religion different from his. And Saint Abraham tried to murder his own son. So the religious murders of the Bible saints led Christian followers during the Dark Ages to murder millions of people in Europe for religious differences also. The Moses religious cult has caused more religious murders than any other religion in the world. So it should not be thought unusual if the saintly Jewish apostles murdered Ananias and Sapphira. They were just following the vicious example of Moses and the other Bible saints.

Note also that the saintly apostles could have told Ananias and Sapphira, "You're not giving the church all your money. Therefore you can't be members." No, they didn't do that. The Bible says that "Ananias . . . . brought a certain part and laid it at the apostles' feet." (Acts 5:1,2) The apostles saw these thousands of dollars and greed took over. Their dark eyes glittered with avarice in their yellow skinned faces. They wanted that money. And they knew that if Ananias was killed, they could keep that money. So they killed Ananias and his wife Sapphira instead of merely rejecting them as members of the church. These saintly Christian apostles, including Saint Peter, were nothing but greedy and vicious murderers, and robbers. A trial judge or jury, faced with the evidence given in the Bible, would come to the same conclusion. Today these Christian apostles, including Saint Peter would be executed.

CHAPTER XXXVI.   A HOLY SCHEME TO GET MONEY FROM NON-JEWS

When the word got around of the deaths of Ananias and Sapphira, it threw a scare into the entire church congregation. They really were afraid to cheat the apostles of any money now. The Bible says: "And great fear came upon the church, and upon as many as heard these things." (Acts 5:11) The apostles smiled grimly. Now maybe this trying to cheat the church would come to an end.

However, the murders of Ananias and Sapphira had an unforseen effect of the Jews outside of the church. Non-Christian Jews were now afraid to join the Christian church. No matter how hard the apostles preached, they could make no new converts. The Bible tells us: "And of the rest durst no man join himself to them." (Acts 5:13)

You can imagine the consternation and chagrin the apostles felt at this turn of events. Without more new converts they would get no more money from new church members who sold their possessions. And with their source of money dried up, how were they going to feed the rest of the church members? It was a disaster. They would all have to go back to work if they couldn't get more new converts into the church.

Then a marvelous though struck the apostles. If they couldn't get more Jews, they would send missionaries outside of Judea and get converts among the non-Jews who hadn't heard about the deaths of Ananias and Sapphira. They could then get money out of those non-Jewish converts among the Greeks and Romans.

But a stumbling block arose. The non-Jews were hard to convert The Romans and Greeks would not consent to having the Jews perform the African fertility rite of circumcision on them. They were too civilized for that. Circumcision was the religious erotic surgical cutting off of the men's foreskins of their penises, and the Greek and Roman men didn't approve of that at all. The Pharisees had made converts of non-Jewish women only, who for perfectly apparent reasons were not required to be circumcised.

According to Abraham, God had told him to circumcise all men in his household, including Gentile slaves, and all Abraham's male offspring. The Bible states: "And God said unto Abraham, 'Thou shalt keep my covenant therefore, thou and thy seed after thee in their generations. This is my covenant which ye shall keep, between me and you and thy seed after thee: Every man child among you shall be circumcised. And ye shall circumcise the flesh of your foreskin; and it shall be a token of the covenant between me and you." (Genesis 17:9-11)

The apostle Saint Paul had been preaching to the non-Jews in Antioch and other foreign cities, and he warned the church leaders that requiring circumcision of the non-Jews would make it impossible to convert many of them.

The Bible says: "But there rose up certain of the sect of the Pharisees which believed, saying that it was needful to circumcise them, and to command them to keep the law of Moses. And the apostles and elders came together for to consider of this matter." (Acts 15:5,6) Moses' Bible law required foreigners who wanted to follow the Jews' religion to be circumcised too. (Exodus 12:48)

However, it was very urgent that they make converts of as many non-Jews as possible, because the congregation at Jerusalem was running out of money for food, and the church members would either starve or have to go back to work. So the practical necessity of the situation forced a compromise, and the circumcision requirement for non-Jewish converts was dropped. The religious laws of Jesus and Moses were fine, but getting money was more important. (Acts 15:23-29)

When Jesus was alive he had specifically told them: "I am not sent but unto the lost sheep of the house of Israel." (Matthew 15:24) Jesus also said, as he sent forth the twelve apostles: "Go not into the way of the Gentiles, and into any city of the Samaritans enter ye not: but go rather to the lost sheep of the house of Israel." (Matthew 10:5,6) The message that Jesus had given was designed specifically to save the Jewish nation from destruction by the mighty Roman Empire. Jesus tried to persuade the Jews to turn from their thoughts of rebellion against Rome, and follow his teaching of pacifism instead. Jesus knew how the Jewish nation had been destroyed when it rebelled against Nebuchadnezzar and the Babylonian Empire, and he had tried to persuade the Jews to avoid rebellion and destruction by Rome. The message Jesus gave was not designed to be presented to Greeks and Romans. It was a message strictly for the Jews, as Jesus repeatedly stated. But now the situation had changed. The members of the Christian congregation at Jerusalem had sold everything they owned and given it to the poor, as Jesus had told them to do. So now they were all poor and desperately needed money. And now they had to go to the non-Jews, the Gentiles, to get it, even though Jesus had forbidden them to do so.

Of course I know that tacked onto the ends of the books of Matthew, Mark, and Luke are revised instructions allegedly given by Jesus after he died. Then Jesus is supposed to have given his disciples new instructions contrary to what he said when he was alive, telling them to convert people who were not Jews. But I don't believe a word of it. "Dead people tell no tales," is the old maxim. I have never known a dead person to say anything. Have you?

Suppose you wrote a will leaving your house to Sam after you died. Then you died and along came Dave with twenty witnesses saying you had changed your mind after you died, and had come back and told Dave you wanted your house to go to him, and the twenty witnesses also heard it, they said. Do you think the probate Court Judge would believe what David and his twenty witnesses said? Any lawyer and any Judge in this country will tell you that Dave and his twenty witnesses testimony would be thrown out of court.

The same is true of this tale that Jesus changed his mind after he died and suddenly sent his apostles out to preach to those who were not Israelites. It is pure hog-wash and rubbish inserted into the life story of Jesus to justify the penniless Jewish Christians in what they were doing to raise money. All four of the Gospels were written after proselyting the non-Jews was begun, so this was easy to do.

In fact, Bible data on the book of Mark will tell you that the last Chapter of Mark beginning at Verse 9, is spurious, and is not found in the earlier ancient manuscripts of Mark. It is nothing but a forgery, where it tells about Jesus instructing his disciples to preach to the non-Jews, and all Bible scholars know this. The Revised Standard Version, and the American Standard Version of the Bible give positive warning of this forgery in their text. The gospel of John has no statement in it either, about preaching to Gentiles. Nevertheless, the missionary effort among the non-Jews then began in earnest. (Acts 15:35-41 et seq.) The entire book of Acts following this point gives an account of the Christian evangelistic campaign.

The Jewish apostle Paul was the leader in the movement to convert the Greeks and Romans. Saints Barnabas, Silas, Mark, Luke and others helped. But in sending them forth, the apostles at Jerusalem gave them a strict admonition not to forget to send any money back to the church at Jerusalem, because they were in dire need. The Bible says: "And when James, Cephas, and John, who seemed to be pillars, perceived the grace that was given unto me (Paul), they gave to me and Barnabas the right hand of fellowship; that we should go unto the heathen, and they unto the circumcision. Only they would that we should remember the poor; the same which I also was forward to do." (Galatians 2:9,10) Again the Bible says: "For it hath pleased them of Macedonia and Achaia (non-Jews) to make certain contribution for the poor saints which are at Jerusalem." (Romans 15:26)

So some money began to flow in to the Jewish congregation at Jerusalem, and they didn't have to go to work after all, thanks to the non-Jews who were talked into parting with their hard earned cash. Such were the devious ways of the devout Bible saints.

However, while contributions of silver and brass may have reached them, it is obvious that the Gentiles weren't foolish enough to give the Jews gold. The Apostle James, who was the leader of the Christian Jews at Jerusalem makes this certain, for James writes in the Bible at James 5:3 that 'gold rusts!' Now anyone familiar with gold knows it never tarnishes or rusts, so obviously Saint James had never seen any gold. But here, allegedly under inspiration of God, he boldly writes that gold rusts. If there is a God he certainly would know that gold does not rust, and therefore would not inspire Saint James to write such a lie.

SEX AMONG THE SAINTS

In the course of Paul's preaching to the Greeks, he found some sexual irregularities in one of the church congregations he had established among them. It seems that one of the church members had married his own widowed mother. This really upset the apostle. He writes in the Bible at 1 Corinthians 5:1:

"It is reported commonly that there is fornication among you, and such fornication as is not so much as named among the Gentiles, that one should have his father's wife."

Saint Paul was very disturbed by this act. He could have pointed out that the Jews never indulged in such outrageous conduct. They had more sense than to marry older women like their mothers. If they were going to indulge in incest, they at least chose younger women.

Saint Abraham, the father of their Jewish nation, when he indulged in incest, had the good sense to marry his own sister, who was at least about his own age. This was a more compatible marriage arrangement; and they were able to have a son, Issac. (Genesis 20:12)

And Abraham's nephew Saint Lot, when he was without a wife, chose his own adult daughters to be his sex partners. That way they were at least young enough to give him children. (Genesis 19:36-38) This was therefore a more practical arrangement for all of them. Whereas if Saint Lot had married his own mother, she would have been so old she could not have borne him any children. You have to be sensible if you're going to indulge in incest, according to the Bible saints. (2 Peter 2:7; Genesis 26:5)

But this Greek member of the church congregation had married his own mother, and she was too old to give him any offspring. Obviously this was an ill-thought-out arrangement, according to the saints. So Paul had no other course than to excommunicate this stupid church member. The Apostle Paul writes in the Bible: "In the name of our Lord Jesus Christ, when ye are gathered together and my spirit, with the power of our Lord Jesus Christ, to deliver such an one unto Satan for the destruction of the flesh, that the spirit may be saved in the day of the Lord Jesus." (1 Corinthians 5:4,5) And so the stupid man was thrown out of the church congregation.

If instead of marrying his mother, this saintly Christian young man had 'joined his body to a harlot' (1 Corinthians 6:16) and caught a venereal disease, and then later married a Christian young woman, she would catch the disease from him. She would then bear him a very defective child, either completely mentally deranged or terribly deformed physically, and with the disease of his parents. Yet in this case the Christian young man would not have been thrown out of the congregation, even though this latter course of action produced far more evil effects than would result from his marrying his mother. You can see the stupidity of the Apostle Paul's order excommunicating this young man and his mother from the church. While no man was ever thrown out of the church because of copulating with whores, which produced far more harmful effects. Common sense would say that if you are going to excommunicate the one, you must excommunicate the others. But Bible saints religion and common sense rarely coincide.

As an example of the spread of disease among men who patronize women prostitutes, in the United States only one state at this time has legalized prostitution, and that state is Nevada. According to Government statistics, the state of Nevada has more cases of syphilis per capita than other states in the Union. Patronizing whores is extremely dangerous and